Is Time out of Joint?

signale|TRANSFER
german thought in translation

Series editor: Peter Uwe Hohendahl, Cornell University

Signale|TRANSFER provides a unique channel for the transmission of critical German-language texts, newly translated into English, through to current debates on theory, philosophy, and social and cultural criticism. *Signale|TRANSFER* is a component of the series *Signale: Modern German Letters, Culture and Thought,* which publishes books in literary studies, cultural criticism, and intellectual history. *Signale* books are published under the joint imprint of Cornell University Press and Cornell University Library. Please see http://signale.cornell.edu/.

Is Time out of Joint?

On the Rise and Fall of the Modern Time Regime

Aleida Assmann

Translated by Sarah Clift

A Signale Book

Cornell University Press and Cornell University Library
Ithaca and London

Originally published as *Ist die Zeit aus den Fugen?: Aufstieg und Fall des Zeitregimes der Moderne* by Aleida Assmann.
© 2013 Carl Hanser Verlag GmbH & Co. KG, München.

Cornell University Press and Cornell University Library gratefully acknowledge the College of Arts & Sciences, Cornell University, for support of the Signale series.

First published 2020 by Cornell University Press and Cornell University Library

Library of Congress Cataloging-in-Publication Data

Names: Assmann, Aleida, author. | Clift, Sarah, translator.
Title: Is time out of joint? : on the rise and fall of the modern time regime / Aleida Assmann ; translated by Sarah Clift.
Other titles: Ist die Zeit aus den Fugen?. English
Description: Ithaca : Cornell University Press : Cornell University Library, 2020. | Series: Signale transfer : German thought in translation | Includes bibliographical references and index.
Identifiers: LCCN 2019032693 (print) | LCCN 2019032694 (ebook) | ISBN 9781501742439 (hardcover) | ISBN 9781501742446 (pdf) | ISBN 9781501742453 (epub)
Subjects: LCSH: Time. | Time in literature. | History—Philosophy.
Classification: LCC BD638 .A816513 2020 (print) | LCC BD638 (ebook) | DDC 115—dc23
LC record available at https://lccn.loc.gov/2019032693
LC ebook record available at https://lccn.loc.gov/2019032694

CONTENTS

Preface   vii

Introduction   1

1. Time and the Modern   12
   Baudelaire's Discovery of the Present   15
   How Long Does the Present Last?   19

2. Work on the Modern Myth of History   30
   Transformations of the Idea of Progress   38
   The Theory of Time Underlying Modern Historiography   47
   Modernization Theory and Theories of Modernity   55
   When Does the Modern Begin? Phases of Modernization
   in Western History   64
   The Golden Door of the Future: Modernization as Culture
   (Using the Example of the United States)   74

3. Five Aspects of the Modern Temporal Regime   92
   Temporal Rupture   93
   The Fiction of Beginning   105

Creative Destruction   116
Destroying and Preserving: The Invention of the Historical   126
Acceleration   135

4. Concepts of Time in Late Modernity   148
Compensation Theory   149
Compensation Theory and Memory Theory—Two Different
Approaches to the Past   170

5. Is Time out of Joint?   175
Total Recall—The Rhetoric of Catastrophe and the Broad Present   177
Connections between the Past, Present, and Future   189

6. The Past Is Not Past; or, On Repairing the Modern
Time Regime   201
Three New Categories: Culture, Identity, Memory   206
The Past Is Not Past: Historical Wounds and the Idea
of Reversible Time   212
Identity Politics—Intersections between History and Memory   217
Two Trends in the Politics of History   220

Conclusion   224
Too Much Past and Too Little Future   224

Works Cited   233

Index   247

PREFACE

This book has a very specific theme: the collapse and reconfiguration of the past-present-future temporal structure. It harkens back to a now largely forgotten time—which was actually not so very long ago—when two key ideas of our own time, dominant both in the humanities and in everyday speech, did not yet exist. Those ideas are "cultures of memory" and "collective identity."

These ideas replaced another one that had a veritable aura surrounding it at first, that of the future. The future was the standard orientation; no one talked about the past. Just as we can no longer imagine people smoking in hospitals, it is now difficult for us to imagine how disinterested people were in the past. Terms like "cultural memory" or "collective memory"—which have since become quite self-evident and standard—were virtually unknown at the time.

This book undertakes a journey into this forgotten past and attempts to gain a clearer understanding of it by exploring its dominant and effective temporal order from a certain distance. Because this temporal order has never been articulated as an explicit argument or unified discourse, I have had to approach it by means of modes of perception, types of activity, and frames of meaning taken from diverse fields. Readers will thus be asked to look at findings from various historical epochs and cultural arenas with the hope that a picture will eventually emerge from out of these fragments of what I, using a somewhat abstract notion, call "the modern time regime."

Because the subject of this book first had to be discovered and delineated, this project could not proceed in as goal-oriented a fashion as other, more clearly defined works might. The impulse for the book initially arose from intuitions and speculation rather than clear facts; to speak metaphorically, the method was less a probe than a divining rod. A clearly established research methodology was replaced by a more tentative search, in which I first had to discover a great deal by happenstance, by the way, in the background, in *soft focus*. Over recent decades, the contours of this initially highly speculative topic have gradually become clearer. Questions I had originally thought I was clarifying for myself alone have increasingly proven to be urgent questions with a collective significance. So, I am now in a position to contribute my own findings to the massive puzzle that this topic presents and, in so doing, trust that I can also benefit from other perspectives and assessments regarding current problems of time.

I wish to thank Michael Krüger for his unwavering support of my work and for his willingness to place this book on his last publication schedule, even though it did not end up, as was once promised, being a book about reading. The "Excellence Cluster" at the University of Konstanz made it possible for me to enlist the assistance of Janine Firges and Ines Detmers in the thorough and prompt revision of the manuscript and the copyediting of the proofs. I am very grateful to both of them.

Is Time out of Joint?

INTRODUCTION

Graham Swift writes in his 1983 novel, *Waterland*: "Once upon a time, in the bright sixties, there was plenty of future on offer."[1] At the time Swift was writing the novel, just two decades after the "bright sixties," the future had lost its sheen; it had already turned into a "past future."

According to Reinhardt Koselleck in his influential work *Futures Past*, it turns out that, indeed, even the future is historical. Though we usually assume that historians work on the past, recent studies show that the future itself is also historical, and that the past has had different possible futures.[2]

---

1. Graham Swift, *Waterland* (London: Heinemann 1983), 20.
2. Reinhart Koselleck, *Futures Past: On the Semantics of Historical Time*, trans. Keith Tribe (New York: Columbia University Press, 2004). This research project came out of his work on the history of ideas regarding time and historicity, which Koselleck's student Lucian Hölscher then assembled into two major studies on the development and trajectory of the notion of the future in Western Europe.

The idea that the future can give us a clear direction or stable horizon for our plans and goals, that it shines as a beacon of their coming fulfillment—that is how it was, "once upon a time." This future has, however, become the past. To take only one instance of this past future: In 1967, the philosopher Ernst Bloch received the *Friedenspreises des Deutschen Buchhandels* (Peace Prize of the German Book Trade) and, in his acceptance speech at the Paulskirche in Frankfurt, declared that a "map on which there is no land called Utopia is not even worth glancing at."[3] For Bloch, utopia serves as a metaphor for visions of the future in which the exploited and downtrodden can anticipate a better and more just world. His notion of utopia is based on the conviction that the revolutions of that time had paved the way for a better and more humane future. For Bloch, these so-called humane revolutions were the opposite of wars motivated solely by the goals of conquest or maintaining power. In contrast to wars, Bloch argues that revolutions function as midwives, helping to give birth to a better world. "Unlike a war," he writes, "the Russian Revolution in particular was in no way motivated by a lust for power but by the vision that emerged of a society no longer torn apart by divisions" (11a).

In view of the millions of lives lost or destroyed under Stalin's regime, Bloch's interpretation of history is no longer tenable in our own time. In fact, its vision of the future collapsed quite abruptly after 1989 in both Eastern and Western Europe, together with the collapse of both the Berlin Wall and the Soviet Union. This future collapsed even for Russians, who certainly did not greet this historical turn with enthusiasm—Vladimir Putin would describe the collapse of the Eastern bloc as the "greatest geopolitical catastrophe of the twentieth century." Russians' history also collapsed: Putin would downgrade the Russian Revolution to a *coup d'état*, and

---

Ten years after Koselleck's pioneering work, Hölscher's postdoctoral thesis, *Weltgericht oder Revolution. Protestantische und sozialistische Zukunkftsvorstellung im deutschen Kaiserreich 1871–1914* (Stuttgart: Klett-Cotta, 1989); *Die Entdeckung der Zukunft* (Frankfurt am Main: Fischer, 1999), followed another decade later, just in time to mark the new millennium.

3. Ernst Bloch, "Widerstand und Friede," acceptance speech for the Peace Prize of the German Book Trade, 1967, 15b.

the commemoration day of November 7 was erased from Russian collective memory. It was replaced by November 4, a recent fabrication of Putin's historians who dug up a forgotten and perhaps largely fictionalized event from the seventeenth century as a temporally proximal substitute for the long-cherished holiday of the Russian people.[4]

Some aspects of the "bright future" of the Cold War and its polarized worldview have only recently come to an end. In October 2011, announcements were made that the United States had dismantled its last remaining B53 thermonuclear bomb, which possessed many hundreds of times the destructive capacity of the bomb that had been dropped on Hiroshima. According to the head of the American Office of Nuclear Safety, the B53 had been developed "in another time, for another world," and its dismantlement was a strong signal that the world had supposedly now become a safer place. In the media, there was talk of a milestone in American President Barack Obama's politics of nuclear disarmament.[5] Before he brought an end to this Cold War future and relegated it to the past, however, Obama reaffirmed another future long familiar to Americans. In 2010, at the NASA space center in Florida, he voiced his intention to send a manned space flight to Mars. He predicted that American astronauts would set foot on the red planet by the year 2035 at the latest, adding: "And I expect to be around to see it!" Moon exploration, by contrast, is old news: "We've already been there . . . ," he said; "there is still a lot more space to explore."[6]

Regardless of how unbroken Obama's spirit of adventure may sound here, it does not detract from the more general sense that the future is no longer much of a motivator in the arenas of politics,

4. Jutta Scherrer, "Russlands neue-alte Erinnerungsorte," *Aus Politik und Zeitgeschichte* 11 (2006): 25.

5. The largest atom bomb in the world, the so-called Russian Tsar Bomba, had 4,000 times the explosive power of the one dropped on Hiroshima and was detonated for test purposes on October 30, 1961, on the Arctic island of Nowaja-Semlja.

6. *Frankfurter Allgemeine Zeitung*, April 4, 2010, www.fax.net/aktuell/gesellschaft/weltraum-programm-obama-will-marsmission-in-jahr-2035-1964515.html.

society, and the environment: Expectations for the future have become extremely modest. Within a relatively short period of time, the future itself has lost the power to shed light on the present, since we can no longer assume that it functions as the end point of our desires, goals, or projections. We have learned from historians that the rise and fall of particular futures is in itself nothing new. However, it is the case not only that *particular* visions of the future have collapsed in our own day, but also that the very concept of the future itself is being called into question.

How did this disenchantment come about? Why have the stakes of the future fallen so drastically in value? Some obvious answers immediately come to mind: The resources of the future have been eroded by a number of complex challenges, such as the depletion of natural resources, the ongoing ecological degradation that accompanies technologically advanced societies, climate change, and water crises. These challenges, along with demographic problems such as overpopulation and aging societies, have fundamentally altered our image of the future. Under these conditions, the future no longer serves as the Eldorado of our hopes and dreams, while at the same time any heady talk about progress has begun to sound more and more hollow. Meanwhile, surveys confirm that the rhetoric of progress has a diminished hold on the public imagination. In a study conducted by Werner Mittelstaedt, when participants were asked the question "Is the world continually getting better?" 70 percent of them responded with a decisive "no"; after some hesitation, 20 percent responded with "yes," and 10 percent offered no response at all.[7] Today we no longer automatically assume that change means change *for the better*. In short, the future has gone from being the locus of expectation and hope to becoming a site of anxiety, prompting ever-new precautionary measures. We can no longer simply rely on the future, but must now tend to it responsibly; otherwise, there might not be a future for coming generations.

---

7. Werner Mittelstaedt, *Das Prinzip Fortschritt: Ein neues Verständnis für die Herausforderungen unserer Zeit* (Frankfurt: Peter Lang, 2008). The study is based on the results of a survey that the author carried out with 200 people between 2004 and 2006.

Alongside the future's eclipse, we are also witnessing another anomaly of our long-held temporal order: the unprecedented return of the past. Historical events that we had long thought were safely behind us are suddenly rearing up in front of us. In this sense, something of a continental shift is taking place in the structure of Western temporality: At the same time as the future has been gradually losing its appeal, the past has an ever greater hold on us, especially in relation to periods of extreme violence. In particular, the burden of the violent histories of the twentieth century weighs heavily on the present, demanding attention and recognition and forcing us to take responsibility and to develop new forms of remembrance and commemoration. Almost two decades ago, the cultural theorist Andreas Huyssen was drawing attention to this remarkable shift in emphasis from the future to the past when he wrote that

> one of the most surprising cultural and political phenomena of recent years has been the emergence of memory as a key concern in Western societies, a turning toward the past that stands in stark contrast to the privileging of the future so characteristic of earlier decades of twentieth-century modernity. From the early twentieth century's apocalyptic myths of radical breakthrough and the emergence of the "new man" in Europe via the murderous phantasms of racial or class purification in National Socialism and Stalinism to the post–World War II American paradigm of modernization, modernist culture was energized by what one might call "present futures." Since the 1980s, it seems, the focus has shifted from present futures to present pasts, and this shift in the experience and sensibility of time needs to be explained historically and phenomenologically.[8]

Huyssen goes on to provide further explanations as to why confidence in the future has been so severely eroded in past decades. In his view, the violent history of the twentieth century is inseparable from a particular understanding of the future; his argument is that certain future-oriented utopias, especially those involving the "new man," played an important role in politically legitimating and unleashing the extreme violence that marked the twentieth century.

---

8. Andreas Huyssen, "Present Pasts: Media, Politics, Amnesia," in *Public Culture* 12, no. 1 (Winter 2000): 21.

This future has become the past. So, the temporal registers of the past and the future are not simply opposites here but are inextricably related to one another. Focusing on the ideologies of fascism and communism, Huyssen complicates the positive image we have of Western modernization by including entirely different and much darker aspects: Being decisively oriented toward the future—the end of which we so often lament—is obviously tied not only to enlightenment, emancipation, and progress, but also to ideological indoctrination, apocalyptic myths, war, and extreme violence. Although *modernization theory* gives us a perspective on the future that is often rosy and optimistic, *critical theorists of modernity* will give us a picture that is bleak and pessimistic in precisely the same measure. We will return to a fuller examination of these opposing perspectives later on.

Huyssen observes that since the 1980s, "the focus has shifted from present futures to present pasts." What initiated this change in focus from the future to the past? What exactly was the status of the past before memory suddenly became, as Huyssen puts it, "a key concern in Western societies"? What problems and opportunities can be associated with this change in our understanding of time and history? In what follows, I will take up these important questions for, as Huyssen states, this "change in the experience and the sensibility of time needs to be explained historically and phenomenologically."

Cultural historians have yet to produce the kind of explanation that Huyssen demands. To my knowledge, no systematic study has been made of this recent shift in the structure of our cultural temporal order.

Before we turn our attention to this question, though, allow me to comment briefly on what personally motivated me to pursue this topic. Though things had already begun to change in the 1980s, such a dramatic shift was unforeseeable at the time, even for those who lived through that period. A further twenty-five years had to pass before the contours of this change would become clear and enter into the "now of recognizability" (*das Jetzt der Erkennbarkeit*— W. Benjamin). As a consequence, this shift in cultural understandings of time was in no way recognized or perceived in a uniform or consistent way. This lack of consensus struck me again and again in discussions with members of the generation of my university professors (particularly those born around 1926). They wanted to have nothing to do with this shift in temporal structure, simply because they held it in such low regard. In particular, the leading lights of postwar modernization—those who had renewed academic life from the ground up with their ideas and questions—had to struggle a great deal with the fact that the return of the past and memory had become key developments in Western societies. Of course, radical cultural changes never remain purely abstract but penetrate right down to the levels of individual experience and subjective interpretations of the world. They also pervade the lives of researchers and affect experiences specific to their generation: their emotions, their investments in their life's work, and their values. This generation of modern reformers is emblematic of an exclusive focus on the future that is incompatible with a return to the past—particularly to one's own past. Because their focus on the future was so clearly incompatible with the premises of research into memory, I found myself repeatedly confronted with a surprisingly strong emotional opposition on the part of my professors.

The clearly emotional character of this defensiveness preoccupied me for some time and motivated my research into historical self-enlightenment that forms the basis of this book. In the context of these tensions and clashes, I delineated the structure of a distinctively modern temporal order, which I then made the focus of a systematic examination. Throughout that process, I was struck by particular aspects of the modern temporal order that, until that time, I myself had lived, thought, and experienced as if they were self-evidently true, understanding them to be neutral descriptions of the world.

In no way did my own historicizing reflections lead to a postmodern rejection of the paradigm of modernization. As absurd as it sounds, my critical interest in shedding light on the temporal foundations of modernization arose out of a socially conservative approach. I admired the excellent work of those among my university professors who had made strong arguments in favor of the modernization paradigm, and I felt deeply influenced by them. My cultural and intellectual socialization made me a product of this intellectual culture. Beginning in the 1980s, however, other cultural voices and intellectual traditions had started to break into the West Germany of the postwar period—among them, Jewish, postcolonial, and feminist—that had previously had no place within the framework of the dominant paradigm of modernization. Because these had been foreclosed by inherited ways of thinking, to turn to them with curiosity and interest automatically became an imperative for the following generation. That was especially the case for the return of the German Nazi past, which theorists of modernization were largely intent on avoiding.[9] In West Germany, this return led to a new interest in "memory as a key concern in Western societies" and in that sense—also outside of Germany—to a shift in focus from "present futures" to "present pasts."

The American historian Charles S. Maier has written that "[t]he twentieth century effectively ended between 1973 and 1989,"[10] indicating just how precise a historian can be when reconstituting and dating a temporal rupture—though only in hindsight. In what follows, I will argue that not only did the twentieth century end in the 1980s, but so too did the unquestioned importance of the modernization paradigm. Yet we cannot speak of this subtle transformation in consciousness as a decisive turn or a sudden upheaval: No intellectual revolution broke out and no border-walls collapsed as the fundamental assumptions regarding the Western notion of time were undergoing change. Neither was this change in orientation an invention on the part of theorists who sought to diagnose a new turn. Rather, it formed one aspect of a more general transformation in the framework of Western cultural development.

Since the 1980s and '90s, the waning of interest in modernization's future has been accompanied, the world over, by increased interest

9. For an outline of this generation and its relation to modernization and the recent past, see Aleida Assmann, *Geschichte im Gedächtnis* (Munich: Beck, 2007), especially chapter 2, "Verkörperte Geschichte—zur Dynamik der Generationen," 31–69.

10. Charles S. Maier, "Two Sorts of Crisis? The 'Long' 1970s in the West and the East," in *Koordinaten deutscher Geschichte in der Epoche des Ost-West-Konflikts (Schriften des Historischen Kollegs 55)*, ed. Hans Günter Hockerts (Munich: Oldenbourg Press, 2004), 61.

in the past and memory. Here I will introduce the notion of a *cultural time regime* to refer to the shift in temporal ordering that accompanies this reorientation. All time regimes provide a groundwork for unspoken values, interpretations of history, and meaningful activity.[11] With the idea of "time regime," I mean to suggest a complex of deeply held cultural presuppositions, values, and decisions that guide human desires, action, emotions, and assessments, without individuals' necessarily being aware of these foundations. François Hartog speaks of a "régime d'historicité" in this regard, by which he means the different ways in which societies position themselves in time and engage with their past. Hartog defines a time regime as "an expression of a temporal experience [that] does not merely mark off time in a neutral fashion, but rather organizes the past as a sequence of structures."[12] Although he clearly adopts the historian's perspective here, he also includes other, more far-reaching perspectives in it:

> More precisely, the concept provides an instrument for comparing different types of history, but also and even primarily, I would now add, highlights methods of relating to time: forms of experiencing time, here and elsewhere, today and yesterday. Ways of being in time. . . . [H]istoricity designates "the condition of being, historically" or even "humankind present to itself as history."[13]

The question concerning cultural time regimes is productive because it opens up the possibility of a comparative study of varying semantics of temporal ordering. It also helps to increase awareness about cultural assumptions that so often operate under the surface as self-evident truths, and indeed are all the more effective as implicit axioms

---

11. Harmut Rosa speaks of "historical-cultural time regimes" in "Jedes Ding hat keine Zeit? Flexible Menschen in rasenden Verhältnissen"; accessed August 30, 2018, http://www.eilkrankheit.de/Textbeitraege/text23.pdf.

12. François Hartog, "Time, History, and the Writing of History: The Order of Time," in *History Making: The Intellectual and Social Formation of a Discipline*, ed. Rolf Torstendahl and Irmline Veit-Brause (Stockholm: Almqvist & Wiksell, 1996), 96.

13. François Hartog, "Time and Heritage," in *Museum International* 57, no. 3 (September 2005): 8.

when they do not become subjects of debate or reflection. The time has now come to examine this cultural complex more closely and to consider both its positive and its negative implications. With the idea of a time regime, we are not only raising questions pertaining to historicity and historicization but are also exploring the more general issue regarding the "acculturation" of time. Placing emphasis on the cultural investments that are made in shaping time is by no means trivial for, in the context of the modernization paradigm, time is often understood to be precisely *not* a product of culture but rather an abstract and purely objective dimension that follows its own internal logic and so is not open to human manipulation. The close proximity of the modern time regime to the natural sciences as well as to new techniques of measurement makes it both very modern and, at the same time, highly resistant to cultural self-reflection or historicization.

What earlier cultural time regimes had in common was the weight they gave to the past. The past was understood to be the site from which both the present and the future took their direction and stability. The time regime of the modern[14] broke away from this traditional form of temporal ordering in that it no longer took its bearing from the past, but from the future. This shift to the future revolutionized the cultural temporal order and restructured its commitment from the old to the new, from the known to the unknown, and from "what was" to what was currently becoming or yet to come. This spreading-out of time along the spectrum of old and new is itself both a symptom of this time regime and an indication of how thoroughly it rearticulates the human experience of time and the historical construction of meaning. In what follows, this "modern time regime," as we will call it from now on, will be examined in detail in terms of its genesis, its shape, and its implications. Because this time regime is both the red thread of an entire era and, at the same time, a catch-all for a whole host of cultural activities, scripts, and interpretations, it becomes necessary to draw on material from

---

14. On this phrase, see Bruno Latour: "The adjective 'modern' designates a new regime, an acceleration, a rupture, a revolution in time." Latour, *We Have Never Been Modern*, trans. C. Porter (Cambridge, MA: Harvard University Press, 1993), 10.

various discourses and cultural arenas to find evidence of this modern temporal bearing, rather than limiting ourselves to an examination of historiography. For, only when the modern time regime no longer confronts us solely as a theoretical concept, but also as a means of giving shape to various cultural activities, can its historical meaning be assessed and described in a differentiated way.

What follows, then, from the modern time regime? Why and under what conditions did it come up against its limits and lose its foundational value or its persuasive force? Which of its aspects are still relevant and which have lost their power through a further change in orientation? What does it mean to bid farewell to these temporal bearings and assumptions of value in our contemporary culture? The following chapters will be concerned with these and other questions. First, we will trace the emergence and trajectory of the modern time regime. Then, we will shed light on some of the symptoms of its demise, and finally, we will conclude by engaging with some critical positions and generating suggestions for further modifications and possible refinements.

1

Time and the Modern

Time and the modern are closely related to one another: The positive connotation of words such as "movement," "change," "transformation," "renewal," and "progress" indicate just how significant the passage of time is for the modern and for understandings of modernization. While time has always been associated with movement and change, it has not always been greeted with enthusiasm; enthusiasm about change and transformation is new and specific to modernity. Within the context of modernity, transition and change are no longer regarded as problems; rather, the fundamental conviction of modernity is that they are to be seized as important cultural resources. This positive evaluation of time and its dynamic understanding of culture brings out new standpoints and pairs of opposites. Hans Ulrich Gumbrecht has worked out three such pairs in his now-classic lexicon entry, "Modern, Modernität, Moderne," found in the *Lexikon histo-*

rischer Grundbegriffe.[1] According to Gumbrecht, "modern" signifies:

1) the standpoint of the present in relation to something preceding and past,
2) the qualification of a thing as "new," displacing something "old," and
3) the experience of the fleeting and the transient over and against something stable and lasting.

The first pair involves a highly conscious positioning of oneself in the present and becomes a characteristically modern experience when the present continually breaks with a past that it deems no longer relevant. The second pair of opposites interprets the difference between what is current and what is past in terms of the dialectical opposites of new/old. As we shall see in greater detail in what follows, the modern concept of time can be understood as a mechanism that produces both the new *and* the old. At the same time, innovation becomes a central cultural imperative. The new is a relative concept that always needs a backdrop against which it can first emerge. Therefore, the production of the new cannot happen without the coproduction of the old. Finally, Gumbrecht's third pair identifies the acceleration of time and the increasingly dynamic mode of perception as a specific feature of modern experience. So, according to him, "modern" means above all an increased awareness of time, a heightened reflection on time, and a heightened sense of how dependent temporal perception is on the condition of accelerated change.

All the meanings of "modern" that Gumbrecht lists—current, new, fleeting—point to a new emphasis on time. According to its own self-understanding, the modern era distinguishes itself from premodern times by virtue of how it leaves behind the temporal

1. Hans Ulrich Gumbrecht, "Modern, Modernität, Moderne," in *Geschichtliche Grundbegriffe: Historisches Lexikon zur politisch-sozialen Sprache in Deutschland*, ed. Otto Brunner et al., vol. 4 (Stuttgart: Metzler 1978), 93–131.

organization of all other cultures and historical epochs, and how it raises the concept of time borrowed from physics—that of a linear and irreversible "time's arrow"—to the level of a binding principle. In so doing, it submits itself to the dictates of a time that continually, steadily, and irreversibly flows through all events and makes them chronologically measurable.[2] What is decisive in this new time is that it is completely detached from natural cycles and human activity. As a consequence, time becomes an objective dimension, in the strongest possible sense; that is, it lies outside of human control and manipulation. The temporal order of physics and its universal application are both modern discoveries. The culture of the modern is, in fact, founded on the temporal order of physics freed from human rhythms and attributions of meaning, and directs itself in accordance with that order. However, as we shall later see in greater detail, the putatively objective character of this temporal order actually becomes imbued with specifically modern cultural meanings, values, and imperatives. Therefore, a more precise formulation would be that modernity has "acculturated" the time of physics.

As we reflect on the cultural connection between time and modernity, we might begin with the first indications of how valuable time was in the context of how little of it there is. This insight became widespread throughout the seventeenth century when Puritans began to reflect on the short lifespan given to them. The time allotted to a this-worldly human existence was no longer understood to be merely a preliminary stage toward the only significant existence in the beyond, but instead a gift that humans had been given—one they had to put to the fullest possible use before the eyes of their divine creator and judge. This new and self-imposed time pressure brought with it a feeling of responsibility for the allotted time span, one that resulted in new forms of planning, self-control, and accounting. Max Weber has clearly shown how this new awareness of time among the Puritan middle-class became

2.   Günter Dux, "Das historische Bewusstsein der Neuzeit. Anthropologie als Grundlagenwissenschaft," in *Saeculum* 39 (1988): 82–95.

not only the foundation for a "methodical way of life" but also the engine for a burgeoning capitalism.[3]

As a point of entry into the connection between time and the modern, however, I have chosen to focus on an essay that appeared two centuries after the Puritans' discovery of finite time. Written by Charles Baudelaire, the essay describes the discovery of the present as an utterly isolated and fleeting moment. The sense of time related to that discovery is, in the most literal sense, borderline. While extremely powerful as a paradigm of artistic perception that disrupts both routinized habits of seeing and conventions of representation, the borderline experience of time encapsulated by it is, however, incompatible with basic human needs like experience, sociality, activity, meaning, or identity. Therefore, we experience the present precisely not as a fleeting "now" but as an already extended span of time that, as will be explained in what follows, can be related to entirely different forms of duration. Following our examination of Baudelaire's artistic determination of the present and the *Zeitroman* as a further, and decisively modern, experiment with time, we will conclude by exploring the connections between time and modernity in more recent historiographical theory.

Baudelaire's Discovery of the Present

Baudelaire was the first to bring together the notions of "time" and "the modern" in a systematic way. In the famous essay "The Painter of Modern Life," he describes a new style of painting that he found and greatly admired in the work of his favorite painter and contemporary, Constantin Guys.[4] Guys had rejected a ponderous style of oil painting on canvas in favor of experiments with lighter techniques such as watercolor and charcoal on paper. And in rejecting time-consuming studio techniques, he also gave up the safe classical

---

3. Max Weber, *The Protestant Ethic and the "Spirit" of Capitalism*, ed. and trans. Peter Baehr and Gordon C. Wells (London: Penguin Books, 2002).

4. Charles Baudelaire, "The Painter of Modern Life," in *The Painter of Modern Life and Other Essays*, trans. Jonathan Mayne (London: Phaidon Press, 1964).

style of academic painting and developed fleeting processes to convey a new quality of the spontaneous and dynamic. In the course of his reflections on this new style, Baudelaire developed important insights on the relation between time and art. The most famous sentence of his essay is the following: "Modernity is the ephemeral, the fugitive, the contingent" (*la modernité, ç'est le transitoire, le fugitive, le contingent*).[5] The word *transitoire* would be better translated as "transitory" here, for the temporal sensibility of the modern that Baudelaire seeks to emphasize is radically different from the Baroque sensibility for the ephemeral. In the context of Baroque *vanitas*, everything sensual and this-worldly was seen as illusory and provisional because it was perceived against the backdrop of a religious promise of eternity. But Baudelaire's transitory moment also differs from the "pregnant moment" of the German Classical period that Gotthold Ephraim Lessing would define as freighted with the past and pregnant with the future. In contrast to the pregnant moment that points beyond itself because it contains both the past and the future and thereby possesses the classical quality of wholeness, Baudelaire's moment is fragmented, fleeting, and splintered, without a before and without an after, without past or future.

Interestingly enough, Baudelaire's definition of the moment also includes a discussion of eternity—not a Christian eternity but an aesthetic one. The more complete citation of the passage in question reads as follows: "By modernity, I mean the ephemeral, the fugitive, the contingent, the half of art whose other half is the eternal and the immutable." Baudelaire understood Guys' achievement to be that he was able to bring out the "strange beauty" of the immediate and living present without forcing it into the corset of a style from a previous epoch, as was so often done. For Baudelaire, only a modernity that can grasp the specific beauty of its own fleeting present deserves to become a formative classic that will be taken up again in the future.

Baudelaire begins his description of the present with another pair of opposites that should be added to Gumbrecht's three pairs we

---

5. Baudelaire, "The Painter of Modern Life," in *The Painter of Modern Life and Other Essays*, trans. Jonathan Mayne (London: Phaidon Press, 1964), 13.

discussed earlier. He distinguishes between *Classical* and *Modern* and, by means of that distinction, contrasts the fleetingness of the modern with the time-resistant solidity of the ancient. What is self-evident in the art world is precisely what the temporal order of physics does not allow: that there are pasts that do not pass away and that, quite simply, some things last. Indeed, all cultures reserve the right to pull carefully chosen objects out from the flow of time to canonize them and give them an enduring present. This detemporalizing is the product of performative activities such as selection, evaluation, and sacralization. No art and no culture are possible without such practices. Canonizing and maintaining specific collections ensure the relevance of those collections for the long term and allow them, as stable vanishing points, to run alongside the horizon of the ever-changing present. Beginning in the Renaissance, artists claimed for themselves the title of a *secondus deus*, a second creator, which gave them quasi-religious status and nourished in them a hope for immortality in the sense of permanent survival in the memory of those who came after them.

In the works of Baudelaire, time and the modern merge in a present that disappears as quickly as it arises. With that focus, he succeeded in developing an entirely new sensibility for the passing moment, for whose artistic expression there as yet existed no adequate expressive possibilities. A generation after Baudelaire, the impressionists sought to capture the fleetingness, the intensity, and the sensual radiance of the moment. One of the new forms of representation they invented in their quest to approximate the moment of the present is the series. Monet's *Haystacks* and Cézanne's *Mont St. Victoire* series powerfully show how the changed lighting of every single moment presents a new motif and, consequently, a chance for a new image.

In the course of his search for an artistic response to the fleeting present, Baudelaire discovered a new type of artist: the flaneur. The flaneur embodies the temporal borderline experience of modernity. He roams the streets of the modern metropolis and, as he does so, is highly conscious of balancing on the tipping-point of the moment. Theorists and writers of modernity have often described this metropolis stroller, led by no particular intentions and needs, as being the idealized embodiment of the modern experience of time. The flaneur lives by his senses and by his floating and evenly suspended attention in the transitory moment. He therefore embodies the thoroughly modern human being who has no memory, no past, and no expectations for the future and who unreservedly gives himself over to the present. Artists of the early twentieth century invented new, nonlinear, collage-like, and cubist forms of representation for their fragmented, kaleidoscopic, perceptual images.[6] Hans Robert Jauß has rightly emphasized that "he who sweeps through the city, who euphorically takes in and enjoys every pregnant sight of current life" at the same time commits himself, unconditionally delivered over as he is to the moment, to the modern "experience of the fragmented, self-effacing I." The flaneur as artist foregoes existential necessities like coherence, continuity, and identity: "The high price paid for the unanticipated expansion of limits in the modern experience of the world is the loss of the identity-guaranteeing *Anamnesis*."[7]

This aesthetic rendering of the modern experience of time not only ignored the dimension of the past, but also foreclosed all notions of utopia, promise, hope, and progress. The fragmented images of the modernists registered the formlessness of life in the modern metropolis and made it out to be a disordered abundance of simultaneous sensory input. In the wake of Baudelaire, artistic reflection aims at capturing a radically modern temporal experience and giving it aesthetic expression. In this endeavor, it repeatedly returns to this idea of a fleeting moment, which has not yet been shaped by any cultural model or become part of any artistic repertoire.

---

6. Cf. Walter Benjamin, *The Arcades Project*, trans. Howard Eiland and Kevin McLaughlin (Cambridge, MA: Harvard University Press, 2003); Franz Hessel, *Walking in Berlin: A Flaneur in the Capital*, trans. Amanda DeMarco (Harvard: MIT Press, 2017); Virginia Woolf, "Street Haunting: A London Adventure" (1927), in *Collected Essays*, vol. 4 (London: Hogarth Press, 1967), 155–66; Harald Neumeyer, *Der Flaneur: Konzeption der Moderne* (Würzburg: Königshausen & Neumann, 1999).

7. Hans Robert Jauß, "1912: Threshold to an Epoch. Apollinaire's Zone and Lundi Rue Christine," trans. R. Blood, *Yale French Studies* 74 (1988): 42.

How Long Does the Present Last?

"Come what come may, time and the hour runs through the roughest day."[8] Macbeth adopts this stance to quell his anxieties about the future; he seeks to fit those anxieties into the standard of a homogeneous empty time. Nonetheless, the regular hourly clang of the mechanical clock and the ticking of seconds—time and the hour— are fundamentally different from the time of human experience. Although the minutes and hours incessantly tick throughout our lives, life is never really mechanically clocked by them. Quantitative time and qualitative life are fundamentally incompatible. To be sure, a controlling glance at the clock constantly reminds us to orient ourselves in time, but we really only follow the movement of the clock's hands in exceptional situations, and even then only for a short time— for example, when we're boiling eggs, sitting in a waiting room, experiencing the overtime of a soccer match, or awaiting the beginning of the new year on New Year's Eve. The human time of experience does not proceed chronologically, but rather concentrates and compresses itself in nonchronological presents that so thoroughly claim our attention that we completely forget the *linear time* that runs through them.

The decisive question is, therefore, the following: How long do these presents last that are not measured by the clock, and who or what establishes the measure for their duration?

The Present as a "Now Moment"

When we imagine time as a stream or an arrow that moves uniformly and irreversibly in one direction, the present is reduced to a nonextended now moment that is nothing more than the change of the future into the past. With every tick of the clock, the clock-hand shifts on the dial and so too does the present. This little slice of time, poised as it is on the cusp of the moment, has already vanished in the blink of an eye. Therefore, the now moment of the present is, as

---

8. William Shakespeare, *Macbeth*, ed. Kenneth Muir (London, New York: Routledge, 1996), act 1, sc. 3.

Baudelaire well knew, pure transition. Nothing rests on it and nothing can be built on it. Because humans are embodied and sensual beings, they are not made for this abstract time. They cannot live in the now moment; therefore, they extend it by means of their memories and their forward-looking expectations and make room for experience, recounting, and remembering and for anticipating, thinking, and existing.

The Present as the Time of Activity

The antithesis to the modern focus on the nonextended now moment is the age-old experience of the time of human activity. According to this schema, the present is always already extended, because time is imbued with human activities and gets its rhythm from them. The multiplicity and variety of these activities constitutes the patchwork of time. No one has summarized this so concisely as Solomon did: "To every thing there is a season, and a time to every purpose under the heaven: . . . A time to cast away stones, and a time to gather stones together; a time to embrace, and a time to refrain from embracing; A time to get, and a time to lose; a time to keep, and a time to cast away" (Eccl. 3).

Even our present is structured largely as a series of active processes: the time it takes to shower, drink one's morning coffee, ride the bus, share a bottle of wine, smoke a cigarette; the time a meeting takes, an evening meal, a card game—the day is an accumulated series of presents, the length of which is composed of these activities and measured according to them. Time is activity and activity is time—that is how we go through time from one present to another. The present lasts for as long as the activity; when it is completed, we prepare ourselves for the next one. Because the majority of these activities are repetitions of fixed routines, this active time always brings in new variations to what is already known and therefore predictable.

The Present as Fulfilled Time

The experience of the present as a precious or fulfilled time is radically different from these routines of daily life. It is based on a modern distinction between empty and full time that Tolstoy brings up in the context of the activity of dusting. After he has been dusting for a while, he suddenly realizes that he does not know whether he has already dusted a particular part of the room or not. Because he was lost in thought and not paying attention to this mindless activity, he no longer remembers the activity he had just completed. This discovery was deeply moving for him: When no memory can call up the time that has just been lived, it is as if it had never happened. For Tolstoy, life that is not consciously experienced is tantamount to an annihilated or unlived life. Virginia Woolf came to much the same conclusion when she distinguished between *moments of being* and *moments of non-being*. According to Woolf, the vast majority of our lives vanishes in the drift of time and in the related condition of *non-being*. The precious moments of the experienced present contrast all the more strongly with this mindless drifting, yet they remain "embedded in a kind of nondescript cotton batten." Like Tolstoy, Woolf also describes this cotton batten (or batting) of a neglected and unlived present: "One walks, eats, sees things, deals with what has to be done; the broken vacuum cleaner; ordering dinner; writing orders to Mabel; washing; cooking dinner; bookbinding."[9] The day is made up of so many presents that, while filled with the time of activity, do not yet amount to a fulfilled present. Indeed, the patchwork of these presents seems to preclude a forceful and definite present. The Russian art theorist Viktor Šklovskij wrote something similar in a famous essay from 1916 in which he examines the negative influence of automatization on perception. "And so life is reckoned as nothing. Habitualization devours works, clothes, furniture, one's wife, and the fear of war."[10] By means of a poetics of deautomatization—that is, art's alienation effect—he seeks to stimulate attention in new ways and, by complicating form, also to prolong perception. For Šklovskij, that is precisely the task of art: to reproduce the fulfilled present

---

9. Virginia Woolf, "A Sketch of the Past," in *Moments of Being* (Fort Washington, PA: Harvest Books, 1985), 70.

10. Viktor Šklovskij, "Art as Technique," in *Russian Formalist Criticism: Four Essays*, trans. Lee T. Lemon and Marion J. Reis (Lincoln: University of Nebraska Press, 1965), 12.

and prolong it. Likewise Woolf's moments of being emerge out of openness to and receptivity for anything that interrupts repetitive routines: the suddenness of surprises, coincidences, encounters. James Joyce spoke similarly of epiphanies—intense and unexpected moments that open a window onto reality and onto the tangible coherence of life.

The Present as Shaped Time

Unlike the epiphanic moments of a fulfilled present, which cannot be planned out in advance, the fulfilled time of aesthetic pleasure *can* be clearly mapped out and delineated. We enter into this present of art not by means of activity but by interrupting it. What is required for this present is bodily quiet: the necessary background for a state of relaxed attention. As an example, let us take a visit to the theater. The theater is a space of another temporality, a heterochronotope. Whereas time continues to flow uninterrupted outside the theater, we enter into another world inside it, one defined by its having a beginning, a middle, and an end. This triad is the sine qua non of how art shapes time—how it expands it and even brings it to an end. By means of this process of artistic or ritualistic enclosure, an expanse of time can be rounded out into a complete picture in a way that is simply not possible over the always open and diffuse course of a lifetime. The properly aesthetic time of an artwork directs the attention of the reader, the listener, and the observer—all of whom are bound to the format, the choreography, the narrative, or the performance. The most important signal that this distinct time frame of the theater is about to begin used to be the curtain, which opened and closed the stage; today it is the announcement to turn off mobile phones.

In the experience of art, attention is shaped, focused, and prolonged under very specific conditions. The theatergoer's ticket might have bought them a seat, but what they actually have to pay is more valuable still: their attention. Theater rests on a pact with the audience member that ensures their undivided attention, commitment, and participation. This is a precarious relationship: Distraction, inattention, and fatigue can take us out of the present of the theater at any moment. All the arts of illusion and participation fail when the reader or audience member does not devote a part or all of their attention. The audience member must therefore agree to a kind of imaginary contract stipulating not only that they will accept the laws of the work without reservation but also will give their undivided attention and become wholly involved in the work. Unlike in film, the theater must produce a common present for the actors and the audience with each new performance. But above all, the experience of time can be directly presented, shaped, and addressed on stage, by using forms that slow it down and speed it up, that purposely compress it or empty it, as well as forms that are exhausting, irritating, or disturbing.

Just as with theater, cinema, or a concert, a sports event in a stadium also offers the promise of a hetero-chronotope, by shaping time to supply a fulfilled present. According to the theorist of presence Hans Ulrich Gumbrecht, mass cultural events, such as spectator sports in huge stadiums, produce pleasurable feelings of wholeness by blurring the boundary between mind and body. The notion of "presence" here refers to the ecstatic state brought about by a complete sensual commitment to the present along with a heightened state of attention. As long as this fulfilled present lasts, the gates to the past and the future are closed and what is being celebrated is the here-and-now of the collective experience.[11]

The Present as Focused Time

The present as it is defined in art is closely connected to another possible way of experiencing it, which depends on how much attention we are willing to devote to something. When measured according to attention, the present potentially involves anything in our surroundings that is directly or indirectly accessible to us. What we focus on, in other words, could conceivably be anything

---

11. Hans Ulrich Gumbrecht, *Our Broad Present: Time and Contemporary Culture*, trans. Henry Erik Butler (New York: Columbia University Press, 2014).

that piques our interest: people, animals, landscapes, signs, or co-incidences.

The philosopher Ludwig Wittgenstein summed up the basic principle of attention in one line: "Where others go on ahead, I remain in one place."[12] Stopping to reflect makes one capable of entering a new present at any time. However, the ability to focus one's attention and, equally important, to engage in periods of quiet and continuous observation are skills that must be learned. On average, a museum visitor spends seventeen seconds in front of a picture, which is why this kind of viewing is ironically described as "walking away from pictures." Museums now provide visitors with audio-guides that captivate them for longer periods of time in front of each picture. The ever-shortening attention span that leads us to walk away from pictures, sounds, words, and information has become a general problem in our culture. It is merely the flip-side of a self-serve culture that has endless streams of media at its fingertips, all of which are desperately and shamelessly vying for that scarce resource: our attention. Anyone in possession of technological devices is flooded with news media of all kinds on a daily basis and is well aware of this competition for their attention. Such competition is particularly acute on the Internet. For instance, most videos on YouTube not only have a title but also a time indicator, and viewers are less likely to click on whatever lasts longer than five minutes. With the Internet, the issue of attention does not so much involve "Where others go on ahead, I remain in one place" as it involves the reverse: "Where others have gone, I too want to go." As such, the present of the Internet tends to be clocked in five-minute intervals. Of course, this interval is not to be confused with time spent surfing on the Internet, which can easily last for over five hours. Time spent surfing online clearly has nothing to do with a focused present, characterized as it is by constant searching, waiting, interruptions, crashes, distractions, and absent-minded clicking.

---

12. Ludwig Wittgenstein, *Culture and Value*, rev. 2nd ed., ed. G. H. von Wright, trans. Peter Winch (Oxford: Blackwell, 1998), 66.

The Present as Contemporaneity

The presents that we have been considering thus far all involve the brief or foreseeable time spans that people experience in their everyday lives. Yet the present can also last a great deal longer than the fulfilled time of the here-and-now. It can last for years, decades, and even centuries. To understand this, we only need to replace the word "present" with "presentness." To give an example of this presentness: In 1967, Heinrich Böll received the Büchner Prize, and his acceptance speech was entitled "Georg Büchners Gegenwärtigkeit" (Büchner's Presentness). Böll explains the phrase in the following way: "The trouble that Büchner caused possesses a surprising presentness; it is right there, present here in the room. It flashes up from five generations ago . . ." (376). Here Böll is both discerning and invoking the contemporaneity between the "revolutionary" Büchner and the youth protest movement of those who came to be known as the '68ers. In this sense, his speech resonates with a statement by Walter Benjamin: "For every image of the past that is not recognized by the present as one of its own concerns threatens to disappear irretrievably."[13] This present arises performatively—that is, when a historical epoch is reclaimed and proclaimed as contemporaneous with one's own, or when one discovers and confirms an inner kinship with something remote in time. The *missing link* that Böll uses to bridge the historical gap between Büchner and the protest movement of the 1960s, and that produces their contemporaneity, is Karl Marx: "It would be to lament one of history's missed encounters between two Germans. The encounter between Büchner and the slightly younger Marx. The powerful language of the 'Hessian Courier,' folksy but true to the material, is political writing which is certainly as powerful as the 'Communist Manifesto'. . . ."[14] By drawing a connection between Büchner and his contemporary

---

13. Walter Benjamin, "Theses on the Philosophy of History," in *Illuminations*, ed. and intro. Hannah Arendt, trans. Harry Zohn (New York: Schocken Books, 1968), 255.

14. Heinrich Böll, "Georg Büchners Gegenwärtigkeit," in *Georg Büchner und die Moderne: Texte, Analysen, Kommentar, Bd. 2: 1945–1980* (Berlin: Erich Schmidt, 2002), 378.

Marx, Böll rescues Büchner from the past—into which every writer risks falling—and pulls him back into the actuality of the present.

In the same speech, Böll also brings a current event to completion; that is, he relegates it to history and rejects it as past. With irony and disdain, he speaks of a great burial. He does not say who is to be buried; indeed, given the Darmstadt audience and what they would have known about the politics of their own time, he does not have to. We, on the other hand, must use Google to find out that on April 25, 1967, Konrad Adenauer was carried to his grave in an elaborate state funeral that took place in the Cologne Cathedral in the presence of international dignitaries. So, at the same time as Böll is signaling the end of the Adenauer era, he is also claiming close kinship with Büchner, a figure distant in time. In that sense, Georg Büchner's "present past" creates a shared space in which he is still relevant as an orientation-point in the present. That is how cultural memory, in which what is past remains present, comes into being: A community of those with common values and shared memories can be produced by canonizing past artists, works, and inspiring leaders. Such a community can be actively invoked over five (and a great many more) generations and serves both to promote self-understanding in relation to the past and to legitimize one's convictions and goals in the present.

The Present as Boundless Simultaneity

We should add one more meaning for the word "present" to our list that is quite different from the ones we have examined thus far. We find it in Gumbrecht again, who builds on a clear opposition between "presence" and "present." As we have seen, he equates "presence" with heightened or fulfilled time, but he uses the word "present" to mean "empty time." In his book *Our Broad Present*, he analyzes how time has changed in our age of electronic media. According to his assessment, in contrast to earlier times, the path to the future is now blocked, while at the same time the floodgates to the past have opened wide. All possible pasts now flow into our present, which as a result is constantly expanding and broadening. Gumbrecht's image for this broad present is a stagnant pond: Everything flows into it, but nothing drains out. His disturbing image is a variation on Nietzsche's image of the past as a tidal wave threatening to submerge the present. As we shall see in what follows,[15] Nietzsche's image is a description of the historicism of the late-nineteenth century, which he bemoans as an era lacking in character (today we would call this a lack of identity), haphazardly accumulating and mixing heterogeneous styles. According to Gumbrecht, new media technologies make it possible for us to save far too much past and maintain it in a state of constant retrievability, so that anything whatsoever can be seized on in the here-and-now. In addition to the media, he also cites museums, monuments, and memorial sites as further evidence for the total presence of the past, insofar as they are sites that make room in the present for more and more pasts. The critical point of Gumbrecht's argument, though, is that media culture and museum culture both produce a simultaneity of the present with any past whatsoever, and thereby destroy the possibility of a deep contemporaneity (for example, of the Büchner and the '68ers variety), because these latter alliances are grounded less on memory than on being forgotten and subsequently rediscovered. In our own time, Gumbrecht argues, things are quite different: The past is now permanently and even monotonously available. I will return to this dystopic idea of the present in greater detail later on, in the context of an analysis of the late-modern concept of time and a discussion of both old and new historicism.

So, there are many possible responses to the question "how long does the present last?" Fundamentally, it is always the case that the present, the here-and-now, is the only site that is lived and experienced and in which one can act and evaluate. Therefore, it is and remains the fundamental and privileged site of the living. As such, the present is the constantly moving position in time between what was and what is not yet. Beyond that, as we have seen, the present is also an experience with varying intensities. The presents that people create and experience last substantially longer than the abstract

---

15. See chapter 5, the section "Total Recall: The Rhetoric of Catastrophe and the Broad Present."

torque of a "now" moment at which future automatically reverses into past. In everyday life, the present lasts only as long as the activity that we are currently performing does, but these activities are apt to supersede each other and, as Virginia Woolf remarked, they do not add up to a more intense experience of the present.

For such an experience to happen, it must stand out from Woolf's nondescript cotton batten of the trivial and the everyday in order to become a presence. Being present happens when, through a sort of active-passive resonance, we give ourselves entirely over to an artistic performance or a sports event. This presence lasts only as long as the narrative arc of the artistically shaped present keeps us engaged and stimulated. Beyond the explicit structure of mediated or live performances, the duration of the present is also determined by our capacity to focus our attention. The present is not the outermost limit of a metronome beating ever more quickly, but instead emerges out of the human capacity to prolong time. Such lengthening can also occur by means of establishing historical connections or reclaiming a contemporaneity that builds a bridge between the past and the time of the now. There are no temporal constraints for this kind of influence that is produced when we recognize shared values and declare ourselves to be contemporaries of an earlier age. Beyond the short-sighted market cycles of coming and going, of becoming and then vanishing, acts of selection and institutions of cultural memory create "present pasts" in history. The canon, as a list of artworks that have no expiration dates attached to them, can be included as an example here, and so can the archive itself. After all, the archive makes it possible to discover ever-renewed and surprising points of entry into the past and then to restage those past moments in the present.

A broad present that records the entire past and completely effaces the temporal-ontological difference between the past and the present is a pure fantasy. To be sure, the fact that more and more of the past can be saved, collected, and deployed has made access to the past more open and democratic and, for that reason, more complicated. But it has certainly not led to a total flooding of the present *by* the past. On the one hand, such a claim overlooks the unremarkable powers of perpetual forgetting and clearing away that are daily features of life in an affluent society. On the other hand, it underestimates the complex selection mechanisms of cultural memory. For, in order for anything at all to remain present, a huge degree of attention and great cultural efforts are required. What is not, by means of a collective effort, selected, appraised, distinguished, staged, reclaimed, and repeatedly represented, will always fall back into a latent state of forgetting, or into that cotton batten in which we are all so deeply embedded.

2

WORK ON THE MODERN MYTH
OF HISTORY

Baudelaire's "now moment" represents an attempt to grapple with time as it is understood to shoot into an open future like an arrow, but also flow uniformly through the present into the past. According to this logic, the present itself does not last but only marks the tipping point where potentiality (future) turns into actuality (present) and then immediately becomes non-actual (past). As we have seen, one way in which this time becomes humanized is through the construction of presents as time-spaces of varying durations, in which sensuality and sense, experiencing and acting, thinking and communicating, remembering, and anticipating all become possible in the first place. By contrast, the representation of time as it is understood in modern physics is completely empty and abstract. It is radically detached from everything that, up to that point in history, had structured human ideas about time: natural cycles, mythic events, activities, cultural celebrations, or religious hopes. As such, it could become the standard that unifies all these cultural expressions.

In the seventeenth and eighteenth centuries, it was frequently emphasized that a new relation to time was being established that broke with traditional cultural time regimes and turned linear time itself into the backbone of Western culture.

Of course, this new temporal standard was neither abruptly nor uniformly established across the board, so the coexistence of different temporal forms continues to characterize even our own era. But research in sociology and history agree on the point that the culture of modernity was founded on the discovery of an abstract, nonsensual, and homogeneous time. As *the time of physics* was being cleansed of all human values, experiences, and cultural meanings, a concept of *historical time*—independent of whatever events and representations filled it—began to emerge as a stable *timespace* with a continuous existence and an unlimited capacity for extension.

A set of linguistic shifts can help us to understand the process of abstraction necessary for this modern concept of time. In 1770, a new concept of "history" in the singular arose and came to replace "histories" in the plural while, at roughly the same time, the abstract idea of "the future" (*zukunft*) came to replace the notion of "prospective" (*zukünftigen*). By virtue of these abstractions, time itself turned into an organizing principle and generated a great deal of long-term clarity; a unified system of world history could record all events as if on a huge world map. From the point of view of the tipping point of the present, the past and the future were extended as open-ended time-spaces, whereupon a great deal of confidence arose that the sciences could extend human knowledge in both directions. As Lucian Hölscher emphasizes, this notion of time is "not an anthropological constant, not a pre-given truth of human existence as such, but rather a specific historical form of thinking." With a view to the concept of the future, he adds in 1999, "we don't know how long this form will persist, but we can recognize how and when it developed."[1]

In the 1980s, a discourse had developed in ethnology and the social sciences that not only looked into the historical development of

---

1. Lucian Hölscher, *Die Entdeckung der Zukunft* (Frankfurt: Fischer, 1999), 10.

the modern concept of time, but also inquired more generally into the cultural production of time as a constitutive dimension of social reality.[2] One aspect of this meta-reflection on cultural orders of time involves looking at the metaphors we use to describe them and how the dominant metaphors, like "arrow" or "river," are directly related to the representation of time as the engine of change. Foundational tropes like these have since become the focus of research for comparative analyses of what Matt Hodges calls implicit "temporal ontologies," by which he means "an implicit or explicit theory of the nature of time and temporal experience that supports a metaphysical paradigm and is an unavoidable element of every social theory."[3] Mikhail Bakhtin's term "chronotope" also describes these temporal ontologies, highlighting the multiple cultural orders of time that establish literary genres, historical epochs, or societies.[4] This turn in the sociocultural analysis of time rests on the premise that we are no longer dealing solely with modernity's universal concept of homogeneous time, but rather with culturally established orders of time that make certain forms of being-in-the-world possible and that marginalize or make other forms impossible. The new questions that arise are as follows: In what ways does a particular temporal ontology influence human experience and activity? What are the implicit values and cultural meanings that inform the respective chronotopes? And, above all, for whom are they useful, and whom do they harm?

The relationship between time and the modern has been the subject of intense debate in many disciplines; in particular, the disciplines of physics and philosophy have made major contributions to these discussions. Here, though, we will sidestep the important work being done in those disciplines and focus our attention on the relation between time, history, and historiography. In the field of historiography, the modern chronotope took on a shape that deeply

---

2. Johannes Fabian, *Time and the Other: How Anthropology Makes Its Object* (New York: Columbia University Press, 1983).

3. Matt Hodges, "Rethinking Time's Arrow: Bergson, Deleuze and the Anthropology of Time," *Anthropological Theory* 8, no. 4 (2008): 417.

4. Mikhail Bakhtin, *The Dialogic Imagination: Four Essays by M. M. Bakhtin*, trans. Caryl Emerson and Michael Holquist (Austin: University of Texas Press, 1981).

informs our sense and awareness of time and, as will be argued in what follows, has had practical consequences for both our thinking and our acting. In this chapter, we will examine the foundations of the modern myth of history. Our examination will include historico-philosophical perspectives and ideas about progress, as well as contemporary theoretical concepts from the areas of systems theory and historiography. Because history and the modern are directly related to one another with regard to the issue of time, we will also bring theories of modernization and the modern to bear on our reflections.

Once again, we will begin with art—this time not from the mid-nineteenth century but from the beginning of the twentieth. At that time, innovative writers all over the world were experimenting with methods of representation to articulate new kinds of temporal experience. They broke away from the narrative conventions of the nineteenth century because they could not fit their new experiences of time into the straitjacket of conventional narrative style. For them, time was something that seemed infinitely more complex and all-encompassing than the notion of time that has it unfolding throughout the course of a narrated history, whose ending would then bring about meaningful and definitive closure. These writers realized that, up to that point, the novel had borrowed its temporal structure from history writing, and so it had remained confined to that structure. The aim now was to explode this confinement in order to make room for other experiences of time: of time as a stream that flows through life sometimes faster, sometimes slower, according to subjective perception; of time that one can leap out of and then gather the fragments through memory and put them together in new ways. Those who sought to explode the conventional framework of time and narrative created the modern *Zeitroman*.[5] Several important novels of this kind emerged just before the

---

5. Dirk Goettsche has kindly indicated to me that my use of the term departs from the more established meaning of the term, which distinguishes the *Zeitroman* (which shares characteristics with the social-realist novel) from other subgenres like the *Bildungsroman* and the family saga. According to Goettsche, it had already emerged as a genre by the end of the eighteenth century, its narrative structure being highly consistent with the basic tenets of the modern time regime. Dirk

First World War and were published shortly after in the early 1920s. Thomas Mann's *Magic Mountain* is one of these novels that no longer follows the destiny of a single family or a single protagonist in the form of a closed narrative arc, as his earlier novel *Buddenbrooks* had done. In *Magic Mountain*, we encounter a character who has no destiny and no clear direction; he functions like a kind of prism, refracting and then gathering together disparate observations and descriptions, conversations and experiences, theories and reflections. In another way, James Joyce abandoned the narrative scheme of the realist novel in *Ulysses*, in which he draws on the foundational narrative of Homer's *Odyssey* not to retell the story but to put it underneath his own text as a kind of template. By means of sharp cuts in focus, speech, and styles from chapter to chapter, Joyce eliminates all narrative structure from his novel. Instead of a time that is generated, shaped, and controlled by means of the narrative framework, this novel takes place over the course of eighteen hours on a single day in Dublin, "Bloomsday" on June 16, 1904, a day during which the various characters of the novel—each with their respective scenarios, issues, and obsessions—cross paths, come up against each other, lose each other again, or get tangled up with one another.

At the same time as these authors, Virginia Woolf also experimented with time in *Mrs. Dalloway*. Her narrative takes place over the course of a single day in London, beginning in the morning and ending late at night. We only see the characters through this short temporal window; whatever happens before or after can be glimpsed solely through what the individual characters remember or anticipate, for no omniscient narrator is present to tie the various scenes of a life to an overarching linear history. For Woolf, too, the clipped frame of a single day, measured by the regular ringing of the bells of Big Ben, offers no guarantee of a stable viewpoint generated by a grand narrative arc or indeed even by the characters' own destinal arc. In the brief temporal window that opens the novel, fictional people are moving along several life paths and toward various destinations, each driven by their respective concerns, memories,

Goettsche, *Zeit im Roman: Literarische Zeitreflexion und die Geschichte des Zeitromans im späten 18. und 19. Jahrhundert* (Munich: Fink, 2001).

and hopes, approaching each other and then losing each other again, brought close together through experiences of sudden encounter but also separated in that disconnected proximity. The experimental composition of this *Zeitroman* and its refusal to rein the characters into a collective, meaningful, and shared history gives Woolf the space she needs for unprecedented innovation in representation: She is able to explore the existential experience of anonymity and isolation among the masses in a busy city; the temporal pathologies of a character suffering from shell shock; the trauma of the First World War; and the suggestion of a tenuous veil mystically relating characters who never meet in their day-to-day lives. Marcel Proust's *In Search of Lost Time*, Andrej Belyj's *Petersburg*, Italo Svevo's *Zeno's Conscience*, and Andre Gide's *The Counterfeiters* are further examples of the modern *Zeitroman* that aimed to capture a more immediate sense of time by breaking away from traditional narrative models. All these novelists broke from the techniques of the realist narrative and invented new ways of representing an abstract but nonetheless lived time that gives their texts rhythm and reconfigures the narrative.

The notion of the *Zeitroman* comes from the work of Hans-Robert Jauß. In his dissertation on Marcel Proust, he argues that these modern experiments are directed "against a myth so lofty that poetic substance can be gained from its dissolution, the myth of history."[6] All the authors named above had a mutual opponent: the myth of history that had dominated the nineteenth century. As evidenced by Darwin's evolutionary theory right up to the emergency of the realist novel, the nineteenth century was obsessed with time as the engine of movement and permanent change. The understanding of history as an overarching process took precedence over all, shall we say, "timeless" truths and lived experience. Alongside biology, history became a leading discipline; all possible phenomena were only to be understood historically, so everything

---

6. Hans-Robert Jauß, *Zeit und Erinnerung in Marcel Prousts "A la Recherche du Temps Perdu": Ein Beitrag zur Theorie des Romans* (Heidelberg: Winter, 1955), 51 (chapters of particular interest are "Abkehr von der Geschichte" and "Kritik der historischen Vernunft").

became dateable. Historical narration dominated all forms of representation: "Historicity . . . immigrated into the very being of things, whose central characteristic became that *they developed*."[7] By 1900, artists began rebelling against this myth of history, along with its narrative structure of the *Bildungsroman*: that is, of progress or decline. They liberated themselves from the ideological implications of historicism and its obligatory narrative scheme so that they could discover new ways of representing experiences of time.

Developing the idea of the "myth of history," Jauß succinctly sums up the temporal ontology that these artists were dismantling. However, we should take care not to equate the word "myth" with "lie" in a critical or ideological sense, but rather translate it as "cultural construct" and understand it as a dateable creation with foundational power, philosophical orientation, and historical efficacy. The task is not only to dismantle such constructs but also to understand them as constructions. What kinds of constructive work has gone into them and what values and meanings do they offer? Historians created—and repeatedly re-created—the chronotope or temporal ontology of the modern myth of history. Yet the reverse is also true: That myth of history also served to create historians. So, what is this myth all about?

The groundwork for the modern myth of history and, by extension, the discipline of academic history goes back to the period of the Enlightenment. As has already been suggested, the discovery of the future and the past happened at the same time. We have Reinhart Koselleck's work to thank for the most important and the clearest description of the groundwork of the myth of history. He argues that in 1770, in the run-up to the French Revolution and its revitalization of knowledge, a successful semantic displacement took place that brought many ideas that had previously existed only in the plural under the singular for the first time. Art replaced the arts, *the* revolution replaced revolutions, *the* people replaced peoples, history replaced histories. Of course, this principle was not entirely new, since ultimately monotheism is itself the result of just

---

7. Albrecht Koschorke, *Wahrheit und Erfindung: Grundzüge einer Allgemeinen Erzähltheorie* (Frankfurt: Fischer, 2012), 278.

such a revolutionary singularization: The one *God* replaced the *gods*. This example makes it abundantly clear that the displacement of the plural by the singular can lead to fundamental changes in the substance of words. The singularization of the notion of art, for instance, made it possible to develop an entirely new aesthetic on the basis of both an abstract notion of art and a new art theory, which then also laid the foundation for a new liberal arts discipline. The same goes for history. Here, too, a new liberal arts discourse emerged that laid the foundation for a new faculty discipline in the universities. With the move from the plural of premodern histories to the collective singular of modern history, the narrative principle that shaped the earlier histories was the first thing to go. "Histories" had to do with occurrences that hang together at the level of narrative. These clear, engaging, concrete, exemplary, and often instructive histories were always histories *of something*; they were replaced in the course of singularization with an abstract and nonsensuous history. In that way, historical narrative lost the character of exemplarity and became a continuous series of events that stimulated curiosity as well as a thirst for knowledge. No longer oriented toward the repetition of something already known, history now sought to capture the new, the different, and the unique.[8] A new understanding of time accompanied this modern idea of history: Whereas until that time, histories had their own narrative-temporal structure inscribed in them, this structure vanished to ever-greater degrees in the transition to the modern and gave way to an "empty" time that would henceforth become the general framework for all histories. "Grasping past and future at the same time, 'history' turned into a regulative idea for all experience and for all that was yet to be experienced."[9] From then on, events not only took place *within* this homogeneous time, but they were also generated *by* this time. Time became the main engine driving historical change, emphasizing the new and

---

8. François Hartog, "Time, History, and the Writing of History: The Order of Time," in *History Making: The Intellectual and Social Formation of a Discipline*, ed. Rolf Torstendahl and Irmline Veit-Brause (Stockholm: Almvqvist and Wiksell, 1996), 102.

9. Reinhart Koselleck, "Geschichte/Historie," in *Geschichtliche Grundbegriffe*, vol. 2, ed. Koselleck et al. (Stuttgart: Klett-Cotta, 1975), 593.

disregarding the old. Following its modern singularization, history consisted of nothing but this singular process. It no longer ran its course up to its narrative end but was opened up to the future of an interminable sequence of stages and events. Once separated from their specific narrative structures, events were then ordered according to overarching points of view and transferred into this homogeneous and continuous time, which could then be accurately measured.

However, this is not quite the whole truth—for the modern idea of "history" did not entirely lose its formal elements or its pretense to wholeness. The process of history indeed took place in an abstract and empty time, yet this time did not proceed in a purely mechanical way; rather, it followed its own logic of development. No longer given in advance by a divine plan of salvation, modern history was certainly directed toward the future, but the dynamic of its development emerged out of itself.[10] These speculations about the logic of how development works its way through history generated both the philosophy of history and, most important, the idea of progress. In the nineteenth century, this idea served to close a now open-ended future by introducing a specific goal or end that could be anticipated. The empty site of the *telos*, or end, of history was thus filled and, from there, took on an all-encompassing meaning. Following the suppression of multiple histories and their narrative structures, a new narrative of progress emerged as the orderly structure of a unified history.

Transformations of the Idea of Progress

The concept of time in the natural sciences is completely divorced from the realm of human perspectives, needs, and experiences. This is as true of the time of astrophysics, which is measured in light-

---

10. Jean-Pierre Wils draws an excellent comparison between *historia sacra*, the Christian story of salvation, and the modern history of progress, in *Wandlungen und Bedeutungen: Reflexionen über eine hermeneutische Ethik* (Freiburg: Herder, 2001), 15.

years, as it is of nanoseconds, used to measure ultrashort processes. The same goes for the biological time of evolution, which grasps internal processes of optimization but contains no overarching teleology. Evolutionary biologists tell us that evolution goes on behind our backs and is basically "blind" with respect to human desires and planning: "Evolution goes nowhere, relatively slowly."[11] This is the fundamental distinction between the idea of evolution and that of progress.

In addition to the modern idea of progress, a traditional one should also be considered. According to the traditional notion, any possibilities that exist for improvement in the lives and the activities of human beings are grounded in the emulation and—where possible—the surpassing of positive models found in history. In other words, the normative reference point remains anchored in the past, for the improvements that become possible by learning from history are not additive and so do not result in an abstract cumulative gain but must always be learned anew in the present. The modern form of progress goes well beyond the activities that arise from individual people's efforts and desires, because the principles and preconditions in accordance with which one acts in modernity are themselves constantly being directed toward an envisioned goal in the future—even if that goal is ultimately unrealistic. This is how time becomes generalized and takes on the form of an overarching process that frames individual actions and gives them direction.

The transition from traditional to modern thinking about progress can be understood by means of a well-known idea handed down from Roman antiquity to the Middle Ages, and then to the modern period. The ancient formulation of this idea goes as follows: We stand on the shoulders of giants. In this form, the idea is perfectly consistent with the traditional time regime in which cultural foundations are anchored in the past. The scholar Bernhard of Chartres takes up this ancient formula again in the twelfth century when he writes: "We see more and further than our forebears did, not because we have better eyes or because we're taller, but because

---

11. Michael Ruse, cited in Eckart Voland, "Die Fortschrittsillusion," *Spektrum der Wissenschaft* (April 2007): 110.

we dwarfs are sitting on the shoulders of giants."[12] We see a particularly vivid expression of this idea in the four church windows of the Chartres cathedral, where the four apostles are sitting on the shoulders of the four prophets of the Old Testament. These images illustrate how the varying traditions of the Old and New Testaments are to be related to one another, according to Christian tradition: The Old Testament represents the roots and the foundation of the church, whereas the New surpasses the Old and develops beyond it.[13] Christian theologians used this image to emphasize that in the framework of Christian exegesis, the difference between the Old and the New Testaments is to be understood in terms of the one surpassing the other. In that way, the Old Testament can be affirmed as the ground and basis for a new future, one that is at the same time far removed from these very foundations. This past and this ancient world are irreplaceable and so must be preserved, though their normative power has clearly been weakened since another beginning has taken place in the interim that hugely diminishes the value of the first one. Because the Old Testament is not dismissed or rejected outright but continues to have value as a prehistory and necessary first step, the New Testament must both compare itself with and distinguish itself from what came before. To accomplish that task, it draws on a temporal dynamic of supersession, fulfillment, and contrast. As a result, the Old Testament is no longer considered an origin, but instead a point of departure for a new development.

---

12.   John of Salisbury, *Metalogicon: A Twelfth-Century Defense of the Verbal and Logical Arts of the Trivium*, trans. D. D. McGarry (Gloucester, MA: Peter Smith, 1971), 167. Bernhard von Chartres is cited here as the crown witness: "Bernard of Chartres used to say that we are like dwarfs on the shoulders of giants, so that we can see more than they, and things at a greater distance, not by virtue of any sharpness of sight on our part, or any physical distinction, but because we are carried high and raised up by their giant size" ("Dicebat Bernardus Carnotensis nos esse quasi nanos, gigantium humeris insidentes, ut possimus plura eis et remotiora videre, non utique proprii visus acumine, aut eminentia corporis, sed quia in altum subvenimur et extollimur magnitidine gigantean").

13.   The image is based on the Medieval hermeneutic tradition of so-called figural interpretation, in which episodes from the Old Testament are interpreted as a necessary prefiguration of the New Testament. See Erich Auerbach, "Figura," *Archivium Romanicum* 22 (1938).

Sir Isaac Newton also draws on this tradition of thinking about progress when, in a well-known letter to his friend Robert Hooke, he explains the temporal order specific to seventeenth-century systems of scientific knowledge: "If I have seen further, it is only because I have stood on the shoulders of giants."[14] Newton takes this idea from Christian biblical exegesis and applies it to the model of progress of the new natural sciences: Here, as well, the Old is permanently surpassed, and Newton expresses gratitude for the foundations that made their systematic overcoming possible in the first place. With a secularized notion of progress, a time frame extending indefinitely into the future would come to replace the competing accounts of salvation in the Hebrew and Christian Bibles. This period would no longer have to rely on religious revelations, but rather on the increase of human knowledge founded on empirical evidence.

Newton assumes the basic ability of humanity to further develop itself and set long-term goals spanning centuries and millennia. According to this model of evolution, the only material from the past worth preserving has already become part of the foundations of the present. We can imagine this cosmos of knowledge as a building constructed on solid foundations, ones that are partly recycled but sections of which are also abandoned and then further built up in new and different directions. The history of progress in the natural sciences has no use for obsolete knowledge or for the curiosity cabinet of scientific errors; these false starts and dead ends are therefore left to historians of science, who display them in their museum of rediscovered perspectives and reconstructed contexts.[15]

For a long time, the modern form of progress was one of the key elements in modern philosophies of history. This progress was not

---

14. Robert King Merton, *On the Shoulders of Giants: A Shandean Postscript* (New York: Harcourt Brace Jovanovich, 1985), 1. This statement became famous because of Merton's book; since that time, it can be found in most quotation anthologies. We should recall that Newton could only write such a thing because he inherited a highly particular Christian tradition.

15. Gaston Bachelard, *The Formation of the Scientific Mind* (Manchester: Clinamen Press, 2006). On this point, see also Hans-Jörg Rheinberger, "Über das Ausblenden," in *Potentiale des Vergessens*, ed. André Blum (Würzburg: Königshausen und Neumann, 2012).

blind, however, but was able to see its way toward particular goals through human planning, aspiring, and desiring. Progress meant interrupting the established order and opening up time in the direction of an unknown but positively evaluated future.[16] Throughout the course of the Enlightenment, the transcendent salvation that many had hoped for from an interventionist divine power gradually started to shift toward a progress that people themselves were capable of planning and executing. At the same time, responsibility for action, as well as its legitimation, also shifted from a religious to a secular framework. In small things as in great, people now became the creators of their own happiness, and of course they also came to bear responsibility for the increasing impact of their activities. In the foreground, though, the heroic opening of the horizon of the future for humankind as a whole stood on its own for a long period. In his essay on Bacon, Thomas Macaulay reads the long list of blessings brought about by science in order to reach the following conclusion: "These are but a part of its fruits. . . . For it is a philosophy which never rests, which has never attained, which is never perfect. Its law is progress."[17]

Hegel extrapolates from these developments in science and applies them to world history, the laws of which he defines as "progress in the consciousness of freedom." Whereas Macaulay's description of the dynamics of science still leaves open the issue of an actual end point or goal, Hegel constructs world history from out of the anticipated end of its completion. While the one argues from the present, prospectively, the other argues retrospectively from the position of a second future, a speculative "end point":

> It is this final goal—freedom—toward which all the world's history has been working. It is this goal to which all the sacrifices have been brought upon the broad altar of the earth in the long flow of time. This is the

---

16. Pierre-André Taguieff, *Du progrès: Biographie d'une utopie modern* (Paris: Librio, 2001). Reinhart Koselleck and Christian Meier, "Fortschritt," in *Geschichtliche Grundbegriffe*, vol. 2, ed. Koselleck et al. (Stuttgart: Klett-Cotta, 1975).

17. Thomas B. Macaulay, "Frances Bacon" (1837), in *Critical and Historical Essays*, vol. 2 (London: Dent, 1937), 376.

one and only goal that accomplishes itself and fulfills itself—the only constant in the change of events and conditions, and the truly effective thing in them all. . . . But as we contemplate history as this slaughter-bench, upon which the happiness of nations, the wisdom of states, and the virtues of individuals were sacrificed, the question necessarily comes to mind: What was the ultimate goal for which these monstrous sacrifices were made?[18]

Hegel's response to his own question is the modern narrative of progress regarding self-consciousness and freedom of spirit. This anticipated goal justifies all victims of history whom, when faced with the overwhelmingly positive pull of the future, one can mournfully disregard and gradually forget. Against the backdrop of this modern idea of progress, it is not difficult to make out the outline of a religious "promised land" of the future, a feature limited to monotheistic religions. The religious opening of new horizons in the future pertains to the destiny of individual people, to the history of a people, as well as to the anticipation of an end time that transcends all temporality. This devotional character still clearly resonates in Hegel's modern notion of progress and his idea of freedom, for "this endpoint is what God will with the world, and God is the most perfect and cannot will anything but himself, his own willing."[19]

The philosopher Karl Löwith has stressed that the "Christian and post-Christian outlook on history is futuristic."[20] His exploration of this hidden connection between the premodern and the modern leads to fundamental criticisms:

Conversely, it is only within a pre-established horizon of ultimate meaning, however hidden it may be, that actual history seems to be meaningless. This horizon has been established by history, for it is Hebrew and Christian thinking that brought this colossal question into existence. To ask earnestly the question of the ultimate meaning of history takes one's breath away; it transports us into a vacuum which only hope and faith can fill (5).

---

18. G. W. F. Hegel, *Introduction to the Philosophy of History*, trans. Leo Rauch (Indianapolis: Hackett, 1988), 22, 24.

19. Ibid., 23.

20. Karl Löwith, *Meaning in History: The Theological Implications of the Philosophy of History* (Chicago: University of Chicago Press, 1949).

In his analysis, Löwith underscores the central paradox of modern thinking about progress: On the one hand, progress is put into the hands of the people who made it and, on the other hand, it recedes as an unattainable good. Koselleck formulates this paradox clearly: "The self-proclaimed authority of 'history' grows with its constructability."[21] Here, the "superiority" of future-oriented history lies in the fact that a steady increase in planning potential is always accompanied by ever-greater degrees of unpredictability.

The narrative of progress—the Western myth of history—would go through quite different phases. For instance, the schema would reverse itself as early as the end of the nineteenth century after the euphoria over progress had reached its high point. For many skeptics and cultural pessimists of the time, the notion of a regressive development came to seem more and more plausible. Furthermore, what began in the nineteenth century as a speculative worldview turned into the ideology and politics of the twentieth century. The difference between the two lies in the ways they negotiate the horizon of the future. The *telos*, whose fulfillment the philosophy of history had pushed into the distant future, was suddenly within the reach of ideology. I call this form of possessing the future "utopianism." It places the end of history within reach of political activity and turns it into something that can be directly translated into reality.

This form of the myth of history is radically different from both a new historiography or an exercise in philosophical speculation; specifically, it is a political program involving unprecedented levels of violence. Under the influence of the left-leaning '68 movement, Odo Marquard speaks in the 1980s of "modern history's desire for fulfillment" and in that context warns of a "dangerous myth of the modern world," of "monomyth . . . of the one and only world history that is not grounded primarily in memory but in a form of expectation by virtue of which humans become the mere instruments

---

21. Reinhart Koselleck, *Futures Past: On the Semantics of Historical Time*, trans. Keith Tribe (New York: Columbia University Press, 2004), 39.

for the completion of progress."[22] Importantly, Marquard privileges a plurality of histories here over a unified world history, which he sees as a dangerous loss of modern checks and balances. With this warning about the monomyth of history and its potentially violent consequences, Marquard is directing his efforts against political appropriations of the future and therefore also against any grand "instrumentalization of anticipation by means of utopian illusions, including turning it into the sole aim of the future." Unchecked by experience and memory, according to Marquard, "expectations [can] become fused into a single great super-expectation: the eschatological expectation of a coming, and entirely different, ideal world" (81). As such, the modern myth of history has had many different phases, interpretations, and translations: from the singularized concept of history in the Enlightenment, along with its simultaneous differentiations and its new academic historical discourse, to the modern historiographical myth of progress and the violent realization of utopian "ends."

No wonder, then, that the word "progress," which rang of such great promise in the eighteenth and nineteenth centuries, has since fallen out of favor.[23] It only continues to be used with any kind of confidence in the areas of science and technology, and that is certainly related to the fact that in these areas, progress is still made up of small and painstaking empirical advances that are impossible to totalize by means of philosophical or political visions. Far from being taken seriously as the objective truth of the historical process, progress is generally considered to be more of an anthropomorphic fiction than anything else today. Why, neurologists have asked, does this idea resonate so strongly? Their answer is that both the linear flow of time and the idea of progress are useful constructions of the human brain "that has preserved itself evolutionarily by

---

22.   Odo Marquard, "Krise der Erwartung—Stunde der Erfahrung: Zur ästhetischen Kompensation des modernen Erfahrungsverlustes," in *Skepsis und Zustimmung: Philosophische Studien* (Stuttgart: Reclam, 1994), 73.

23.   "Only very few American writers in recent years have been concerned with social progress." Werner Mittelstaedt, *Das Prinzip Fortschritt: Ein neues Verständnis für die Herausforderungen unserer Zeit* (Frankfurt: Peter Lang, 2008), 12.

mastering life."[24] In this regard, the philosopher of biology Ernst Mayr speaks of a "final worldview" and emphasizes "that people are spontaneously inclined to be development-directed, and to interpret in light of a goal. Not least, religions become very attractive in light of such final worldviews."[25]

Nietzsche was a staunch critic of the idea of progress and thought little of such final worldviews. He challenged the historians of the nineteenth century with his highly untimely claim that world history had no goal. Hubert Cancik comments: "Game, not purpose; periods—orbit, circle, not goal: that was, for Nietzsche, a physical, historiographical pronouncement. It confirmed his doubt in the usual phrases used in the late-nineteenth century about the 'meaning of history' and 'progress of culture.'" Nietzsche summarizes his rejection of notions of progress in two clear statements. The first: "[W]orld history is not a unified process. Its goal is perpetually achieved."[26] He condemns progress and its fixation on the future in order to restore meaning and weight to the present. The second: With "time without all aim," Nietzsche rejects visions of the future; it is his way of lingering in the present. At the same time, then, he is also rejecting the construction of linear time. And here we come back to Baudelaire's discovery of the moment. For, like Baudelaire, Nietzsche also articulates an essentially modern sense of time that distinguishes itself from past and future in order to embrace the sensual experience and numinous quality of the present. Unlike with Baudelaire, however, Nietzsche's moment here has nothing to do with the transitory and everything to do with the mysticism of an eternal moment:

> Here I sat, waiting—not for anything—
> Beyond Good and Evil, fancying
> Now light, now shadows, all a game,

---

24. Voland, "Die Fortschrittsillusion," 108.
25. Cited in Voland, "Die Fortschrittsillusion," 113.
26. Friedrich Nietzsche, cited in Hubert Cancik, *Antik. Modern. Beiträge zur römischen und deutschen Kulturgeschichte*, ed. R. Faber et al. (Stuttgart: Metzler, 1998), 26ff.

All lake, all noon, all time without all aim.
Then, suddenly, friend, one turned into two—
And Zarathustra walked into my view. . . . [27]

The Theory of Time Underlying Modern Historiography

Now that we have established an overview of the dominant ideas related to progress, let us return to the modern myth of history, including the intellectual construct that arose around 1770 and laid the groundwork for a new kind of history writing. What were its historical preconditions, and which elements and preliminary decisions made it up?

Abstraction through Denaturalization and Deculturalization

The abstract measurement of time gradually spread with the invention and widespread use of mechanical clocks. This brought about two far-reaching changes. First, it represented a huge leap of abstraction that made it possible to distinguish time and event from one another and to decouple them. Second, the implementation of a mechanical measurement of time led to a uniform *universal time*. Before these momentous leaps of abstraction, time existed only in terms of the coexistence of different cultural orders of time that sometimes complemented and sometimes competed with one another. For instance, in the social sphere, the time of the church or the convent coexisted with that of the market, and there were also the parallel temporal universes of individual cultures, such as we still see today in the various festival calendars in China, or those of Judaism, Christianity, or Islam. The radical dissolution of cultural understandings of time created a new form of time in which different social and cultural systems of time all found a place and could therefore also be compared and coordinated. The sociologist

---

27. Friedrich Nietzsche, "Sils-Maria," in *The Gay Science*, trans. W. Kaufmann (New York: Vintage, 1974), 371.

Niklas Luhmann has proposed the concept of "world time" to describe this development of a "dateable temporal sequence" that is void of events, is abstract, is measurable, and that "progresses homogeneously, independently of observers."[28]

From the Now Moment to the Present—The Social Construction of Time

Luhmann was intensely engaged with the theme of time, though sociology as a discipline is primarily interested in the present, which is why one speaks of the notorious "presentism" among sociologists.[29] Luhmann's theory of time is chiefly synchronic; his interest lies in the social construction of the present. While the time of physics supplies an indifferent measure for the flow of events in which the present manifests itself simply as a "now moment" without extension, social time opens up a space of the present that has extension and in which simultaneous perceptions can be made, information can be exchanged, and activities can be coordinated with one another. Luhmann describes in depth how a nonextended now moment gets transformed into a lived social present. This social time is first brought about through human interaction; the extension of the present is defined through the range of people's actively pursued goals and the media by means of which they communicate. According to Luhmann, a socially constructed time that resists perpetual transience arises with the development of a system of social action—in the form of reciprocal expectations, through open channels of communication, and by maintaining identity through a series of changing conditions. The overriding sense of constant temporal loss is not eliminated by means of these stabilizing frameworks of meaning, value, and relevance; it is, however, given a relatively permanent shape and is thereby

---

28. Rudolf Schlögl, "Zeit und Ereignisse in der frühneuzeitlichen Vergesellschaftung unter Anwesenden," in *Systemtheorie und Geschichtswissenschaft*, ed. Thomas Kisser (Paris, 2013), 4. Niklas Luhmann, "Weltzeit und Systemgeschichte," in *Soziologische Aufklärung*, vol. 2: *Aufsätze zur Theorie der Gesellschaft* (Wiesbaden: Verlag für Sozialwissenschaften, 2009), 104ff.

29. See Edward A. Shils, *Tradition* (Chicago: Chicago University Press, 1981).

adapted to meet human needs. Storage techniques and communication media, such as memory and writing, play important roles in the development of social time by virtue of how they store otherwise fleeting voices and make them available or repeatable as communication.

The Separation of Past and Future—The Historical Construction of Time

Oriented toward the synchronization of past, present, and future in the context of social action, this approach differs markedly from the concept of time used in the discipline of history. Historians do not ask how what happened in the past is preserved in social time, nor do they ask how the future is anticipated; rather, they rely on the "natural course of time" that "continues into the past" and then disappears. Their understanding of time is diametrically opposed to the way people normally experience it:

> The need to appropriate the past and the future to one another even to be able to live is inherent to every person. . . . Every person and every human society has a sphere of experience which acts as a point of reference for further action and in which what is present only transitorily is or can be remembered, as well as specific horizons of expectation in relation to which courses of action are decided upon.[30]

The historian's profession undermines what people routinely depend on: The historian must do everything he or she can to prevent the different temporal modalities from intersecting. For historical time can only arise in the context of this difference between the realm of experience and the horizon of expectation—namely, in the context of the separation of present, past, and future. In that sense, the historian focuses exclusively on the past and, in order for him or her to be able to do this, the past must be clearly distinguished from the other temporal registers. Which temporal ordering forms the basis

---

30. Reinhart Koselleck, cited by Kari Palonen, *Die Entzauberung der Begriffe: Das Umschreiben der politischen Begriffe bei Quentin Skinner und Reinhart Koselleck* (Münster: LIT Verlag, 2004), 278.

of their research? And what role do the dynamics of modernization play in that ordering?

Systems-Time

The historian Rudolf Schlögl draws on Luhmann's theory of the social construction of time (or the present) to address these theoretical questions. In vivid detail, he describes the socialization of time, in particular, in terms of how articulations of memory and predictability determine the range of possibilities and produce the terms of engagement that make sense within particular historical parameters. Schlögl writes: "The social brings forth time and conversely, the social presupposes time—not the time of physics, but a phenomenon connected to the medium of sense."[31] However, as a historian, he must take another step: He must temporally contextualize these social "presents" and historicize them. Ultimately, he is engaged with *past* presents that form part of a reconstructed historical process. To gain a perspective on this overarching historical process, as a modern historian, he can neither draw on historico-philosophical speculations regarding progress nor rely on otherwise linear narrative schemas. For, in the post-historico-philosophical epoch, the open-ended historical process generates its own time and its own teleology. The abstract and invisible "systems-time" has since taken the place of the idea of progress, a systems-time that also structures the process of modernization. According to Luhmann, the dynamics of the temporal logic consist of a process of steadily increasing abstraction, rationalization, differentiation, and functionalist increases in efficiency. In that sense, it corresponds exactly with the basic requirements of systems theory, also called modernization theory. Since Max Weber and Niklas Luhmann, the "differentiation of cultural spheres of value" is considered to be the engine driving the modernization process. Modern societies are characterized by autonomous domains like economy, law, art, science, or religion. These fields have produced institutions with their own rules of operation that give each of them a high degree of autonomy.

---

31. Schlögl, "Zeit und Ereignisse," 3.

Modernization in this sense is nothing other than the increased checks and balances that arise as a consequence of the continual establishment of new and autonomous subsystems.

From the perspective of theorists of modernization, what is decisive in this regard is that this engine of the modern is certainly initiated by people, but it need not be further supported or maintained by them. The logic of these dynamics functions, namely, as an autopoetic (or self-reproducing) system, and the same goes for all systems that arise throughout the course of differentiation.

This process of modernization is likewise the historical process. For Schlögl, that process not only concentrates on increasingly complex stages, but it also produces an increasingly clear demarcation of temporal registers. In fact, the two—the separation of cultural spheres of value and the separation of temporal registers—are entirely consistent with one another: "The more diversity is produced in the models of differentiation of a society, the clearer the differences between and the de-couplings of the temporal levels of past, present, and future *must* be and the more abstract the concept of time *must* be" (emphasis added). The imperative of this temporal ordering is to decouple past, present, and future: "The present *must* be disconnected from the past so that action becomes possible" (emphasis added).

The organization of temporal modalities into future, present, and past is itself nothing new in Western culture. Rather, it had already been firmly anchored in the tense system of the Latin language, which is why, following Plato, Augustine could philosophize so eloquently about it in the famous 11th book of his *Confessions*. However, what is specifically modern about it is the cultural interpretation given of these temporal registers since the beginning of the monetary economy in the Renaissance and the Enlightenment. The future was freed up as a space of planning, foresight, and speculative transaction, and it also contained the promise of a lasting renewal and transformation of all relations. Simultaneously, the present was appreciated to a tremendous degree and, as we saw in Baudelaire's reflections on time, so too was life itself, which stirred the senses and mobilized attention. As well, the past was given a new cultural definition as that into which the present permanently changed, namely the "past" in the sense of out of date, gone, or obsolete, something from which one can definitively turn away. Whereas sociologists place the *present*—as the current space of action—at the forefront of their theory and research, historians define their subject, the *past*, as fundamentally over and cut off from any present. This clear distinction of the three temporal registers from one another seems to be a central structural element and feature of the modern time regime. But this has not always been the case. In his analysis, Schlögl acknowledges that with respect to the temporal logic of the modern, "the temporal registers of past, present, and future were not completely separated from one another" (16). This began to change in the early modern period when the future gradually started to become independent of religious hopes for the end time and Christian typological models of expectation. As a consequence, the future became increasingly available for this-worldly planning and speculative action—for instance, in a credit economy. A further push in the direction of rationality and system complexity arose with the historicism of the nineteenth century. Since that time, "the societies of Europe have at their disposal an idea of world time that not only clearly separates past, present, and future from each other, but that also for its part historicizes this trio to the extent that any by-gone present has its past and its by-gone future. Every current present will be the past of a future present" (5ff). According to Schlögl, the more developed a society is, the more consistently will it achieve the separation of the different temporal registers.

According to the account given by systems theory, since modernization is identified with this autopoetic systems logic, it acquires the status of an absolute force of nature. In that sense, the functional logic of the "system," as Chris Lorenz remarks, "becomes raised virtually to the level of the 'engine' of history. History was primarily understood to be the *evolution of this system*, an evolution that could be explained by theories of modernization. . . . So, *systems* advance to the rank of their *actual historical agents*."[32] The system

---

32.   Chris Lorenz, "Wozu noch Theorie der Geschichte? Über das ambivalente Verhältnis zwischen Gesellschaftsgeschichte und Modernisierungstheorie," in *Kol-*

that produces its own dynamic is both the engine driving modernization *and* the engine driving history. The difference between the two magnitudes becomes negligible, indeed impossible to measure. But that is only a question of perspective. Recently, it is more often the case that this systems logic and the logic of modernization are understood as cultural options and not as forces of nature, since we have begun to recognize that this system privileges certain possibilities for action and interpretation to the advantage of some while excluding other options to the disadvantage of others.

So, what *is* the modern myth of history? Let us briefly summarize. The consolidation of many histories into one single history opened up a new and unified perspective on the entirety of world history. World time was given a teleologically directed arrow, thereby becoming "world history." This systematization provided a universal axis on which different cultures could be arranged and hence grasped together at a glance, and it also made it possible to compare different cultures to one another, in accordance with which they could be ranked as more or less developed or undeveloped. A unified world time thus already contained the idea of progress. That is to say, according to Koselleck's argument, the basic experience of progress already has its roots "in the knowledge of non-contemporaneities which exist in a chronologically uniform time," a knowledge that becomes "a constant impulse leading to progressive comparison."[33]

In the newly emergent temporal scale of world history, it became possible to place different historical trajectories in relation to one another, but the one thing one could not do was learn lessons from history for the future. Modern theories of history provide a justification for the end of this possibility with two frequently repeated arguments: one involved the singularizing of history and the other had to do with the *historia magistra vitae* (an issue to which we will return in greater detail). Koselleck develops these arguments in great

---

loquien des Max Weber-Kollegs XV-XXIII, ed. Wolfgang Schluchter (Erfurt: Universität Erfurt, 2001), 107; emphases in original. Armin Nassehi's book *Die Zeit der Gesellschaft: Auf dem Weg zu einer soziologischen Theorie der Zeit* (Wiesbaden: Verlag für Sozialwissenschaften, 2008) is also based on systems theory.

33. Koselleck, *Futures Past*, 238.

detail, both of which enjoyed a kind of sacrosanct status in historiography. Evidently these arguments were closely related to one another insofar as both functioned to distinguish modern historiography from its predecessors. According to the premodern conception, histories in the plural still contained lessons that could be learned for the benefit of life and the future. That is, histories in the plural were written in such a way—with a worldly relevance, along with a colorful narrative style—as to be preserved in memory and heeded in the future. In other words, they had a forward-looking dimension in that they were directed toward the future. Modern history writing categorically rejected this orientation toward the future in terms of continued relevance or narrative structure. This forward-looking articulation of meaningfulness came to be replaced by the soundest possible reconstruction of past events. While the many narrated histories as well as the philosophy of history were directed toward the future, the science of history in the singular concentrated exclusively on the past. To ensure this exclusive focus at the level of institutional methodology, the past therefore had to be radically cut off from the present *and* the future. Temporal permeability in the account, whether in the form of historical lessons, worthiness of remembrance, or other kinds of interpretation, was no longer tolerated. Insofar as academic history turned toward the past, it had to shut down the collective horizon of the future, in relation to which premodern historians and their readers still understood themselves.

As well, the past had to be made distinct from the present. This separation of the past from the present is connected to the work of consciously bringing an earlier epoch to an end and inaugurating an emphatically modern time. To achieve this new freedom, there was only one possibility: "the subversion of the traditional experiential space, which had previously appeared to be determined by the past, but which would now be disrupted."[34] Subversion and disruption—this sentence captures something of the revolutionary mood in which modern historiography tore asunder existing links between temporal registers.

---

34. Ibid., 39 (from the chapter "Historia Magistra Vitae: The Dissolution of the Topos into the Perspective of a Modernized Historical Process").

On the one hand, the modern myth of history intended that historiography would radically separate the present from the future and the past and, by virtue of that separation, would empty the past of any future-oriented significance. On the other hand, all signs of the future vanished from society's temporal horizon. It is the argument of this book, as well as the motivation for writing it, that the categorical separation of the "space of experience" from the "horizon of expectation"—canonized in the academic world and repeated in liturgical fashion in practice—is not only a maxim of academic history, but has also been raised to the level of a foundational principle of modern temporal culture. The fundamental connection between past and future on which every person and every society depends is severed in modern culture, addicted as it is to distinctions and differentiations. The academic historian was prevented from building bridges between different temporal registers, and this differentiation has been adopted by the modern time regime as a whole. That is, the methodological restriction of historiography to a purely backward-looking science is directly related to its integration into an obsessively forward-looking sociotemporal milieu. The more radically the past as academic history is cut off from the temporal structure, the more could history as a whole move exclusively, and in an unrestricted fashion, in the direction of the future. The modern myth of history as was reconstructed and confirmed by the theorists of historiography of the 1960s and '70s ends up being both a reflection of, and a requirement for, the cultural time regime of modernity.

Modernization Theory and Theories of Modernity

The time regime of modernity remained indiscernible for as long as it could operate without being questioned. Throughout the last decades of the twentieth century, however, several pointed intellectual controversies shook the most basic cultural assumptions of the West's self-understanding. For example, in 1979, the philosopher and cultural theorist François Lyotard made his famous declaration regarding the end of "grand narratives," a phrase that held broad appeal as an expression of underlying skepticism about the modern myth of history. The grand narrative that he declares to be at an end was predominantly the one that recounted the (exclusive) progress of humanity in Western history. In the 1990s, a debate took place among historians, philosophers, and sociologists who sought to question certain aspects of the thinking around modernization. In a nutshell, the debate had to do with the question of whether terms like "modernity" and "modernization" are purely descriptive or whether they also contain implicit normative values and political orientations that are now open to scrutiny for the first time. In an essay from 2005, Riccardo Bavaj offers an overview of this debate and argues that the "classical theory of modernization," borne on an optimism regarding progress, was much more than an academic paradigm.[35] Rather, he understands it to be related to the wide range of cultural options that followed the American example of "competitive democracy, the market economy, the welfare state and mass consumerism."[36] Indeed, well before Bavaj, the Bielefeld historians Hans-Ulrich Wehler and Jürgen Kocka had already incorporated elements of nineteenth-century evolutionary theory and twentieth-century functionalism into modernization theory and, on that basis, had developed their own form of social history that met with wide acclaim in the late-1960s and early-'70s. As a rigorous scholarly application of modernization theory, this academic direction in social history also played a powerful role in the modernization of West German universities.

The obligation to modernize during the period of the Cold War was a norm that brooked no alternative: The stark choice was between Western democracy and the socialism of the East. However, many studies have subsequently shown that modernization theory

---

35. Riccardo Bavaj, "'Modernisierung, Modernität und Moderne': Ein wissenschaftlicher Diskurs und seine Bedeutung für die historische Einordnung des 'Dritten Reiches,'" *Historisches Jahrbuch* 125 (2005): 413–51.

36. Ibid., 414. Bavaj argues that in the United States—the land of modernization's utopia—theorists such as Immanuel Wallerstein had been arguing for a more critical understanding of modernization since 1979, whereas the German social historian Jürgen Kocka interprets the political turmoil of 1989–1990 as a historical "confirmation of the theory of modernization" (414).

was the common denominator shared by the two competing political systems. During the Cold War, "a dynamic" ruled "not of extermination but of competition; not of absolute enmity, but of similarities in the ideological origin and the social outlines for the future."[37] With the discrediting of communism, however, the modernization paradigm of the East was decisively rejected.

In general, modernization theory refers to a description of history that focuses on the emergence and development of Western industrial societies. Accordingly, modernizing development is understood as a far-reaching autonomous dynamic that sets in motion a sequence of so-called basic processes. In part, it is accomplished by individual people, but it also partially takes place behind their backs, as it were.[38] The central logic of these basic processes consists in what we have already described as the differentiation of cultural spheres of value such as law, religion, politics, economy, science, and art, and their development into autonomous systems and fields of action on the basis of new historical institutions. Administrative, economic, and scientific-technological developments belong to such basic processes of modernization, ones that initiate the dynamics of Western societies and keep them going. In turn, they generate specifically modern phenomena, such as "urbanization, literacy, [and] educational expansion," as well as the emergence of "classes and nations as new forms of political association" and the "emergence of individuals from out of their primary group-connections and modes of belonging."[39]

Seen in this way, modernization theory is nothing other than the "structural-functional" self-description of modern societies; their technical-abstract idiom focuses on "problems and solutions" as

37. Tim B. Müller, "Innenansichten des kalten Krieges: Über ein glückliches Zeitalter," *Zeitschrift für Ideengeschichte* VI/3 (2013): 27.

38. Wehler discusses six "subsystems": economic growth, structural differentiation, changes in values, mobilization, participation, and institutionalization of conflicts. Hans-Ulrich Wehler, *Modernisierungstheorie und Geschichte* (Göttingen: Vandenhoeck und Ruprecht, 1975), 16ff.

39. Lutz Raphael, "Ordungsmuster der 'Hochmoderne'? Die Theorie der Moderne und die Geschichte der europäischen Gesellschaften im 20.Jahrhundert," in *Dimensionen der Moderne: Festschrift für Christof Dipper*, ed. Ute Schneider et al. (Frankfurt: Peter Lang, 2008), 78.

well as "structures and functions" (to deploy some of the terms favored in the 1970s) that uncover, from a macro-perspective, tendencies of both this developmental dynamic and its template. The decisive factor in modernization theory seems to me to be the inseparability of analytical descriptive language and implicit normative premises: One can (almost) not speak about modernization without affirming the values attached to it. In brief, this has to do with a deep confidence—strengthened by rationalization, calculability, and feasibility—in the "growing mastery of humans over their natural and social environments" and, in that sense, with "the sustained expansion of its steering and performance capacities."[40]

This description of the modernization project comes from Hans-Ulrich Wehler's 1975 *Modernisierungstheorie und Geschichte* (Modernization Theory and History), a book that laid the groundwork for a new kind of social history based on American modernization theory. However, several revisions and corrections first needed to be made to historicize and contextualize modernization theory. So, in the book, Wehler undertakes a critical and penetrating examination of modernization theory with the goal of "developing an improved variant" through corrections and "immanent reforms." First of all, he replaces the idea of social progress with that of social change and warns against defining modernization strictly "as a normative theory, for example, of industrial, mass democratic, Western social states" or to equate it overly hastily with rationalization, industrialization, or secularization (44–47). In particular, he distances his theory from a one-directional developmental logic in the form of "chain reactions" and an automatic increase in interdependence, and he points out—"in the interests of greater historical accuracy"—that historical processes proceed largely by way of detours. In Wehler's view, the logic of modernization processes is an abstract matrix that does not allow for a one-to-one mapping onto the messy reality of historical processes. "To grasp the tension of real historical processes, we need to replace linear progression and victory of the new with an understanding of how the new coexists with the old, how they blend together, collaborate

---

40. Wehler, *Modernisierungstheorie und Geschichte*, 17.

with one another, and change each other in subtle ways. In short, how the traditional strengthens the modern and vice versa" (41).

Twenty years later, Wehler was forced to revise the close alliance between social history and modernization theory in even more fundamental ways. In particular, he detected a complete change in values in which "characteristics that had been seen as the strength of this theory in the optimistic 60s and 70s . . . started to be seen as weaknesses in the more skeptical 80s."[41] The strong integration with the West and the phenomena of Americanization were, in his view, perfectly consistent with the political climate of the Cold War and the game of modernization "catch-up" that the Federal Republic of Germany was playing. By affirming the forward-looking elements of Western modernization, West Germany "become anchored in the camp of Western modernity as a society that had learned the lesson of National Socialism."[42] After the end of the Cold War, Jürgen Kocka, a prominent cofounder of the Bielefeld School of social history, also noted that "the winds have changed direction." It had become more and more difficult to transmit the fundamental values of modernization to a new generation: "The language of the sixties or seventies sounded strange to many."[43] Kocka surmises that the turmoil of his generation was connected to the attempt—and the possibility—"to practice history as a form of enlightenment and learn from it. But now, people are also taking something else from history that is ultimately much more powerful: ownership of the past, memory, guarantees of identity, now and then also even entertainment" (18). That said, he then goes on to introduce a whole series of concepts and ideas that had no place in modernization theory. Kocka's idea of an enlightened learning from history was obviously meant to indicate something entirely different from "ownership of

---

41. Wehler, cited in Lorenz, "Wozu noch Theories der Geschichte?," 111.

42. Thomas Welskopp, "Westbindung auf dem 'Sonderweg': Die deutsche Sozialgeschichte vom Appendix der Wirschaftsgeschichte zur historischen Sozialwissenschaft," in *Geschichtsdiskurs, Bd. 5: Globale Konflikte, Erinnerungsarbeit und Neuorientierungen seit 1945*, ed. Wolfgang Küttler et al. (Frankfurt am Main: Fischer, 1999), 210ff.

43. Jürgen Kocka, "Historische Sozialwissenschaft heute," in *Perspektiven der Gesellschaftsgeschichte*, ed. Manfred Hettling et al. (Munich: Beck, 2002), 6.

the past." In an essay entitled "Rückblick und Ausblick, oder: Arbeiten, um überholt zu werden" (Hindsight and Outlook, or Working
in Order to Be Surpassed), Wehler also discusses "the weakening
belief in progress and the increasing doubt in the project of Western
modernization" as well as "how attractive the idea is that culture
could be an independent field of action enabling change and intervention in highly complex societies."[44] For Eric Hobsbawm, this momentous intellectual and academic-political turn of the 1980s could
be recognized in the fact that "things were going downhill for structure, and uphill for culture."[45] The academic dispute regarding
schools of thought, fought out around the battle cries of "structure"
and "culture," was essentially a controversy over the validity and
applicability of modernization theory. This aspect, which implicitly
fueled these academic controversies, has subsequently become the
subject of explicit reflection and discussion.[46]

In his manifesto on modernization theory and history, Wehler
had already warned against repressing "ambivalences, dissonances,
downsides of the 'dialectic of enlightenment,'"[47] precisely the ambivalences and dissonances that became important themes in critical

---

44. Christoph Conrad, "Die Dynamik der Wenden: Von der neuen Sozialgeschichte zum *cultural turn*," *Geschichte und Gesellschaft. Sonderheft, Vol. 22,
Wege der Gesellschaftsgeschichte* (2006), 154. Conrad is referring here to Wehler's
lecture "Rückblick und Ausblick, oder: Arbeiten, um überholt zu werden?" (Bielefeld: Universitätsverlag Bielefeld, 1996). Wehler makes no secret of the fact that he
is suspicious of the approaches taken in the field of cultural studies and thinks little
of the "adepts of the memory cult." On this point, see Wehler, "Was uns zusammenhält: Zum Auftakt des mehrbändigen Projekts über 'Deutsche Erinnerungsorte,'" *Die Zeit*, March 22, 2001, 28.

45. Christoph Conrad has examined this trend reversal in historical research
by tracing the use of the terms "modernization," "the modern," and "postmodern"
in academic journals between 1955 and 2005. For the term "modernization," he
registers a rapid increase in its use in the 1960s with a high point in the first half of
the '70s, followed by an abrupt drop that intersects with a rise in the use of the
terms "the modern" and "postmodern" in the middle of the '80s. The drop-off in
use of these latter ideas coincides with a rise in the use of the terms "culture" and
"identity." Conrad, "Die Dynamik der Wenden." The citation from Hobsbawn is
from p. 136.

46. See Bavaj, "Modernization, Modernity, and the Modern," and Lorenz,
"Wozu noch Theorie der Geschichte?"

47. Wehler, *Modernisierungstheorie und Geschichte*, 44.

theories of modernity.[48] In using the phrase "theories of modernity," I am referring to a cultural, historical, and philosophical perspective that confronts phenomena that the concept of modernization leaves untouched including, for instance, radical political ideologies, fanaticism, violence, and trauma. Seen from this perspective, the unleashing of an unprecedented potential for violence and destruction during the two world wars no longer appears as a departure from modernity, but rather as one specific phase of it, namely the "high modern" (Ulrich Herbert). The critical theory of Theodor Adorno and Max Horkheimer (to which Andreas Huyssen is also committed) had already developed the concept of a "dialectic of enlightenment" to probe the modern at the level of deep psychology and to work out its ambivalences and inner contradictions. "The curse of irresistible progress is irresistible regression," state the authors in *Dialectic of Enlightenment*.[49] As was also the case in the work of Walter Benjamin, Adorno's notion of "barbarism" appears as the flipside of modernity whose end can never be guaranteed; his claim was that the patterns of totalitarian violence that civilization engenders from out of itself therefore arose "not at the moment when [modernity] collapses but as part of its proper functioning."[50]

---

48. Max Miller and Hans-Georg Soeffner, eds., *Modernität und Barbarei: Soziologische Zeitdiagnose am Ende des 20.Jahrhunderts* (Frankfurt am Main: Suhrkamp, 1996).

49. Theodor W. Adorno and Max Horkheimer, *Dialectic of Enlightenment*, ed. Gunzelin Schmid Noerr, trans. E. Jephcott (Stanford: Stanford University Press, 2002), 28.

50. Bavaj, *Modernisierung, Modernität und Moderne*, 431; see also Jan Philipp Reemtsma, "Das Implantat der Angst," in *Modernität und Barbarei: Soziologische Zeitdiagnose am Ende des 20.Jahrhunderts*, ed. Max Miller and Hans-George Soeffner (Frankfurt am Main: Suhrkamp, 1996), 31; Gertrud Koch, *Bruchlinien: Tendenzen der Holocaust Forschung* (Vienna: Böhlau, 1999). H. D. Kittsteiner's work is closely affiliated with Benjamin's *Urgeschichte* (deep history) and also with Horkheimer and Adorno's in-depth analyses, in that his primary concerns are the visions and images central to modernity's cultural repertoire. Creating what he calls a "layered history of modernity," he is able to track the historical changes of the modern project, in addition to showing the underlying continuity, the *subplot*, of the "modern project" that runs throughout the different epochs and has left behind a problematic legacy in the cultural unconscious. Heinz D. Kittsteiner, *Wir werden gelebt: Formprobleme der Moderne* (Hamburg: Philo & Philo, 2006).

In his provocative work *Modernity and the Holocaust* (1989), Zygmunt Bauman confirms Horkheimer and Adorno's pioneering argument regarding the theory of modernity from a sociological perspective. His book integrates the crimes against humanity committed in the twentieth century into a history of civilization.[51] According to Bauman, "[t]he holocaust was not an antithesis of modern civilization and everything (or so we like to think) it stands for." It is much more the case that this historical event revealed another face of modern civilization and shows that "[e]ach of the two faces can no more exist without the other than can the two sides of a coin" (7). The Holocaust has taught us that a bureaucratic rationality committed to a pure principle of efficiency is ethically blind and could easily be associated with any aim whatsoever. Therefore, within a modern climate of reification, anonymity, discipline, and classification, the rules of instrumental rationality could also turn the factory-like massacre of European Jews as a perverse form of "social engineering" into an overriding process that paralyzes individuals' capacity to experience empathy or exercise moral judgment. Bauman's analysis represents a decisive turn in the discourse about modernization and modernity, insofar as he exposes the ethical blind spot in the structural-functional basic processes of "modernization." His work is therefore situated between two different perspectives: between the affirmative perspective implicit to modernization theories, whose discourses depict the system as a quasi-natural process of problems and solutions, of structures and functions in ever-increasing degrees of complexity, and the more pessimistic outside perspective of critical theories of modernity that exposes contradictions and ambivalences using in-depth psychological and cultural arguments and that opens up possibilities for some critical distance.

While modernization theory is based on the modern myth of history in the sense of a progressive self-empowerment of people through science and technology, critical theorists of modernity radically call this idea of progress into question. Indeed, in light of the

---

51. Zygmunt Bauman, *Modernity and the Holocaust* (Cambridge, UK: Polity Press, 1989).

catastrophes of the twentieth century, the instrumental rationality integral to modernization theory takes on an entirely different aspect: Critical theorists of modernity hold that this logic can also be connected to a dangerous ideological hubris regarding the total operationalization of history or to the presumption of certainty and control vis-à-vis its planning. As such, it can lead to unimaginable excesses of violence and the greatest catastrophes in human history. With the collapse of communism, the utopian dream about the human ability to plan and project also collapsed. In place of grand narratives, visions, and utopias, a deep skepticism and a cautiousness arose regarding all ideological projects promising a "new humanity" that would be carried out with no regard for human victims, posterity, or even the environment.

As part of this intellectual confrontation with aspects of modernity, any normative interpretation of classical modernization theory that "canonized, as it were, the status quo of Western industrial nations" should be rejected.[52] But, unlike with postmodernity, this new impetus toward self-critique did not lead to a radical break from the modern project. The heirs of Western cultural development could not simply make a clean break from the premises of the modernization project because they are, as before, the inheritors and beneficiaries of a world that was created on the basis of those premises. Moreover, they remain dependent on the expert knowledge of this culture for the solutions to many of the problems that arose as a consequence of the modernization process in the first place. The radical skepticism regarding modernization can therefore neither undo the Western route of modernization nor simply reject it. Particularly in the areas of science and technology, the thinking about modernization that created and continues to create the basic requirements for our lived world—ones that we could not and *would not want* to do without—still constitute an important part of the core inventory of Western thinking. At the same time, this thinking has meanwhile been subject to serious challenges by other cultural models—and some of these challenges have even been acknowledged

---

52. Bavaj, *Modernisierung, Modernität und Moderne*, 447.

by public apologies—yet it is also the case that it has submitted its own premises to critical examination and modification. What is therefore needed is a historical exercise in self-reflection regarding particular aspects and premises of the tradition of modernization that can form the basis of a more critical and prudent engagement. The present study can be understood as a contribution to just this kind of historical self-examination. To that end, we shall focus on a single, yet decisive, strand of this web—namely, the time regime of modernity.

When Does the Modern Begin? Phases of Modernization in Western History

At the very center of the time regime of modernity, we find a decisive turn toward the future that simultaneously involves the devaluation of the past and tradition. This very abstract description concerns a turning point in the history of ideas that did not appear once and for all but rather has repeatedly taken place under varying historical conditions and in many different forms. Historians have repeatedly tried to represent the history of this conceptual breakthrough of the modern as a one-time event that becomes incorporated, in clearly dateable fashion, into the course of a history—a historical course that, at the same time, it structures. Reinhart Koselleck has proposed such an approach with his idea of a "saddle period." He is referring to a caesura around 1770 that marks a one-time, irreversible, and all-encompassing new direction for all fields of cultural life, knowledge, and action. This proposal has been generally accepted in historical scholarship, since it has the advantage of establishing a clear starting point for the history of modernization. There is, however, something to be said for unsettling this established beginning and replacing the collective singular term "modern" with a plurality of "phases of modernization" that have taken place at various times and under different conditions. Therefore, we shall consider modernization here less as a one-time historical turning point and certainly not as a narrative, and more as an impulse or energy of Western culture that gets released or implemented, in one way or another, in different historical contexts.

In what follows, examples will be given of such phases of modernization. Only when taken together do they represent the phenomenon of modernization that, even in terms of a latent potential ready to be awakened and deployed, has largely determined the dynamics of Western cultural history. The implication here is that the modern is not a stable characteristic of Western culture but is above all a process that has the character of an injunction and continually renewed goals. However, at the same time, this also implies that it can have extremely varied qualities: Aside from decisively active phases of innovation, it also includes stable and institutionalized forms, or the simple preservation and—in the sense of dialectical countermovements—reproduction of nonmodern structures. The following summary of the important phases of modernization in history is organized chronologically. However, what finds expression here is less a clear linear development than a cluster of heterogeneous impulses, values, programs, and practices, all of which build on one another in the history of modernization in direct or indirect ways. As modernization is so often identified with secularization and the separation of church and state, the foundation of modernization within Jewish and Christian monotheism may come as a surprise. But when we automatically assume that religion falls on the side of an ossified tradition and an obsolete past, we underestimate a crucial source of energy in Western culture from which even secular modernization movements continue to draw.

(1) Modernization's "big bang" took place in the break of Jewish monotheism with, and its departure (exodus) from, the world of polytheistic cultures. In the course of this departure, movements of delimitation and lines of demarcation emerged that were utterly decisive for the history of Western culture. In this sense, more significant even than the "mosaic distinction" (Jan Assmann) between true and false religions was the ontological distinction between God and world. The strong connection that bound the gods with the world in all polytheistic religions was severed in the biblical myth of creation, which

introduced a clear distinction between the creator and his work. The Jewish monotheistic God no longer resides in the world but has withdrawn from it into new and abstract spheres, such as scripture, cult, the people, or history. In the course of this withdrawal, the world was suddenly reduced to the profane, the disenchanted, the objectified, the materialized, and the site of human responsibility. Analogous to the distance between creator and creation, a division arose between matter and spirit that developed in Jewish monotheism and Greek philosophy at the same time. This division finds stark expression in the prohibition against images.[53] The worshipped "living God" is disembodied and is thereby sharply distinguished from the "dead graven images" representing the pagan gods.[54]

Monotheistic religions break ranks more or less systematically with polytheistic religions that are animated by the immanence of the divine and establish no clear boundary between the gods and the world. The revolutionary step from "the gods" in the plural to "god" in the singular is related to this turn toward monotheism, which Koselleck will later trace in notions such as histories/history or arts/art, in relation to which he showed how singularization creates entirely new meanings and discourses. Even more decisive for religion than the step from plural to singular, which was already present in polytheistic religions, was the step from cosmos to scripture as the fundamental medium of religious revelation. Just as the Israelites left Egypt, the land of polytheism, so too did the biblical God leave the pantheistic world in order to reveal himself exclusively in the medium of scripture, which at the same time established the basis for the mobility of this religion. By means of the Torah, the Jews created a "portative fatherland" (Heinrich Heine) for themselves, which allowed them to distance

---

53. Striking examples of the confusion of boundaries between the divine and the material in pagan religions can be found in the satirical accounts of such cultural practices. These can be found in Jeremiah 10 and Isaiah 44.

54. This revolutionary division was an irreversible step that propelled history in the direction of scientific research and technologized progress.

themselves from local sacred sites and overcome territorial boundaries.

The biblical God mysteriously defines himself as "I am, that I will be" (Exodus 3:14). A new dimension of the future is developed in this sentence, one that also opens the course of history and releases it for the process of becoming. Jan Assmann has characterized religion in Thomas Mann's *Joseph* novels using the formulation "God is the future," highlighting their distinctly modern character. Here we have a god in a state of becoming, "cutting across the mythical time of the eternal return and circling simultaneity. . . . God's time is the linear time of becoming, promise, fulfillment. With 'God,' directionality and the future enter into human time. The direction of this future time is no better characterized than by Sigmund Freud's 'progress in spirituality,' or by Max Weber's idea of 'rationality and world disenchantment.'"[55]

(2) Christianity undercut a number of the basic premises of monotheism: the becoming-flesh of the word as the transmission of the Holy Scriptures; the introduction of the trinity; the cult of images; and the (occasional) recognition of nature as the domain of divine revelation. But for all that, Christianity profoundly strengthened the dimension of futurity and expectation active in history, given the imminent eschatological expectation of the end of the world and the return of the Messiah. For example, Luke recounts an episode in which he describes the situations of Christ's disciples and emphasizes how destructive their radicalism is for culture: "And he said unto another, Follow me. But he said, Lord, suffer me first to go and bury my father. Jesus said unto him, Let the dead bury their dead: but go thou and preach the kingdom of God. And another also said, Lord, I will follow thee; but let me first go bid them farewell, which are at home at my house. And Jesus said unto him, No man, having put his hand to the plough, and looking back, is fit for the kingdom of God" (Luke 9:

55. Jan Assmann, *Thomas Mann und Ägypten: Mythos und Monotheismus in den Josephsromanen* (Munich: Beck, 2006), 197ff.

59–62). This radical expectation of the future, accompanied by a break from the past and the prohibition of memory, has often been reinvoked during revolutionary historical movements. In a letter written to Arnold Ruge, for instance, Karl Marx anticipates the breakthrough of a new time and says the following: "Let the dead bury the dead and mourn them. In contrast, it is enviable to be the first to enter upon a new life: this shall be our lot."[56] A less radical orientation toward the future, borne by the feeling of certainty regarding a gradually higher development, relates to the concept of time within Christian typology. In this instance, the paradigmatic instance of progress is the overcoming of the Old Testament and its replacement by the New Testament. This normative foundation would also set the stage for the Enlightenment optimism about progress in terms of its dominant ideas of time and development, which took its inspiration from that foundation. To sum up: With the emergence of Jewish and Christian monotheism, an entire set of crucial boundaries was being redrawn, such as those of matter/spirit, dead/living, past/future, and old/new. At the same time, these new boundaries created the decisive prerequisites for modernization in that they form the hot nucleus (and, indeed, one never to be extinguished) of the modernization project.

(3)   Although there were certainly important phases of modernization throughout the period of the Middle Ages, historical scholarship most often depicts the epoch of early modernity as an example of the first important social phase of modernization. The notion of "modern" (*Neuzeit*) first appeared in the nineteenth century and was not yet being used as a self-description.[57] However, it cannot be denied that this epoch is characterized by a great deal of innovation: mechanical clocks, the compass, gunpowder, and the printing press had all radically changed the

---

56. Karl Marx, "To Arnold Ruge" (May 1843), in *Early Writings*, trans. R. Livingstone and G. Benton (London: Penguin, 1992), 200.

57. Reinhart Koselleck, "Wie neu ist die Neuzeit?," in Koselleck, *Zeitgeschichten: Studien zur Historik* (Frankfurt am Main: Suhrkamp, 2003), 227.

known world. Newly opened transportation routes made new raw materials available and expanded territories on the other side of the Atlantic, which led to the establishment of worldwide colonial powers. In this epoch, which saw the invention of the literary genre of utopianism as well as new forms of strategy and planning, the idea of the future was being subject to fundamental changes. The distinction Koselleck introduces between "space of experience" and "horizon of expectation" (a distinction we will come back to in greater detail) is thus based on precisely this sixteenth-century phase of modernization. Lucian Hölscher writes that during that time, "'[s]paces of experience'—in the sense of the dominance, in the lived world, of traditional, and above all, religious certainties about and attitudes toward being—are gradually being devalued as a consequence of multiple processes of rationalization and secularization . . . and are being replaced by 'horizons of expectation' in the sense of open options regarding decisions and action."[58] One aspect of the way the future was understood—the one framed by religious hopes and expectations and by perspectives on the totality of things—was neutralized and opened up for the purposes of practical action and strategic planning within the purview of human responsibility. Members of the expanding middle class would be the ones to profit most from this phase of modernization, which had hardly any effect at all on the aristocracy, and even less on rural populations. As well, the middle class of the early modern period established itself as a newly active subject and quite self-consciously entered onto the stage of history. Indeed, it became the most important sponsor of the modernization program; the middle-class goals and values of innovation, adventure, and risk, but also planning, self-discipline, and self-formation, were all being constituted on the basis of the new temporal order. In the context of expansionist politics, colonialization, modern warfare,

---

58. Alexander Schmidt-Gernig, review of Lucian Hölscher, "Die Entdeckung der Zukunft," in *H-Soz-u-Kult*, February 10, 2000; hsozkult.geschichte.hu-berlin.de/rezensionen/252.pdf.

and an increasingly speculative capitalist and market economy, an abundance of what Peter Burke calls "practices of the future" emerged in which the dangers and threats associated with the sudden opening of the horizon of the future were interpreted as either chances or calculated risks.

(4)   In no way were all signs pointing toward the future during this time, however. Seen from the perspective of artists and humanists, this was the era of a Renaissance informed by two complementary developments. On the one hand, there were the new values of originality and self-conscious innovation. On the other hand, philological and historical standards were being developed for engaging with tradition, including its professionalized critique, its interpretation, and its stabilization. Over the temporal distance of the Middle Ages, Roman and Greek antiquity were being newly discovered and assessed and their legacies philologically reworked. So, the future-oriented discoveries that were taking place were supplemented by the rediscovery and the reappropriation of a supposedly timeless past. This connection to antiquity, alongside the Bible, created a place in Western cultural memory for the secular worship of images and texts. While, on the one hand, role models from the classical period were celebrated as unsurpassable, on the other hand, a new artistic practice arose that was making its own claim to innovation and to its own form of immortality.

(5)   Koselleck considers the actual modern period to be the age of Enlightenment insofar as, like the American and French revolutionaries, it had developed a discourse that was highly conscious of the novelty or newness of its own time. One no longer imagined oneself at the end of an old age but at the beginning of a new period; "the future was opened up, and an independent humanity—at least a literarily and intellectually self-determining one—prepared itself to gradually master this future or, as one began saying at that time, to make history."[59] Koselleck describes this historical phase as a saddle period that marks an epochal line between the premodern and modern

---

59.   Koselleck, "Wie neu ist die Neuzeit?," 227.

worlds and gives to that period the overarching law of the modern dynamics of history. The discovery of universalistic concepts like "humanity" belongs to this phase of modernization. Similar to Jasper's notion of "axial age," Koselleck's saddle period also generates the notion of the autonomous and self-determining individual, a notion with which we still live. On the one hand, the historiography of the saddle period suggests that this new individual arose at the end of the eighteenth century like a phoenix out of the ashes and was permanently enshrined as a stable norm in Western culture. On the other hand, we have meanwhile developed a rich understanding of the challenges and difficulties associated with the autonomous individual—in the face of which this universalist norm must be constantly reclaimed and newly asserted.

Like his Bielefeld colleague Reinhart Koselleck, Hans-Ulrich Wehler too has modernization begin with an "epochal break in the out-going eighteenth century." At the same time, he emphasizes that "the caesura, the breakthrough of the 'modern,'" must be further clarified on the basis of an adequate historical theory. The American and French "double revolution," he argues, when taken together with the industrial revolution in Great Britain, constituted a "specific starting point" that introduced a new type of social change. This epochal change was provoked through the "economic and political advance of some pioneer societies and the processes of change that followed on the part of late-comers," who at that point had gotten caught in the maelstrom of modernization.[60]

This phase—this "maelstrom of modernization"—was also tied to a new classical period in which a focus on the future was once again dialectically paired with a safeguarding of the past. While every additional phase of modernization causes the present to vanish with increasing speed, complementary phases of the canonization of "classics," most notably in the subsystem of art, work to suspend the iron law of ever-faster rates of change and also to establish new phases that embrace

---

60. Hans-Ulrich Wehler, *Modernisierungstheorie und Geschichte*, 59.

a timeless continuity. Between the "hot" periods of modern development, the "cold" periods validate art in terms of its "sacred" claim on continuity and immortality. Religion was inherited through the religion of art, with its claim to timeless validity. The canonization of those eighteenth- and nineteenth-century classics that were to be considered timeless occurred in the interest and in the name of the nation and an economically stable middle class, whose social status was secured with the help of an educational canon.

(6) A further phase of modernization followed in the nineteenth century with the industrial revolution, whose new means of production had revolutionary effects on people's living conditions. At the same time, rapid population growth and new technologies of transport engineering (and the increased speeds associated with them) served to increase awareness about irreversible changes that were taking place to landscapes as well as ways of life. Pasts fell away as a consequence of innovations in the economy, technology, and social dynamics. As a result, attention was increasingly being paid to the engine of this change as well as to the processes of disappearance. The accelerated push for innovation was one side of this phase of modernization, the other side being the romantic reimagining of what had been lost and the literary archiving of what was no longer valid or had disappeared. The temporal dynamic of becoming and then passing away in the long process of evolution constituted the mental backdrop of a world in which everything had become historical and nothing could escape the fundamental law of change. The revolutionary movements of the nineteenth century tied this perspective to extensive political projects, with the expectation that people could first discern and then control the laws of both evolution and historical change. The project of nation-building stood at the center of the nineteenth-century phase of modernization as a territorially delimited political collective that would bind the various social levels and classes to an overarching collective identity and a sense of belonging. This self-image of the nation was grounded either in a revolutionary act of liberation or in the imagination

of a heroic history that reached far back into the past and was recuperated in the present through historical museums and building styles.

(7) At the beginning of the twentieth century, another important phase of modernization took place, this time instigated by European artists and their vanguards in both the East and the West. At the time, modernist art movements arose all over the place and ranged from modernist works that would go on to become classics to the futuristic avant garde. This wave of modernization was staged by the authors themselves, inspired as they were by a certain heroics of innovation, as well as by activists whose provocative manifestos called for the total liquidation of the past. Some artists broke with traditions in order to release or rediscover other pasts. At the center of all these turning points, as Hans Robert Jauß has expressed it, we hear "the renunciation of the old world of the entire Western past."[61]

(8) The final phase of modernization that we will touch on here has to do with the German postwar period and the era of the Cold War. In the aftermath of the Second World War—with its further development of the technologies of war, the unleashing of violence, and the factory-like organization of mass murder—the past was consciously set aside, and once again all bets were placed on the future. The postwar modernity of the economic miracle was tied to an "Americanized" way of life. In West Germany, deficits in modernization were made up for with a rise in standards of living. This was also the time in which the face of German cities was radically modernized, including the reckless destruction of historical buildings. This phase of modernization leads us into the past of the 1960s and '70s when there was "still a whole lot of future on offer." That future included an economic upswing with new social roles and outlooks on life, the international propagation of new styles in architecture, and—not least—the founding of new universities in which

---

61. Hans Robert Jauß, "1912: Threshold to an Epoch—Apollinaire's *Zone* and *Lundi Rue Christine*," trans. Roger Blood, *Yale French Studies*, no. 74 (1988): 40.

theories of modernization were raised to the status of a new mainstream discourse.

The examples of modernization sketched out here include intellectual, social, economic, political, technological, and artistic innovations. Rather than a linear development of modernization, I prefer to speak of a dynamic of heterogeneous phases, each of which has entirely different causes and thereby brings about very different innovations. All these phases of modernization have helped to shape the Western consciousness of time through their specific cultural evaluations of past, present, and future. In what follows, I will situate each of the examples that more closely illustrate the genesis and trajectory of the modern time regime within one context or another of the phases of modernization presented here.

Modernization—this is the upshot of the section—did not happen continuously or uniformly but rather took place in discontinuous phases. However, there is one culture in particular whose development is tied more powerfully to the modernization program than any other, and whose temporal orientation is focused more strongly on the future than any other temporal register. In the following section, we will focus our discussion on this culture.

The Golden Door of the Future: Modernization as Culture (Using the Example of the United States)

> Genius looks forward; the eyes of man are set in his forehead,
>
> Not in his hindhead; man hopes; genius creates.
>
> —*R. W. EMERSON*[62]

By means of a historical example, we shall now look more closely at how the cultural foundations of the modern time regime were

---

62. Ralph Waldo Emerson, "The American Scholar" (1837), in *Selected Writings of R. W. Emerson*, ed. W. H. Gilman (New York: New American Library, 1965), 228.

implemented in history. The time regime of the modern can be understood as a cultural framework that gives direction to activities, mobilizing some values, desires, and visions and, as we shall see, excluding others. Its foundations, which extend from the Bible and the pre-Socratics to early modern Europe, have made history in the Western world (in the most literal sense of the word "Western"). We shall examine what the future can mean as a concrete and politically mobilizing promise of continual innovation and social dynamism by looking at the example of the self-understanding of the American nation. Here, I will be relying on an essay by the American Studies scholar Ulfried Reichardt appropriately entitled "The 'Times' of the New World: Future-Orientation, American Culture, and Globalization."[63] In it, the author describes the cultural values and continuing effects of the radical future-directedness of the United States since its historical inception.

In the essay, Reichardt begins with the observation that since the end of the twentieth century, American ideas and products that have been most successful at the level of global competition are those found in the areas of the economy, technology, culture, and politics; they have been exported throughout the entire world, where they have dominated global markets and been adapted to other contexts. The concepts of globalization, modernization, Westernization, and Americanization are all closely related to one another, and this close connection suggests that, as regards technologies of the future, the United States is the most important global instigator. In the course of this appraisal, Reichardt raises the interesting question of how to account for the incredible success that the United States has had in its quest to become the most important engine of globalization. To answer it, he goes far afield and examines the history of the American mindset, the particular roots of which

---

63. Ulfried Reichardt, "The 'Times' of the New World: Future Orientation, American Culture, and Globalization," in *REAL* 19 (Tübingen: Gunter Narr, 2003); Ulfried Reichardt, *Globalisierung: Literaturen und Kulturen des Globalen* (Berlin: Akademie Verlag, 2010). In 2003, Reichardt was still describing this development (despite its blind spots) as an unmitigated success story. The present work will perhaps contribute to a historicization of this history, insofar as the framework goes beyond that single perspective.

he discovers in the development of a uniquely American culture of time.

Reichardt's analysis demonstrates that the American culture of time is inseparable from the discovery of a "new world" and the program of modernization. While, generally speaking, the modern culture of time played a central role for the development of all Western nations, the United States has an intensified and therefore exemplary relation to the modern time regime, so much so that one can examine it there in its most undiluted form. Mainstream ideas in that nation—such as the "American dream," the possibility of financial success for everyone regardless of their social positions and ethnic origins, or "manifest destiny"[64] (a historical plan driven by divine providence)—all exemplify this uniquely American sense of time: "It can be summed up in a shift from the past (including memory and tradition) to the *future* as the main and dominant modality of time which organizes, and, importantly, legitimizes life and action."[65] While in Europe this change from a traditional to an emphatically modern temporal consciousness first became prevalent in the eighteenth century, the "signs of the times" on the continent of North America had already shifted toward the future a century earlier with the arrival of the Puritans. Once this radically individualistic protest movement had entered the phase of populating the new transatlantic colonies and the Puritans had severed their ties with the Old World, the newcomers had to adjust to the radically new in every possible area of their lives. There was, however, a good map along with a reliable itinerary for this uncharted territory: the first settlers took their most significant cues from the spirit of the Old Testament prophets. Interpreting their own destiny as the final fulfillment of the promise originally issued to the Israelites, they saw and cast themselves in the role of a "chosen people" in a new Jerusalem. In the New World of the colonies, the Puritans redeployed biblical history in such a way that they consciously inaugurated a

---

64. Lawrence H. Fuchs, "Thinking about Immigration and Ethnicity in the United States," in *Immigrants in Two Democracies: French and American Experience*, ed. D. L. Horowitz and G. Noiriel (New York: New York University Press, 1992).

65. Reichardt, "The 'Times' of the New World," 249ff.

new phase of human history with their politics of exodus, their self-liberation, their independence, and their acceleration of the new. According to Reichardt, this self-understanding of "the elect," grounded in religion, has survived its secularization and remained authoritative both for the cultural orientation of the nation and for its missionary zeal. He refers to classic authors such as Ralph Waldo Emerson and Walt Whitman, who would reaffirm a self-reflective American culture in the nineteenth century and would again decisively direct it toward the future. During this phase, the colonies no longer dissociated themselves solely from the English motherland; rather, "new America" was dissociated from all of "old Europe." In precisely this sense, Hegel had also already described America as "the land of the future. . . . It is the land of longing for all those who are weary of the historical arsenal that is old Europe."[66]

Being radically oriented toward the future, America likewise relied on a politics of open horizons, of permanent technological change, and of unrestricted mobility—all of which are values of modernization aimed at traversing national borders. According to Reichardt, the reason why that country has played both the role of trailblazer in the West and the engine of globalization is its exclusive focus on the future and on modernization.[67] American exceptionalism has most radically achieved the program of modernization and, at the same time, has also helped to shape the processes of globalization in decisive ways. The concept of time that underlies these developments is based on the optimistic belief in an evolutionary-linear development that promises continuous progress, as well as a positive

---

66. G. W. F. Hegel, *The Philosophy of History*, trans. J. Sibree (New York: Dover, 1956), 86–87.

67. "My thesis now is that this constitution of the time of modernity described by Koselleck cannot be merely *also* found in America, but rather that it took shape faster and more consistently in America than in Europe and that it helped constitute the American identity because of the forms of thought which had already evolved first in Puritanism, then in the framework of the enlightenment and finally in the context of the historically early foundation of a republic" (Reichardt, "The 'Times' of the New World," 257ff). "Globalization, thus, is the globalization of modernization (including individualization and modern forms of the economy), with all its costs and benefits" (ibid., 261).

definition of the "new" as the site of productive unfolding and creativity.[68] In the first edition (1837) of a newspaper in which journalist John O'Sullivan proclaimed his democratic creed, he reminded his readers that the history of progress arose out of experiments, the most dramatic of which was the American Revolution. To which he added the following explanation: "The eye of man looks naturally *forward;* and he is carried onward by the progress of time and truth, he is far more likely to stumble and stray if he turn his face backward, and keep his looks fixed on the thoughts and things of the past. We feel safe under the banner of the democratic principle, which is borne onward by the unseen hand of Providence, to lead our race toward the high destinies of which every human soul contains the God-implanted germ."[69]

Here I would like to add that this radical future-orientation of the American self-image and of its temporal sensibility is not to be confused with the revolutionary ideas of young artists who wrote futuristic manifestos in Italy or Russia at the beginning of the twentieth century. The latter wanted nothing to do with the past and declared war (in the aftermath of Nietzsche) on the cultural institutions of historicism: "We will destroy the museums, libraries, academies of every kind, will fight moralism, feminism, every opportunistic or utilitarian cowardice." These youthful and wild "culturo-clasts" campaigned to "free this land from its smelly gangrene of professors, archaeologists, *ciceroni* and antiquarians," and reveled in images of burning and flooded libraries: "Set fire to the library shelves! Turn aside the canals to flood the museums! . . . Oh, the joy of seeing the glorious old canvases bobbing adrift on those waters, discolored and shredded! . . . Take up your pickaxes, your axes and hammers and wreck, wreck the venerable cities, pitilessly!"[70]

68. Reichardt, in "The 'Times' of the New World," points out that the open future contains not only promises of success but also contingencies and risks, ones that can be countered by the American spirit of experimentation and its pragmatism.

69. John O'Sullivan, "Introduction," *The United States Magazine and Democratic Review* 1, no. 1 (October 1837): 9.

70. Filippo Tommaso Marinetti, "The Founding and Manifesto of Futurism," trans. R. W. Flint, in *Futurist Manifestos*, ed. Umbro Apollonio (New York: Viking

The inclination toward the future that characterizes American culture can in no way be associated with such a cultural revolution. To the contrary, it must be associated with its libraries, museums, and its historical research, ideally with a strong interest in conservation. For America is at the same time also a stronghold of historicism.[71] The calls of John O'Sullivan or Ralph Waldo Emerson to the writers and thinkers of America to pursue an American "special way" and, finally, to cut the cord with England and old Europe ("We have listened too long to the courtly muses of Europe")[72] are wholly compatible with the particular love, care, and competence with which this "old Europe" is collected, cared for, and interpreted in the New World.

Reichardt colorfully sums up the attitude toward life based on belief in the future: it, he writes, "is internally dynamized and thus in motion, in process, never fixed or finished, such that an identity, the meaning of one's life or the mission of the nation is always projected into the future, never completed, yet to be achieved, and thus conceived of as emergent."[73] Over the course of centuries, the individual, social, and national optimism regarding the future has become part of a process of self-understanding as well as a central aspect of American identity. This cultural trust in the future has a particular history that begins with the first Puritans to land on the

---

Press, 1973), 22–23. The manifesto declares the renunciation of all canonized authors who "should be pummelled by the 'steamer of the present.'" Renate Lachmann, "Mnemonische Konzepte," in *Arbeit am Gedächtnis*, ed. Michael Frank and Gabriele Rippl (Munich: Fink, 2007), 132.

71. According to the cultural critic George Steiner, America has spawned "an absurdly hybrid culture": at one end of the spectrum, it accelerated the decline of high culture through democratization, mass media, and the market principle, and "at the opposite end of the spectrum, these same products are salvaged out of life and put in the museum vault." American libraries, universities, archives, museums, and research centers "are now the indispensable record and treasure-house of civilization. It is here that the European artist and scholar must come to see the cherished after-glow of his culture. Though often obsessed with the future, the United States is now, certainly in regard to the humanities, the active watchman of the classic past." George Steiner, *In Bluebeard's Castle: Some Notes Towards the Redefinition of Culture* (London: Faber and Faber, 1971), 110.

72. Emerson, "The American Scholar" (1837), 240.

73. Reichardt, "The 'Times' of the New World," 262.

coast of the new world, and it continues today. On November 7, 2012, that trust would be renewed once again in a powerfully emotional way when the newly reelected President Barack Obama announced that "[t]he best is yet to come." Here we see how a normative system of values and a cultural habitus connect earlier historical eras to later ones, both of which ensure that each generation is oriented toward the new and puts it into practice.

The American Politics of Immigration

The importance of the future for the American national myth has exerted a particularly strong influence on American immigration policy. Up until the 1980s, a model of integration known colloquially as the "melting pot" regulated the influx of immigrants.[74] The premises of this traditional model were directed toward rapid assimilation—an attractive offer, to be sure, but one for which immigrants nonetheless had a high price to pay. The offer consisted in a package of citizen rights and the prospect of economic advancement under the conditions of the American ethos of competition and performance. In the 1960s, the literary critic Leslie Fiedler emphasized that the American nation, unlike the English or French, would not be held together by means of a collective inheritance but rather by a collective dream. "As Americans," he says, "we are inhabitants of a collective utopia and not of a collective history."[75] He was of the opinion that Americans were fundamentally different from Europeans, insofar as they were encouraged to forget their origins.

The heterogeneous ancestries of the migrants could not be allowed to introduce divisions into the new body politic. Forgetting one's ancestry was therefore the price immigrants had to pay for the heady prospects of rights and opportunities. Of course, their memories

---

74. The image of the melting pot goes back to the end of the eighteenth century. However, it became iconic at the beginning of the nineteenth century because of a play of the same name by the British playwright Israel Zangwill, following another wave of immigration from Eastern Europe.

75. Leslie Fiedler, "Cross the Border—Close the Gap," in *Cross the Border—Close the Gap* (New York: Stein & Day, 1971).

could not simply be taken away from them at the border like a piece of luggage, but they could be systematically washed out through the national immigration rituals of the "melting pot." In the kindergartens, schools, and companies of the nineteenth and twentieth centuries, the symbolic conversion from ancestry to the future that went along with an immigration policy of assimilation was celebrated and performatively executed through changes in clothing and flags.[76] There was good reason for such rituals of forgetting that accompanied immigration, closely associated as those rituals were with the revolutionary program of modernity: The postulate of the equality of all citizens demanded the abolishment of any privileges and distinctions that might be grounded in one's ancestry in favor of a successful implementation of the principle of personal achievement and individual merit.[77]

This change of identity, which often began with a change in name, was not understood as a prescriptive forgetting, but rather—and entirely in keeping with the modern time regime—as a blank check written for the future. The promise of social advancement was a national narrative that made the shift in focus from the past to the future a mobilizing value and a goal. This goal is also articulated in the "The New Colossus" (1883), a sonnet written by a Jewish immigrant, Emma Lazarus, about the Statue of Liberty standing in New York Harbor. Lazarus puts the words of welcome uttered by the Mother of Exiles into the mouth of the statue, words that are now engraved on its base:

---

76. Conversation with Michael Holquist; see also Alison Landsberg, *Prosthetic Memory. The Transformation of American Remembrance in the Age of Mass Culture* (New York: Columbia University Press, 2004), 49ff.

77. Of course, the promise of equal opportunities of advancement was not always actualized. For example, in his autobiography, the novelist Philip Roth describes how in the 1930s his Jewish father was systematically prevented from moving up the ranks in his career as a manager in a white Christian context. While his father had to suffer under "the company's deep-rooted reluctance to allow a Jew to rise too high" (22), his own history of integration as Jewish and as American filled him with patriotic gratitude: "growing up Jewish as I did and growing up American seemed to me indistinguishable." Philip Roth, *The Facts: A Novelist's Autobiography* (London: Vintage Books, 1988), 122.

"Keep, ancient lands, your storied pomp!" cries she
With silent lips. "Give me your tired, your poor,
Your huddled masses yearning to breathe free,
The Wretched refuse of your teeming shore.
Send these, the homeless, tempest-tossed to me:
I lift my lamp beside the golden door."[78]

Those immigrants ravaged by poverty, oppression, and persecution long for freedom and well-being. They see a golden door opening up in front of them that offers them the promise of a new beginning and a new identity—a promise that, in a great many cases, was also kept. Therefore, for the "homeless, tempest-tossed" masses, there was very little occasion to look back and affirm a point of origin that was not itself marked by pogroms and poverty.

Lazarus came from a respected Jewish family that had immigrated from Brazil to the American colonies as early as the seventeenth century. She enjoyed a life-long friendship with the philosopher Ralph Waldo Emerson, a friendship that also included her sister Josephine. Following her sister's death, Josephine Lazarus campaigned for a modern Judaism that was inspired by Emerson's notion of natural piety and the future-oriented spirituality of "transcendentalism," and was geared toward an enlightened universalist humanism.[79] She was personally convinced that it was possible to overcome the divisive borders of religion and develop a new modern identity. More radical still was the outlook of a Russian-born immigrant named Israel Zangwill, whose play *The Melting Pot* was a triumph on Broadway in 1909. In it, he articulates a philosophy of immigration that eliminated not only the ethnic divisions between Jews and Christians but also those existing between old and new immigrants. He criticized the white Christian "Mayflower aristocracy" that had tacitly been established as a ruling class in the United States. At the same time, he could draw on the core of

78. Emma Lazarus, "The New Colossus" (1883), in *Selected Poems*, ed. J. Hollander (New York: Library of America, 2005), 58. These are the final two tercets of the sonnet.
79. Josephine Lazarus, *The Spirit of Judaism* (Cambridge, MA: John Wilson University Press, 1895).

American self-determination as reflecting a nation that "always projects itself into the future and is never closed, is always still to be fulfilled in a constant process of emergence." The utopia and magic of his melting pot went to the very heart of American self-understanding, its temporal awareness, and its immigration politics: "What is the glory of Rome and Jerusalem where all nations and races come to worship and look back, compared with the glory of America, where all races and nations come to labor and look forward!"[80]

A young immigrant named Mary Antin, who had emigrated with her family in 1894 from a Jewish shtetl in Czarist Russia to Boston, met both the Lazarus family and Israel Zangwill. Under the influence of her Jewish friends, the barely thirty-year-old Antin wrote her autobiography, *The Promised Land*, which was published a year after the death of her mentor Josephine Lazarus and dedicated to her.[81] The book's overnight success cannot be attributed to its literary merits alone: It also has to do with its patriotic support for the American politics of immigration, a politics that, as the editor suggests in the preface, "cuts the individual off from their past and assists them in their blossoming as an individual. The trip from the Jewish ghetto to America led to a discovery of her own self on the way from the Middle Ages into the modern."[82] Antin wrote her immigration story as an exemplary story of progress: "I began life in the Middle Ages, as I shall prove, and here I am still, your contemporary in the twentieth century, thrilling with your latest thought" (xxii). By writing her autobiography and recalling Jewish life in the small town of Polotzk, she is able to take leave of her past. In effect, her book voices a personal commitment to the modern way of life; she describes her life's journey as the fulfillment of this vision:

---

80. Israel Zangwill, "The Melting Pot" (1908), cited in Werner Sollors, *Beyond Ethnicity: Consent and Descent in American Culture* (New York/Oxford: Oxford University Press, 1986), 68.

81. Mary Antin, *The Promised Land* (1912), ed. Oscar Handlin (Princeton: Princeton University Press, 1969). The book first appeared in installments in *Atlantic Monthly*.

82. Ibid., "Preface," xii.

> In that moment I had a vision of myself, the human creature, emerging
> from the dim places where the torch of history has never been, creeping
> slowly into the light of civilized existence, pushing more steadily forward
> to the broad plateau of modern life, and leaping, at last, strong and
> glad, to the intellectual summit of the latest century (364).

The modern narrative of emancipation describes the immigrant's life
as a journey from darkness into the light and expresses pride at having liberated oneself from self-incurred immaturity and thereupon
becoming an individual. Antin is prepared to discard the heavy garb
of the past and, as is expected and required of her, wants to rely
solely on the future. But this is more difficult than it sounds:

> I can never forget, for I bear the scars. But I want to forget—sometimes
> I long to forget. I think I have thoroughly assimilated my past—I have
> done its bidding—I want now to be of to-day. It is painful to be con-
> scious of two worlds. The Wandering Jew in me seeks forgetfulness. I
> am not afraid to live on and on, if only I do not have to remember too
> much. A long past vividly remembered is like a heavy garment that clings
> to your limbs when you would run. And I have thought of a charm that
> should release me from the folds of my clinging past. I take the hint from
> the Ancient Mariner, who told his tale in order to be rid of it. I, too, will
> tell my tale, for once, and never hark back any more. I will write a bold
> "Finis" at the end, and shut the book with a bang![83]

Clearly, the imperative to leave the past behind on the path to the
future was easier said than done. Antin's testimonial is therefore an
invaluable document of the inner turmoil she experiences as she
moves along the path from what she calls the Jewish Middle Ages
to the modernity of America.

The act of immigration involved acquiring a new ideal, but in
no way did this entail an overnight change in cultural identity
(whether in language, morals, memories, loyalties, relationships, or
values). In those days, one assumed that the process of assimilation
took time; as a general rule, a transitional time was estimated of

---

83. Ibid., xxii.

two to three generations.[84] This delay was not considered a problem, though, since time itself would certainly encourage this change. According to this melting pot model of immigration, time and the future were powerful factors in processes of integration, since expectations of progress were such a crucial part of the temporal regime. This prevailing mood changed abruptly when the "salad bowl" replaced the old metaphor in the 1980s. The contrast is obvious: in a salad bowl, nothing is cooked and nothing melts; the ingredients retain their color, shape, and taste, and remain recognizable as distinct elements. As the modern time regime and the future associated with it began to erode, the values and key ideas associated with immigration underwent change: rather than "assimilation" and "melting" along the lines of *"e pluribus Unum,"* now it was a question of "cultural difference" and "ethnic identities." Throughout the course of this change, stories and cultures of origin that had been widely forgotten were again dug up and reanimated. This change is reflected not least in the character of the Ellis Island National Museum of Immigration, near the Statue of Liberty in New York Harbor, which opened in 1990. Before that time, there was clearly no demand for such an institution. Ellis Island, it says on the museum's home page, "our most potent symbol of the American immigrant experience, had become sadly deteriorated."[85] This changed dramatically when, in the course of the renovation of the Statue of Liberty, the decision was made to reconceive this important American "site of memory." In the intervening period, the museum began to offer an entire spectrum of memory services, including an Oral History Recording Studio and an American Family Immigration History Center, in which visitors can identify the names of the ships that brought their forebears and can view the files of some 25 million arrivals in a digital

---

84. The sociologist Robert E. Park developed a theory of "American assimilation" that remains influential. Under this umbrella term, he distinguishes four phases in the history of migrants (he himself talks about a "Race Relations Cycle"): contact, competition, mutual adjustment, and assimilation.

85. Accessed September 7, 2018, http://www.libertyellisfoundation.org/about -the-foundation.

archive. The present-day desire for family histories and genealogies has breathed new life into the museum.

American immigration policy in the nineteenth and, to a large extent, in the twentieth centuries meant choosing the future and intentionally forgetting the past. Tellingly enough, it was in the 1980s that this paradigm came under critical scrutiny, precisely at a time when confidence in the time regime of the modern period had begun to wane, along with its optimistic future. Following the dominance of a future-oriented forgetting, a strong interest in the past arose that manifested itself, for instance, in a new boom in historical novels.[86] But most notably, different waves of reclaimed memory took place in the context of unmastered pasts. As the focus shifted from the future to the past, the contours of ethnic identities, group loyalties, and minorities—many of which had no place in the great melting pot of American culture—again became visible; some that had obviously not disappeared entirely were now being reconstructed and reclaimed with a positively explosive power. At one time, future-directedness had driven the pendulum in the direction of the harmonized or "unified people," but now it has rebounded in the opposite direction, that of fragmentation. This cultural fragmentation has meanwhile become a social and historical fact that raises the question of how national consensus and social solidarity are to be reestablished in light of these differences and retrenchments.[87]

---

86. Ina Bergmann, "'To You, Perceptive Reader, I Bequeath My History': Die Renaissance des historischen Romans im 21.Jahrhundert," in *Amerikaniches Erzählen nach 2000*, ed. Sebastian Domsch (Munich: Text & Kritik, 2008).

87. At the time, defenders of the political right developed solutions that were as simple as they were dangerous: They attempted to establish ethnic boundaries in their states by invoking the values of pride or heroic suffering, or they relied on a diffuse collective sense of threat aimed at consolidating societies by means of xenophobia and exclusion. By contrast, more constructive solutions have also been developed, including attempts to redefine the concept of cosmopolitanism and consider the relation between the national and the transnational in new ways. Charles Taylor, "Multiculturalism and 'The Politics of Recognition,'" in *The Politics of Recognition*, ed. Amy Gutmann (Princeton: Princeton University Press, 1992); Martha C. Nussbaum, *For Love of Country?* (Joshua Cohen, ed., Boston: Beacon Press, 2002).

African American Countermemory

At this point, we need to listen to the voices of those for whom the American image of the "golden door" of the future had never held appeal. For this reason, we now turn to that segment of the American population that could not possibly experience the national history as "manifest destiny" or as a secularized story of salvation because, for them, it carried the burden of paying the highest price for this national project of the future.[88] These voices did not make themselves heard for the first time in the 1980s: in fact, they make up a coherent body of work throughout the entirety of the twentieth century, one that grew substantially following the Second World War. However, their voices initially became distinctly audible in mainstream American society in the 1980s. Reichardt cites the African American author Ralph W. Ellison (who was named by his parents after the American philosopher Ralph Waldo Emerson) as someone who never tired of pointing out the ways in which American optimism about the future was predicated on forgetting a violent past. What Ellison was demanding in the United States in the 1950s has since become an urgent and timely imperative for states that are attempting to adapt their cultures to the new challenges of immigration: "A people must define itself, and minorities have the responsibility of having their ideals and images recognized as part of the composite image which is that of the still forming American people."[89]

---

88. In the previously cited essay "The 'Times' of the New World," Ulfried Reichardt includes the African American countervoices that were informed by the trauma of slavery and continued to be excluded from the blessings of the American dream through racist oppression. Mention is made in his essay not only of black voices but also of the culture of the American South. Following the Civil War, the nation was divided into two cultures: a "culture of victory" and a "culture of defeat" (to make use of an idea from Wolfgang Schivelbusch's work). The intellectuals and artists of the American South could not engage in any simple way with the mainstream culture of forgetting, and so grappled with the past in very different (nostalgic, critical, reflective) ways. Alongside Margaret Mitchell, we must above all mention William Faulkner and Tennessee Williams here, novelists whose involvement with an unmastered past became a source of literary inspiration.

89. Ralph W. Ellison, "Twentieth Century Fiction and the Black Mask of Humanity," in *Shadow and Act* (New York: Random House, 1953).

In the 1940s and '50s, other black authors were making arguments similar to Ellison's. For example, Richard Wright was demanding a new and more critical relation to American history, one that included the African American experience in the national memory of Americans:

> We black folk, our history and our present being, are a mirror of all the manifold experiences of America. What we want, what we represent, what we endure is what America *is*. If we black folk perish, America will perish. If America has forgotten her past, then let her look into the mirror of our consciousness and she will see the *living* past living in the present, for our memories go back, through our black folk of today, through her recollections of our black parents, and through the tales of slavery told by our black grandparents, to the time when none of us, black or white, lived in this fertile land.[90]

James Baldwin's battle for the social integration of blacks also included the demand that African American experiences be included in the white narrative of history. He reports that he grew up with the lesson that neither Africa nor he had a history. "I was a savage about whom the least said the better, who had been saved by Europe and who had been brought to America. Of course, I believed it. I didn't have much choice."[91] Baldwin was convinced that this story, "yet to be told and which no American is prepared to hear," must finally be told. "As is the inevitable result of things unsaid, we find ourselves until today oppressed with a dangerous and reverberating silence."[92]

The black civil-rights movement of the mid-twentieth century revealed blind spots in the modern orientation toward the future, along with gaping holes in American memory. It was in a particularly good position to do this, since for those who had been the vic-

---

90.   Edwin Rosskam and Richard Wright, *12 Million Black Voices: A Folk History of the Negro in the United States* (New York: Thunder's Mouth Press, 1988), 146.

91.   James Baldwin, "The American Dream and the American Negro" (1965), in *Collected Essays*, ed. Toni Morrison (New York: Penguin, 1998), 717.

92.   James Baldwin, "Many Thousands Gone" (1955), in *Collected Essays*, ed. Toni Morrison (New York: Penguin Books, 1998), 19.

tims of violence and racism, the officially sanctioned forgetting could bring about no promise of renewal, much less a new innocence: rather, forgetting would merely serve to normalize and prolong the repressive relations of power in mainstream society that continued to be characterized by racism. Only after optimism about the future had begun to erode was it more broadly recognized that the victims of history had a right to be included in the national narrative. The author Toni Morrison stands at the very threshold of this turning point; three decades later, listening to this "reverberating silence," she wrote about the trauma of slavery from the perspective of a black woman. As she puts it in an interview, she composed *Beloved*, her novel from 1987, explicitly *against* the erasure of the past in American memory:

> We live in a land where the past is always erased, and America is the innocent future in which immigrants can come and start over, where the slate is clean. The past is absent or it's romanticized. This culture doesn't encourage dwelling on, let alone coming to terms with, the truth about the past.[93]

If we shift our attention from public statements made by well-known black writers and intellectuals to the informal lived worlds and domestic interactions of African American families, we gain another perspective on the continuity of this black countermemory. For instance, an important aspect of many of the plays of twentieth-century African American dramatists consists of the more unofficial memories of family life: what family members complain about, what they preserve, and what they transmit. This perspective affords us a view of the complex issues pertaining to the effect of slavery on familial ties and the renewal of black (mostly female) identity. This subculture replaced the Puritanical vision of the future as a New Jerusalem with the "Africa myth" as the imaginary site of origin for African American identity, beginning with the trauma of abduction and extermination of their forefathers and foremothers

---

93. Toni Morrison, "Living Memory: A Meeting with Toni Morrison," in *Small Acts: Thoughts on the Politics of Black Culture*, ed. Paul Gilroy (London: Serpent's Tail, 1993), 179.

("the middle passage"). Above all, these plays shed light on subjective experiences of slavery that, though officially obliterated or silenced, were nonetheless passed on within black families throughout the entire twentieth century as a collective past and countermemory that was decisive for the development of identity.[94] Here we discover that generations of the family are counted since the era of slavery, and the future generations in the plays are encouraged to take their place in this genealogical chain. In stark contrast to the American orientation toward the future, here we see the ancestors' fates function as both warning and motivation: their suffering must be remembered, and they are examples to be emulated. As Morrison often emphasizes, in contrast to mainstream society's celebration of the individual as free-standing and always open to opportunity, in black society, ravaged as it has been and still is by oppression and racist violence, no one can do without the warm laps of parents and grandparents: "They are a sort of timeless people whose relationships to the characters are benevolent, instructive, and protective, and they provide a certain kind of wisdom."[95]

These works of theater are very far away from the ethos of the future as a "golden door" that had defined orientation of the modern American mainstream, including its immigration policy, from its beginnings in Puritanism, through the Enlightenment and right up to the 1980s. When Salman Rushdie went over this jubilant message again in his novel *Fury* (2001), it had already lost its charm and sounded bitter and forced. The protagonist of this novel is from India and came "to America like so many before him to receive the benison of being Ellis Islanded, of starting over":

> Give me a name, America, make of me a Buzz or Chip or Spike. Bathe me in amnesia and clothe me in your powerful unknowing. . . . No longer a historian but a man without histories let me be. I'll rip my lying mother

---

94. On this point, see Simone Paulun, *Enacting Cultural Identity: Time and Memory in 20th Century African-American Theater by Female Playwrights*, PhD diss., Konstanz Universität, 2011.

95. Toni Morrison, "Rootedness: The Ancestor as Foundation," in *Black Woman Writers (1950–1980): A Critical Evaluation*, ed. Mari Evans (New York: Anchor Press, 1984), 343.

tongue out of my throat and speak your broken English instead. Scan me, digitize me, beam me up. If the past is the sick old earth, then, America, be my flying saucer. Fly me to the rim of space. The moon's not far enough.[96]

This discussion of countermemory and the importance of the past as a cultural resource in the lived experience of African Americans shows that many different, even irreconcilable, cultures of time conflict with one another in American society. These conflicting perspectives make abundantly clear what is only now gradually sinking in: namely, that the modern time regime is in no way a neutral or natural framework of human activity but instead represents a very particular "politics of time."[97] This excursus into black countermemory takes us back to the cultural turning point of the 1980s with which we began the book. Before we again take up this theme of the return of the past, we must first examine in greater detail the components that make up the modern time regime—and how it came to have such a formative influence on Western cultural history and on everyday life.

---

96. Salman Rushdie, *Fury* (London: Jonathan Cape, 2001), 51.

97. The notion of "the politics of time" is one that I borrow from Berber Bevernage, though I am using it in a more general sense than he does: "I propose to analyze the function of history, or rather of a particular discourse on history in the field of transitional justice from the perspective of a politics of time—'a politics which takes the temporal structures of social practices as the specific objects of its transformative (or preservative) intent.'" Berber Bevernage, *History, Memory, and State-Sponsored Violence: Time and Justice* (New York: Routledge, 2011), 11.

3

FIVE ASPECTS OF THE MODERN
TEMPORAL REGIME

How did the modern time regime come into being, and what were the values associated with it that started Western civilization on its particular trajectory?[1] How has that regime been translated into action and collective self-awareness, historically and politically? Where did the values of Western culture come from, and how do they inform its sense of the rest of the world? Which of these values are worth safeguarding and which have become too problematic? To answer these questions, we must first reconstruct and critically examine the history of the modern time regime.

The worldview associated with modernity's time regime rests on various presuppositions, five of which we shall examine in greater

---

1. In this context, see "From Popular Goethe to Global Pop," in *Suchen nach dem Westen zwischen Erinnerung, Ermächtigung und Entmachtung*, ed. Ines Detmers and Birte Heidemann (Amsterdam: Rodopi, 2013).

detail here. These issues are closely related and directly build on one another:

1) temporal rupture,
2) the fiction of beginning,
3) creative destruction,
4) the invention of the historical, and finally,
5) acceleration.

Temporal Rupture

> Caesuras cut out material from the past of a present
> that should not be considered in its future.[2]

With the first and most fundamental issue, "temporal rupture," we return once more to the issue of the differentiation of temporal registers that, according to systems theory, is the decisive characteristic of the process of modernization. In fact, the borders between temporal registers play a decisive role in how a society understands itself. With temporal rupture, the present and the future are foregrounded at the cost of a devaluation of and a breaking-away from the past. As we shall see, this temporal ontology can also be summed up using phrases like "the invention of the new" or "a new beginning."

We can begin to clarify what is at stake in temporal rupture by means of a literary example. In an essay by Virginia Woolf, we find the following, quite incredible statement: "[O]n or about December 1910, human character changed."[3] With this unequivocal claim, Woolf is establishing a caesura to mark the beginning of a new era of artistic modernism. As a writer and active member of a modernist group of artists, she felt authorized to make such audacious performative statements. Yet, in the very next sentence, pulling back from such adamancy, she continues in a somewhat

---

2. Schlögl, "Zeit und Ereignisse," 11.
3. Virginia Woolf, *Mr. Bennett and Mrs. Brown* (London: Hogarth Press, 1924), 4.

more conciliatory tone: "The change was not sudden and definite like that. But a change there was, nevertheless; and, since one must be arbitrary, let us date it about the year 1910" (ibid.). Since then, critics have come to define the year 1912 as "a highpoint in European art." About this, Hans Robert Jauß observes: "The year 1912 can be perceived however not just from the retrospective of what has happened since, but in the consciousness of its contemporaries—the avant-garde Italian futurists, who were prominent at the time, the French cubists or Orphists, and the German expressionists, Anglo-American imagists and Russian cubo-futurists."[4]

In 1923, Virginia Woolf made good on her claims about an epochal shift, at the very high point of the movement of artistic modernism. James Joyce's *Ulysses* and T. S. Eliot's *The Waste Land* had appeared the year before, followed in 1923 by her own novel, *Mrs. Dalloway*. Woolf's decision to date that epochal shift at 1910 made sense, because an event took place that year in which she herself, as a member of the Bloomsbury Circle, actively participated. It involved the exhibition on "Post-Impressionism" that showed important works by Cézanne to the London public for the first time. This exhibit gave the London artistic avant-garde scene of the early twentieth century the opportunity to define and display the premises of their own creativity.[5] Thirteen years later, when the new movement had reached its high point, Woolf looked back and searched for its beginning. So, what she had proclaimed as an epochal shift in human character was actually something much more specific—namely, the beginning of an artistic movement that would later enter into cultural history as "classical modernism." This notion designates the heyday of artistic innovations in music, painting, and literature in the first decades of the twentieth century.

Big differences certainly can be observed between an aesthetic movement like modernism on the one hand and, on the other, a pro-

---

4. Hans Robert Jauß, "1912: Threshold to an Epoch," 54. It has recently been suggested that the year 1913 is also a threshold year: Florian Illies, *1913: Der Sommer des Jarhhunderts* (Frankfurt am Main: Fischer, 2012). In this context, see also Felix Philipp Ingold, *Der große Bruch* (Munich: C. H. Beck, 2000).

5. See Karolina Jeftič, *Literatur und modern Bilderfahrung: Zur Cézanne-Rezeption der Bloomsbury Group* (Munich/Paderborn: Fink, 2011).

cess of modernization that tends to penetrate all areas of life in Western society. Similarly, there are major differences among artists, revolutionaries, and historians in terms of how they view temporal rupture. Woolf was defining the identity, the values, and the relevance of a new art movement to which she herself belonged. To give definition to this identity and viewpoint, she had to insert a beginning into the continuum of time and, at the same time, had to bring that continuum to an end. Her gesture involved nothing less than conducting an impassioned examination of old and new social values, making claims, and establishing spheres of influence, all of which necessarily involved exclusions, devaluations, and departures.

The temporal boundaries of an era are always established in hindsight; in the moment of the here and now, though, they are proclaimed (as did the futurists) or consolidated through epoch-making works or events. Because of that, they are always the outcome of conscious position-taking; on the one hand, they emerge through a dramatization of their difference from earlier eras and, on the other hand, they arise by leveling the differences internal to any given era. Niklas Luhmann once described the newness of eras as "exaggerated," suggesting that it functions primarily to reduce or eliminate historical complexity.[6] According to Luhmann, adopting the "rhetoric of epochal caesura" works to mobilize attention and produces "a strengthening effect in the course of its being communicated" (26). Such rhetoric, he admits, is by no means ineffectual and can in fact have a profound historical impact. As a consequence, in our own day, we are increasingly interested (along with Luhmann) in "the extent to which such epochal self-understandings, that articulate and over-articulate differences in experience, are grasped as facts in the course of history, and continue to have an impact on it" (ibid.).

Periodizations are also ways of marking caesuras in the course of history. The word *caesura* comes from the Latin "caedere" ("to fell," "to kill") and means "to cut" or "cut into" in schools of

---

6. Niklas Luhmann, "Das Problem der Epochenbildung und die Evolutionstheorie," in *Epochenschwellen und Epochenstrukturen im Diskurs der Literature- und Sprachhistorie*, ed. Hans Ulrich Gumbrecht and Ursula Link-Heer (Frankfurt am Main: Suhrkamp, 1985), 11–33.

thought, movements, and music. Caesuras can be hard or soft. Hard caesuras are created by revolutions and wars; they establish a new worldview, a new ideology, a new consciousness, a new status quo. In that respect, they also generate firm boundaries in relation to which it is impossible to "go back." Soft caesuras offer an indispensable means of structuring the stream of time with markers and making it rhythmic. This is particularly true of historical periodization (indeed, the English word "period" also means "point" [*punkt*]); by introducing punctuation into time, caesuras give shape and direction to the continuum of history. Historians do not use periodization to make claims and establish markers that actively intervene in the course of events, as Woolf did; rather, they use them to clarify and understand historical sequences in hindsight. Historians have always hotly debated questions that arise in relation to the practice of periodization (when does something end, and when does something new begin?), especially when suggestions are made to replace one periodization with another. But they do not reflect on the practice of demarcation as such in any fundamental way.[7]

Reinhart Koselleck and Christian Meier took a decisive step in the direction of precisely such a fundamental reflection. In a comprehensive study of the basic ideas of historiography, they examine the notion of "progress." In their article, they describe with almost anatomical precision how progress always takes place "in the temporal breaks of hiatus-experiences that are constantly being reproduced."[8] The word *hiatus* (like the word *caesura*) can mean opening, fold, chasm, gap, and interruption.[9] By emphasizing its technical formulation, the authors sidestep the positive rhetoric regarding progress that attaches to ideological self-understandings in order to focus exclusively on its temporal structure. Their references to temporal in-

---

7. For a recent examination of this theme, see Berber Bevernage and Chris Lorenz, eds., *Breaking Up Time: Negotiating the Borders Between Present, Past, and Future* (Göttingen: Vandenhoeck & Ruprecht, 2013).

8. Koselleck and Meier, "Fortschritt," 392.

9. The idea has a special place in the terminology of medicine and geology; in everyday language, it has become a synonym for the winter and summer breaks in television series.

terruptions and what they call "hiatus-experiences" lead straight to the heart of the modern time regime. More specifically, according to their description, progress does not simply involve starting something on its course but rather involves an operation that must be constantly repeated. In other words, this differentiating power must be constantly reactivated. In general, we could therefore say that, ever since the French Revolution, the engine of progress has drawn its energy from a dividing, splicing, and differentiating power that constantly introduces ruptures and emphasizes differences. Along with the differentiation of cultural spheres of value like politics, law, religion, science, and art, we could also think of differentiations of human groups into generations, social classes, or nations. In the language of systems theory, we could say that such divisions introduce new levels of complexity and accelerate developmental dynamics.

The modern time regime does not rely on continuity; it relies on change. More precisely: it depends on the hiatus between the past and future, which it dramatizes as a hiatus and, in so doing, produces it in the first place. Here is what Koselleck has to say: "Finally, the divide between previous experience and coming expectation opened up, and the difference between past and present increased, so that lived time was experienced as a rupture, as a period of transition in which the new and the unexpected continually happened."[10] His historical claim is as follows: "My thesis is that during *Neuzeit* [the modern period—trans.] the difference between experience and expectation has increasingly expanded; more precisely, that *Neuzeit* is first understood as a neue Zeit [new time—trans.] from the time that expectations have distanced themselves evermore from all previous experience" (263). Since its publication, Koselleck's thesis has become the generally accepted way of formulating the gap between a "space of experience" (the past) and "horizon of expectation" (the future) (255–76). Were there a Nobel prize for a historical theory of time, as there is in physics, Koselleck would surely have won it. Yet at the beginning of the 1970s, other formulations were already being made that were going in similar directions. The philosopher Joachim Ritter suggests that "[t]he future that began with

---

10. Koselleck, *Futures Past*, 246.

[modern] society relates to the past in the mode of discontinuity."[11] It is safe to assume that his formulation regarding what he called a "splitting of past and future" was also known in Bielefeld. Though Ritter did not have the historical process specifically in mind, he was in fact interested in the exclusive focus on the future as a necessary precondition for the liberation of human subjectivity.

The rupture between the space of experience and the horizon of expectation did not necessarily reduce the present to a nonextended "now moment" that had so interested Baudelaire as the uniquely "modern" quality of the instant. It was much more a question of liberating the present from any past claims, experiences, or examples so that it could be all the more closely tied to the future-oriented potentials of projection, imagination and planning. "The emergence of society from its self-imposed dependence on the past" was the Enlightenment clarion call for this break between past and future, one that Koselleck also explains in the context of the rhetoric of *historia magistra vitae*. The more it became clear that time itself acted as the engine and agent of historical change, the more obvious it was that history did not repeat itself and that the practice of "learning from history was over."[12] There had, of course, always been change in time; indeed, one of its more striking images is the allegorical figure of Fortuna. The rotation of her wheel results in radical disruptions, reminding people that in this fallen world one cannot count on any stability whatsoever, let alone have any certainty regarding planning or prediction. But in the end, even the image of change-inducing Fortuna could become adapted to a predictable cyclical model under the temporal regime of the inconstant moon, which brings forth practically nothing new under the sun, so to speak. During the Renaissance, therefore, the modern notion of time as the agent of change and the engine for bringing forth the "new" also fundamentally changed the image of Fortuna.[13] This

11.   Joachim Ritter, *Subjektivität: Sechs Aufsätze* (Frankfurt: Suhrkamp, 1974).
12.   Hans Ulrich Gumbrecht, *In 1926: Living at the Edge of Time* (Cambridge, MA: Harvard University Press, 1997), 411.
13.   On this issue, see also Klaus Reichert, *Fortuna oder die Beständigkeit des Wechsels* (Frankfurt am Main: Suhrkamp, 1985).

"revolutionary" knowledge did nothing less than retrospectively give the entire era its name: the modern era [*Neuzeit*].

As we have just emphasized, a clear separation of temporal registers is vitally important to the modern time regime. The paradigmatic modern experience of hiatus led to a reconfiguration of the present between the past and the future, one that also had a direct impact at the level of individual experience: "The social and moral present in all its aspects becomes an arena for articulating one's expectations of the future, but these must be continually redefined in light of the dynamics of change. This pushes the past ever further away from the actors."[14] By pushing the past away, space is made for new projects and planning in the ongoing history of human improvement. At the same time, this liberation from the past for the sake of newness and risk also produces a state of crisis, because longer-term security gets lost when expectation is cut off from experience. The particular trajectory of the modern time regime, which consists of dramatizing and accelerating the break from the past, contrasts with that of premodern temporal ontologies, where it was chiefly a matter of continuities and connections between the past, the present, and the future. Of course, traditional societies were also familiar with radical hiatus-experiences, such as the death of a ruler, the end of a dynasty, or natural catastrophes. But, in confronting such breaks, they adopted the opposite strategy: they mended or covered up such breaks or, better still, they prevented them from ever happening in the first place. Serious breaks, such as the death of important individuals, the constant change of generations, or the change of a political regime, are therefore compensated for by using fictions of continuity that stabilize power, thereby avoiding the danger of a crisis of meaning and legitimacy. The task of premodern and non-Western temporal cultures alike is thus to counter the fundamental experience of breaks and discontinuities with something more powerful.

Within the framework of modernity's concept of time, this stance had to be fundamentally reevaluated. What had earlier represented a threat to be removed or avoided at all costs was now conceived as both an opportunity and a resource. At the same time, that implied

---

14.   Raphael, "Ordnungsmuster der 'Hochmoderne?,'" 80.

a far-reaching break with older or different cultural presuppositions. In the framework of this revolutionary thinking, whose origins perhaps lie in the monotheistic religions, it amounted to a radical reevaluation of existing cultural norms and values. The past, which up to that point had been a cultural reservoir of binding norms and orientations, was now interpreted as a burden and a constraint. The revolutionary break freed up new historical actors who could bring an end to the rule of the past over the present. Even though the revolutionary reorientation away from the past and toward the future was staged in a thoroughly secular context, the modern rhetoric of liberation had religious overtones of epochal and apocalyptic conversion. It was nothing less than an act of human self-empowerment over and against all transcendent powers. This self-liberation took place with the intention of "expung[ing] from human beings all that came from the past and hindered their complete self-regulation and expression."[15] Therefore, the rhetoric of modernization not only involved a break with religion but also resulted in the devaluation of the idea of "tradition." From then on, tradition was assessed in a negative way and was generally understood as an obstacle to progress. In his evolutionary-historical model of society, Max Weber defined tradition solely in terms of an early stage of, or an impediment to, social development, which he often equates with an "automatic reflex":

> Strictly traditional behavior, like the reactive type of imitation discussed above, lies very close to the borderline of what can justifiably be called meaningfully oriented action, and indeed often on the other side. For it is very often a matter of almost automatic reaction to habitual stimuli which guide behavior in a course which has been repeatedly followed.[16]

Since, in the eyes of modernization theorists, the past tends to harden into the form of an "almost automatic reaction," a one-off break

---

15. Edward A. Shils, *Tradition* (Chicago: University of Chicago Press, 1981), 43.

16. Max Weber, *Economy and Society*, ed. Guenther Roth and Claus Wittich (Los Angeles: University of California Press, 1978), 25. In this context, see also Shmuel N. Eisenstadt, *Tradition, Change, Modernity* (New York: Wiley, 1973) and Aleida Assmann, *Zeit und Tradition: Kulturelle Strategien der Dauer* (Cologne/Weimar/Vienna: Böhlau, 1999).

will not suffice: what is needed is a continual breaking from it. In such acts of break or rupture, cultural goods must be permanently filtered out of the present, discarded, and declared irrelevant. This repeated dropping of ballast takes place through a performative "relegation to the past" of that which, up to that point, had continued to exert a claim on the present and so was still considered relevant. A particularly striking rhetorical strategy used to produce such hiatus-experiences within the continuum of time is the repeated declaration of the "death" of every possible cultural institution or value. For a late example of this once-widespread way of speaking, we can cite from the American literary critic Leslie Fiedler. Today his statement reads like a parody of what in 1972 was an attitude that was meant to be taken very seriously: "As certainly as God, i.e. the Old god, is dead, so the Novel, i.e. the Old Novel, is dead."[17] Fiedler made this claim at the height of the Cold War, during a time of great confidence in the modernization paradigm. A decade or so later, his enthusiasm had already become either incomprehensible or intolerable. For instance, the French philosopher Paul Virilio could only react allergically to such language: "We have all had enough of hearing about the death of God, of man, of art and so on since the nineteenth century. What in fact happened was simply the progressive disintegration of a faith in perception."[18]

Modern time becomes dynamic by means of what Koselleck and Meier call temporal ruptures and is expressed not solely through the course of history and its continual overturning of ideas and convictions, but also in relationships between generations. Within premodern contexts, the relation between fathers and sons was understood to be consecutive and continuous. The son had the task of learning from the father, representing him, burying him, inheriting from him, and when necessary also justifying him, walking in his footsteps, and continuing to carry out his plans. Above all, he had the task of ensuring the (presumably good) name of his

---

17. Fiedler, "Cross the Border, Close the Gap," 65.

18. Paul Virilio, *The Vision Machine*, trans. J. Rose (Bloomington, IN: British Film Institute, 1994), 16. The notion of "faith in perception" is a reference to Maurice Merleau-Ponty, who understands it as a pre-reflexive belief in the reality of a shared world.

father after his death. In that way, the son inherits a huge cultural responsibility: His succession became the guarantee, genealogically and religiously, of the father's immortality. In the cultural time regime of the modern, this relation between the generations has changed dramatically. Indeed, they became antagonistic, even oedipal. Modern sons no longer listen to their fathers: they set other goals for themselves, seek out their own paths, and break with traditions that have been handed down. When Freud, as one of the chief advocates and architects of modernity, declares patricide to be the foundational myth of culture, he surely had the particular trajectory of Western culture in mind, and not culture in general. The same goes for his discovery of an oedipal tension between the generations, which is likewise no universal law but rather the mark of modern culture and an important engine of its temporal dynamic.

We must therefore ask ourselves: Since when have there been sons and daughters who engage in revolt?[19] When did it become acceptable to rebel against the authority of the fathers? And when was a cultural narrative established that approved of this rebellion and even required it? The most important cultural condition for such a family revolt is the self-understanding of the era as a new time [*Neuzeit*], one that has turned away from what it sees as the Middle Ages or as the premodern and that places great emphasis on difference and innovation. Since that time, the basic values of this culture no longer involve continuity and duration, but rather caesura and rupture. So, not only do innovation and change come to be privileged, but at the same time youth also comes to be valued over parents or the elderly. Sociologists insist that generational breaks "have the consequence of producing innovation in our culture. . . . Cultural change happens in the first instance through the dissolution of one generation by the next."[20] Karl Mannheim describes this dissolution as the process by which "[n]ew participants in the

---

19. Peter von Matt, *Verkommene Söhne, missratene Töchter: Familiendesaster in der Literatur* (Munich: dtv, 2001).

20. Andrea Heubach, *Generationengerechtigkeit—Herausforderungen für die zeitgenössische Ethik* (Göttingen: Vandenhoeck und Ruprecht, 2008), 45.

cultural process are emerging" and "former participants in that process are continually disappearing."[21] Of course, this innovation does not come about simply by virtue of genealogical succession, but rather through the cultural norm of rupture that is articulated differently, depending on historical and political conditions. Before the Enlightenment, this norm was not viable at a practical level. According to the assessments of historians and sociologists alike, the first generation to break from their fathers (which also means from their teachers and masters) and be admired for it is the *Sturm und Drang* (Storm and Stress) generation. This generation escaped the dictates of their fathers around 1770, so at a time before the French Revolution and roughly simultaneous with the American Revolution. This is the era that Koselleck calls the "saddle period," and historians have repeatedly confirmed it to be the epitome of the hiatus experience. And indeed, there has been a great deal of cultural pressure to break with the norms of society and familial allegiances ever since. Even when this imperative is only acted on in certain milieus, it still has direct consequences for the cultural value of parents and the elderly, who must come to the following realization: "We sense our passing from the lived experience of our generation into the time of history as we ourselves become a historical object."[22]

This temporal ontology privileged a new concept of generations in which the temporal depth of the family, created by successive generations of grandparents, parents, and children, can be disregarded in favor of the charged relation between only two social generations: a younger and an older generation. Whereas multiple ties would work to ensure a three- to four-tier coherence of family generations living at the same time, social change takes place exclusively through what we term the "young" and the "old," the latter constantly being replaced by the former. With this dismantling of a three-tiered to a two-tiered generational model, the temporal rupture constitutive of modernization is accelerated and, as a result, Western culture is

---

21. Karl Mannheim, "The Problem of Generations," in *Essays on the Sociology of Knowledge*, ed. and trans. Paul Kecskemeti (New York: Routledge, 1952), 292.

22. Christopher Bollas, *Being a Character: Psychoanalysis and Self Experience* (New York: Hill & Wang, 1992), 272.

made increasingly dynamic. The emphasis here is placed on masculinist and middle-class youth, since this generational model in no way reflects an anthropological universal but has to do with "youth" as a central notion of Western culture: "This transitional phase 'youth,' a stage of life between childhood and adulthood that implies certain privileges and possibilities for development but also involves exclusion and powerlessness, is one of the hallmarks, a product—in many respects also, a precondition—of the modern."[23] One educator even speaks of a "Youth Project" that is "closely tied to the project of the modern."[24] What he means can be illuminated by means of a distinction between *initiation* and *individuation*. While in traditional societies, the child is taken up into the world of adulthood at the threshold of sexual maturity by means of symbolic initiation rites and rites of passage, the cultural task of youth consists in individuation. In contrast to initiation, which makes it possible for the youth to share in and be assimilated into their new cultural status, "individuation implies in many respects a painful process of separation, one often accompanied by grief: an 'inner' and 'outer' break with tradition.'"[25] What is imposed on modern individuals, or what is expected of them, corresponds almost exactly with the process carried out in society as a whole throughout the course of its history. The ontogenesis of youth repeats the phylogenesis of modern society. Jürgen Habermas draws attention to this connection when he remarks that adolescence is "like an echo of the developmental catastrophe that historically once devalued the world of traditions."[26] Habermas gives this development a tragic spin: the catastrophe carried out in the modern period through the dissolution of earlier traditions and life-worlds *must* be repeated in every generation! Studies in the sociology of development often em-

---

23. Vera King, *Die Entstehung des Neuen in der Adoleszenz: Individuation, Generativität und Geschlecht in modernisierten Gesellschaften* (Wiesbaden: Verlag für Sozialwissenschaften, 2002), 38.

24. Werner Helsper, ed., *Jugend zwischen Moderne und Postmoderne* (Opladen: Leske und Budrich, 1991), 77.

25. King, *Die Entstehung des Neuen*, 42.

26. Jürgen Habermas, *Moral Consciousness and Communicative Action*, trans. C. Lenhart and S. Weber Nicholsen (Cambridge, MA: MIT Press, 1990), 126.

phasize the systematic character of this rupture: "To enter adolescence first means to perceive a rupture in one's life that will never be closed. For better or worse, the world of the family loses its authoritative and its protective power. . . . The adolescent experience . . . is characterized in all its phases through the mode of catastrophe, of a sudden break."[27] The same also goes for the older generation: "When a new generation is formed, this inevitably sends shock waves through earlier generations. . . . For there is generational conflict when one's own cultural potency [and the power to define meaning—A.A.] is defined by successive generations that have other perspectives on social reality."[28] As reality, norm, and phantasm, this predetermined breaking point—so emblematic of generational conflict within the modern time regime—has become a source of "continually reproduced hiatus-experiences." In that regard, it serves not least to strengthen the notion of self-dramatized beginnings, as we shall see in the next section.

The Fiction of Beginning

Without that envelope of the unhistorical he would never
have begun or dared to begin.

—*FRIEDRICH NIETZSCHE*[29]

The denial of tradition as an endowment—doubts raised
about its legitimacy—leads to the hypostatization of
innovation and originality, the idea of "without presupposi-
tion," and the construction of an unprecedented beginning.

—*RENATE LACHMANN*[30]

---

27. Christian Schneider et al., ed., *Trauma und Kritik: Zur Generationenge-schichte der Kritischen Theorie* (Münster: Westfälisches Dampfboot, 2000), 63.
28. Bollas, *Being a Character*, 250.
29. Friedrich Nietzsche, "On the Uses and Disadvantages of History for Life," in *Untimely Meditations*, ed. Daniel Breazeale, trans. R. J. Hollingdale (Cambridge, UK: Cambridge University Press, 1997), 64.
30. Lachmann, "Mnemonische Konzepte," 132.

Why does the modern time regime privilege the break and not continuity? The answer is simple: to allow for a new beginning. For, as we know from Hermann Hesse's poem "Stages," in which he articulates the dynamics of the modern sense of time in lyrical form, every beginning possesses a magical quality:

> In all beginnings dwells a magic force
> For guarding us and helping us to live.
> Serenely let us move to distant places
> And let no sentiments of home detain us.
> The Cosmic Spirit seeks not to restrain us
> But lifts us stage by stage to wider spaces.[31]

This poetic statement reads like a variation on Hegel's vision of progress. What the world spirit experiences throughout world history is also possible in the life of every individual: to ascend to even greater heights of freedom. To make this happen, individuals only have to affirm the progressive movement into an open future and accommodate themselves to this law of eternal becoming. The view is exclusively directed ahead and cannot get caught up on any past ("sentiments of home"). Of interest in this notion of time is the connection between the beginning and progress, which are obviously not incompatible. The magic of the beginning is renewed at every stage, for it is tied to forgetting or overcoming the earlier stages.

In the history of Western culture, the magic of the beginning also consists in the ever-present chance to get rid of the accumulated weight of history and be able to start again from scratch. In such contexts, beginning is not connected to progress but rather to the *tabula rasa* or *zero hour*. A word or two about this latter notion: the expression "zero hour" comes from the language of military planning. It establishes a due date, at which point an important operation alongside a new chain of events should begin. D-Day, June 6, 1944, the date on which the large concerted Allied offensive began with the landing at Normandy, is just such a zero hour. May 8, 1945,

31. Hermann Hesse, "Stages," in *The Glass Bead Game*, trans. R. Winston and C. Winston (New York: Holt, Rinehart & Winston, 1969), 444.

the day of German capitulation after the Second World War, was also a zero hour, the point at which Europe's new political order had begun. The zero hour also plays an important role in scientific experiments: countdowns to the zero hour were broadcast worldwide when rocket-launch experiments in space began. Epidemiologists establish the emergence of a new and previously unknown illness with the terminology of "index patient O." The religious zero hour that organizes the Western calendar has widespread significance: the epochal threshold of Christ's birth that divides the entire history of humanity into a "before" and an "after." This temporal division has long been decontextualized and generalized, since:

> The new zero-point used to measure time was not only able to avoid the serious mistake that arose out of the uncertainty of trying to give the exact date for the beginning of the world. It also dissolved the boundaries—a soon to be unavoidable necessity for historical research—of historical chronology in a new and more fundamental way, in that it no longer established arithmetic boundaries for the historical outlook, which now receded into an ever more distant past and future.[32]

After this initial beginning that established our world-historical chronology, new beginnings have been repeatedly established. Some examples are the French Revolution and its introduction of a new calendar, and the American Revolution, which was widely understood as an opportunity for a radically new beginning. Thomas Paine, one of the spiritual founding fathers of the United States, expressed this idea with perfect clarity:

> We have in our power to begin the world over again. A situation, similar to the present, hath not happened since the days of Noah until now. The birthday of a new world is at hand, and a race of men, perhaps as numerous as all Europe contains, are to receive their portion of freedom from the events of a few months. The reflection is awful—and in this point of view, how trifling, how ridiculous, do the little paltry cravings of a few weak or interested men appear, when weighed against the business of a world.[33]

---

32. Hölscher, "Die Entdeckung der Zukunft," 31ff.
33. Thomas Paine, *Complete Works of Thomas Paine: Containing All His Political and Theological Writings*, ed. Calvin Blanchard (Chicago: Belford & Clarke, 1885), 49–50. I thank Philipp Fraund for this reference.

The claims Paine is making about a new beginning are of a cautionary sort: the American people must become aware of the burden of their current moment and the responsibility they are carrying for world history. Not only were the colonial shackles of the motherland dissolved with the American Declaration of Independence, but the problematic legacy of Puritanical roots was also lifted. Therefore, a "young American nation [arose] that had recently parted from Europe politically and from Calvinism spiritually chose Adam, the prototype of an *innocent* man [freed from the doctrine of original sin], as the symbol and ideal of its destiny."[34] This "Adam" is one of many variations on the so-called "new man," who would later take on more dangerous qualities in the political ideologies of the twentieth century. Whereas, according to Christian interpretation, Adam's original sin could only be removed by an act of divine mercy, the innocence of the American Adam within a secular framework could be attained by eradicating or even forgetting the past. From the first Puritan newcomers who had left the Old World behind right up to the present day, the American Adam has thus become the prototype for the immigrant who breaks with everything from the past and starts anew from the very beginning.

This "will to begin" is not the exclusive achievement of the early-modern period but, as we have suggested, already manifests itself in a revolutionary way in the monotheistic religions. Every history, including religious histories, can start again at any time from the very beginning. This idea of a new beginning was literally unthinkable for the polytheistic religions, since they understood themselves as existing from time immemorial, *not* as being "founded" at a specific point in time.[35] Whereas Judaism sets its own beginning with

---

34. Ursula Brumm, *American Thought and Religious Typology*, trans. J. Hooglund (New Brunswick, NJ: Rutgers University Press, 1970), 199; R. W. B. Lewis, *The American Adam: Innocence, Tragedy and Tradition in the 19th Century* (Chicago: Chicago University Press, 1955).

35. This difference between founded religions of the beginning and religions of origin corresponds to Theo Sundermeier's distinction between "primary" and "secondary" religions. Theo Sundermeier, "Primäre und sekundäre Religionserfahrungen," in *Was ist Religion? Religionswissenschaft im theologischen Kontext: Ein Studienbuch* (Gütersloh: Chr. Kaiser, 1999).

the creation of the world, the monotheistic religions that follow it establish a new beginning in historical time and are highly conscious of their hindsight perspective. For the monotheistic religions, there is no time frame that fades into the mists of a mythic "time immemorial"; they all situate themselves within the same calculable historical chronology. Thus, Judaism, which reckons from the creation of the world, is now 5,779 years old; Christianity, which begins with the birth of Christ, is 2,019 years old; and Islam, which is dated from the year of Mohammed's departure from Mecca to Medina in 622 CE, is, according to its lunar calendar, 1,440 years old.

The modern time regime replaces a mythical origin in time immemorial (*in illo tempore*) with a beginning in the "here and now." In an important book about beginnings, Edward Said articulates the same distinction. Whereas *origins* are defined as "divine, mythical and privileged," *beginning*, on the contrary, is defined as "secular, humanly produced, and ceaselessly re-examined."[36] According to Said's view, whereas in myths the origin of the world order is relegated to another order of time and so is fundamentally protected from human intervention, beginnings are rational and empowering constructions that legitimate human experience, knowledge, and art. The source of inspiration is no longer to be found in earlier authorities, epochs, and traditions, but rather in the rationality, ingenuity, and creativity of the authors themselves. In the seventeenth and eighteenth centuries, the bold practice of consciously establishing a new beginning in philosophical and literary texts occurred many times.[37] For instance, René Descartes' *Meditations on First Philosophy* established a new beginning by fundamentally challenging the conditions of knowledge and reconstructing the world on paper *more geometrico*. However, the most striking depiction of a radical beginning is and remains Daniel Defoe's novel *Robinson Crusoe* (1718). The eponymous hero of this story proves that it is possible for the resilient, hardworking, and ingenious

---

36. Edward Said, *Beginnings: Intentions and Method* (New York: Columbia University Press, 1985), xii.

37. Albrecht Koschorke et al., eds., *Der fictive Staat: Konstruktionen des politischen Körpers in der Geschichte Europas* (Frankfurt am Main: Fischer, 2007).

individual to begin the world and its history all over again. Through experimentation and experience, Crusoe repeats the accumulated history of humanity all on his own and, in so doing, ends up organizing his life with the aid of the rational, temporal framework of a calendar (the fact that he names the first human being he meets on the island "Friday" is an expression of the colonizer's excellent modern time-management). "A beginning," writes Said, "not only creates but is its own method because it has intention."[38]

We could generalize by saying that the fiction of the beginning is the central foundational myth of modernity. That is also Albrecht Koschorke's assertion in his research into the philosophical and literary narratives of beginning in the early-modern period.[39] For example, Robinsonades, named after Daniel Defoe's 1718 novel, "tell of a new cultural beginning from out of its own resources and in that sense, belong to a wide field of European mythologies of origin. But Robinson's shipwreck in no ways marks a clear distinction between the old, poor life and a new, reformed world: In fact, Crusoe devotes a great deal of energy to salvaging usable goods from the shipwreck and dragging them onto his utopian island." Koschorke recognizes in this detail an important structural characteristic of all narratives of beginning: "On the one hand, they construct a kind of baseline so that the new beginning can appear absolute and pure; on the other hand, they cannot do it without a maneuver that crosses over this line of origin. Wherever a line is drawn, dubious figures gather, illegitimate border crossers, smugglers, etc. who violate boundaries like parasites."

In *Faust*, Goethe stages the paradigmatic new beginning both as a foundational moment and as the crux of the modern. While in his study, Faust, driven by the search for certain knowledge, reaches for the foundational text of his own cultural inheritance, the New Testament, to "[p]roperly translate / the sacred Greek original / into

---

38. Said, *Beginnings*, xxiii.
39. With reference to Descartes' writing, Albrecht Koschorke also shows that even Descartes' systematic philosophical refounding of philosophy "does not avoid such impurity/contamination." "On Epistemological Smugglers (Defoe, Descartes)," Lecture for POLNET Summer School at the University of Konstanz, 116 (August 2004).

my own dear native tongue."[40] With this conscious act of translation, a hiatus emerges, a gap, that cannot be closed again. Cast out of the richness of the original and its revelations, Faust finds himself in the realm of words where one is (almost) as good as another. With the act of translation, a proliferation of signifiers necessarily arises; no word can remain at a standstill any longer. But the modern Faust (read "Luther") was not the first to engage in this act of translation—he only advanced it. The Greek New Testament was already the translation of the original Hebrew bible, and it had already transformed the origin of genesis (*b'reshit* in Hebrew—"In the beginning, God created the heavens and earth") into a new Christological beginning: "In the beginning was the word and the word was with god and god was the word." Faust continues this chain of metamorphoses associated with the establishment of a beginning: From "word," he lands on "mind," and then "power," and then, finally, "deed." Goethe's scene in the study brings to the stage what it means, in Edward Said's sense, to go from a divine, mythical, and privileged origin to a secular beginning, one that is generated by humans and so is endlessly variable.[41]

Genealogy and Autogenesis

The modern fantasy of a new beginning will be illustrated here by means of another famous literary example. It has to do with the monologue in Shakespeare's *Hamlet* in which the eponymous hero reacts to the appearance of the ghost of his dead father. At the same

---

40. J. W. Goethe, *Faust I and II*, trans. S. Atkins (Boston: Suhrkamp/Insel, 1984), 33.

41. A collection that came out of a Munich lecture series takes up this inexhaustible movement: Inka Mülder-Bach and Eckhard Schumacher, eds., *Am Anfang war . . . Ursprungsfiguren und Anfangskonstruktionen der Moderne* (Munich: Fink 2008). The volume explores the fiction of beginning as a procedure: "Starting out with the intention of demystifying the mythological body of narrative beginnings, the clarification itself became a radically new beginning, and became enmeshed in the very gestures of self-foundation and self-creation, in large narratives of origins, developments, and progress, that had been subject to a radical critique in the twentieth century under the banner of différence, supplementarity, belatedness, and repetitions" (7).

time, he also reflects on what a radical beginning might mean in the context of generational change and on the epoch-making caesura of the modern period [*Neuzeit*].[42] This son does not (yet) have an Oedipal complex; it has not occurred to him to sever ties with his father, much less to get rid of him so that he can wed his mother. However, that is precisely what his Uncle Claudius has done. In Freud's interpretation, of course, Claudius would become a sub-stitute for the secret Oedipal desire of the young Hamlet. In the monologue in question, however, it is not a matter of a father–son conflict but rather of the "modern" will to an absolute and new beginning.

Prominent themes of the modern—such as revolution, innova-tion, and individuality—involve the staging of a radical beginning and so must also include the staging of a break with tradition. As a result, the modern involves what Peter Sloterdijk calls the "stress of self-starting."[43] In Hamlet's monologue, we see precisely how such a rupture is carried out. After the ghost has taken his leave with the words "Adieu, adieu, adieu. Remember me,"[44] the son becomes obsessed with *one* sole desire: He longs to preserve in memory the moment he has just experienced. Hamlet has a thoroughly "mod-ern" sense of the ephemeral transience of the present, which, as soon as it happens, has already vanished or become passé. His monologue thus focuses entirely on memorizing what has just happened. In it, he transforms his memory into a symbolic table on which to write his ghost's dispatch:

Remember thee?
Ay, thou poor ghost, whiles memory holds a seat
In this distracted globe. Remember thee?
Yea, from the table of my memory
I'll wipe away all trivial fond records,

42. Koselleck on the term *Neuzeit*, in *Futures Past*, 222ff.
43. Peter Sloterdijk, *Zur Welt kommen—zur Sprache kommen: Begleitheft zu Peter Sloterdijks öffentlicher Vorlesung* (Frankfurt: Frankfurt City and University Library, 1998), 42.
44. William Shakespeare, *Hamlet*, ed. Cyrus Hoy (New York: W. W. Norton, 1963), (I, v, 91), 22.

All saws of books, all forms, all pressures past
That youth and observation copied there,
And thy commandment all alone shall live
Within the book and volume of my brain,
Unmixed with baser matter (I, 5, 95–104).

To make room for his father's words, everything else must be erased. In this monologue, Shakespeare stages the modern desire for a new beginning as a *tabula rasa*. But, in contrast to the table that can be erased and to white paper that can be written on for the first time, human memory is always *already* written on. In the case of human memory, in other words, there can be no absolute beginning or complete erasure, but only ever acts of rewriting and overwriting. Here, Shakespeare is introducing the necessary precondition for every radical beginning: frenetic erasure as an act of intentional forgetting. In this sense, Hamlet's monologue can be read as a primal scene of modernity that grounds its own act of innovation (as would happen a century later in the philosophy of John Locke) on a tabula rasa. Shakespeare stages this performative act, and Hamlet's endeavor makes it clear—*ex negativo*—that there are no absolute beginnings or completely blank sheets of paper, either in memory or in culture. The radically new beginning turns out to be no more than a phantasm, one that can never be realized without destructive violence. The fivefold repetition of the tiny word "all" in Hamlet's speech emphasizes the radicality and the unconditioned nature of this desire to erase. For him, it is a matter of "all" and nothing; this absolutely new beginning depends on the purity of this nothing, "unmixed with baser matter." To put it in psychoanalytic terms, Shakespeare is pointing toward the "anal character" of any radical innovation that invests in the quality of "purity," such as the Puritans, who committed themselves to this program, even through their choice of what to call themselves.

In this monologue, Shakespeare exposes the constructivist and performative character of a modern break, yet he does so—paradoxically enough—in the context of a character who fully adopts the law of the father and precisely does not break with him. Whereas one hundred years later, Defoe's hero Robinson Crusoe would become an individual by breaking with his father—he defies the latter's explicit command *not* to go to sea—for Hamlet, rather, what is at stake is a model (prevented because of murder) of initiation. A significant symbol of these ties is the very name of Hamlet, which is shared by both King and Prince. The son walks in the footsteps of the father and makes himself into a willing vessel for the King's will. Whereas Crusoe rebels against his living father, the supremacy of Hamlet's dead father will not be broken. Hamlet philosophizes in his monologue about the potential for emotion, purity, and violence hidden in the act of beginning, yet he is himself anything *but* a revolutionary.[45]

The paradigmatic revolutionary in the history of Western literature would be created three-quarters of a century later. Here I am referring to the figure of Satan in John Milton's epic *Paradise Lost*. The Romantics saw and celebrated Satan as a revolutionary, though Milton himself would certainly not have approved of this, even though he put his own talents at the disposal of the revolutionary Cromwell. To be sure, the Puritan revolution violently broke with the human institutions of monarchy and church, though the intention was not to bring about a new beginning but to reestablish the direct rule of God on the model of the Old Testament. In that sense, Milton's "revolution" is closer to the older meaning of the word, indicating the movement of stars as they continually revolve back to their predetermined place in the cycle of a natural cosmic order. Though Satan does rebel quite brutally against God in the epic, for Milton the Puritan, Satan was still no revolutionary—we will come back to this change in the meaning of the word in the next chapter— but instead a heretic possessed by envy and hubris. Of course, Milton does portray him as a lone fighter, which certainly encourages the Romantic reception of him. However, the poet's intention notwithstanding, what is decisive for our purposes is the later reevaluation of this literary figure who captures the pathos of modernity

45. For him, generational duties and genealogical loyalties are (as is also shown in Ulysses' famous speech in *Troilus and Cressida*) the only way to avoid catastrophe. As one caught between innovation and tradition, he can reveal the radical preconditions of modernity all the more clearly.

and leads us back to the key question regarding beginnings. Of particular importance in this regard is the following speech that Satan makes as leader of his seditious army, before the great war in heaven:

> Who saw
> When this creation was? remember'st thou
> Thy making, while the Maker gave thee being?
> We know no time when we were not as now;
> Know none before us, self-begot, self-raised
> By our own quick'ning power, when fatal course
> Had circled his full orb, the birth mature
> Of this our native Heav'n, ethereal sons.
> Our puissance is our own, our own right hand
> Shall teach us highest deeds, by proof to try
> Who is our equal (V, 856–66)[46]

For Milton, Satan is the arch-heretic because he denies his divine origin. For precisely the same reason, the Romantics see him as a Prometheus-like liberator who anticipates human responsibility and thereby founds the modern. With his positing of the new *beginning* of "our own quick'ning power," he severs the tie to a mythical *origin*. In this case, nothing must be forgotten, for a new law henceforth applies involving the evidence of empirical perception ("who saw?") and human memory ("remember'st thou?"). With these words—blasphemous for Milton, courageous for the Romantics— not only are mythic origins dissolved, but genealogical claims are called into question. Since the Enlightenment, the principle of self-creation (autogenesis) was understood in terms of each person's task of educating themselves. For the Romantics, this principle was epitomized most impressively in the exceptional phenomenon of the artistic genius, who no longer owed anything to a tradition and created only from the sources of (their own) nature: "self-begot, self-raised." In the context of this aesthetics of genius, the word "original" underwent a profound reinterpretation. No longer tied

---

46. John Milton, *Paradise Lost* (London: Penguin Books, 2000), 123.

so closely to the negative Christian anthropology of original sin, "original" now came to be understood in relation to the idea of nature as a positive transcendent source of creativity. With that, for the first time, the two meanings of the word "original"—that is, "of the origin" and "unique"—became entangled. Like his work, the artist himself would now be venerated as an "original," one who carries his origin (Lat. *origo*) within himself.

Creative Destruction

In his monologue, Shakespeare's Hamlet embodies the unconditioned modern will as a tabula rasa, and in the process draws attention to the adverse and even potentially violent or destructive features that inhere in the modern project of beginning. Utopias are a modern genre in which radical projects run counter to what already exists. In the context of this counterproposal, an important difference can be discerned between, on the one hand, literary fictions meant to assist in a reflection on what already exists and, on the other, what comes to be understood as directives for action at the level of politics. Revolution is a political medium for implementing utopian counterprojects. Its goal is to force an irreversible break with the existing order and establishing an inevitable new beginning. Just as with the idea of the "original," whereby the meaning shifted from "of the origin" to "unique," the word "revolution" also underwent an important historical shift in meaning. As was just mentioned, the word in the premodern period refers to the cyclical revolutions of the stars within the cosmic order. That revolutions would be made by humans and would take place in history rather than in nature is another direct consequence of the cultural time regime of modernity. Utopias and revolutions belong closely together; they are philosophical as well as political means of forcing a temporal break and then establishing and staging the new.

Karl Marx summarized the aversion of the modern toward the past in his famous phrase: "The tradition of all the dead generations weighs like a nightmare on the brain of the living."[47] For him, a human being is free and sovereign only once he or she can move freely without "recollections of past world history" (99) and "forgets" the historical paragons and models of the past. Whereas Cromwell's English revolution still took its inspiration from the prophets of the Old Testament, and the French Revolution of the middle-class still relied on the dress of Roman heroes, Marx claims that "[t]he social revolution of the nineteenth century cannot draw its poetry from the past, but only from the future. It cannot begin with itself before it has stripped off all superstition in regard to the past" (99). To which he adds: "In order to arrive at its own content, the revolution of the nineteenth century must *let the dead bury their dead*" (99, emphasis added). The inclusion of the citation from Matthew (Matt. 8:22) indicates that Marx's commitment to a pure present and future draws its force from the immanent eschatology of the evangelists. The past must be broken off from the present and, for that to happen, it must first be devalued wholesale and declared to be junk, superstition, a nightmare. With his devaluation of the past as the "realm of the dead" that threatens the living, Marx situated the binary opposition of "death versus life," so common since the Enlightenment, on a temporal axis and, at the same time, raised it to the level of a nightmarish phantasm. The only solution to this threatening burden was a revolution capable of driving out the ghosts of the past and clearing the air. Nietzsche, another critic of historicism, also emphasized the crippling burden of the past. At the same time, however, he acknowledged that the use of history can also be oriented toward life and the future, including the monumental forms and their inspiring role models that Marx held in such disdain. Another form of the use of the past that Nietzsche recommends comes much closer to Marx's thought, and that is "critical" history, by which Nietzsche means a break from and the destruction of the past in the service of a new future. Whoever chooses this

47. Karl Marx, "The Eighteenth Brumaire of Louis Bonaparte," in *Karl Marx and Frederick Engels: Selected Works in One Volume* (New York: International Publishers, 1968), 97.

form of using the past, Nietzsche claims, "must possess and from time to time employ the strength to break up and dissolve a part of the past: he does this by bringing it before the tribunal, scrupulously examining it and finally condemning it."[48] However, Nietzsche also suggests that this kind of breaking-free is not without its dangers since in the rush of its dissolution, one's own foundations are also sometimes destroyed.

However important these positions are, the key notion for this particular aspect of the modern time regime is not so much "critical destruction" as "creative destruction." It took shape in the mid-nineteenth century (the decade immediately before Marx's *Eighteenth Brumaire*) in the hands of a professional revolutionary, Mikhail Bakunin, who was preoccupied with his task as a destroyer of existing structures. He understood his task, however, not as *destructive* but as *creative,* and in a famous formulation he even arranged these opposites into a relation of interdependence: "The passion for destruction is a creative passion, too!" This statement is possibly the most radical expression of the time regime of modernity.[49] A century later, the Russian anarchist Bakunin's impulse coalesced once again, but under another name and under entirely different circumstances; namely, at the heart of American capitalism, which just proves that this particular aspect of the modern time regime has the same relevance even for opposing political ideologies such as communism and capitalism.[50] In the 1930s, the econo-

---

48. Friedrich Nietzsche, "On the Uses and Disadvantages of History for Life, 75–76.

49. This statement is found in Mikhail Bakunin's article "The Reaction in Germany," which he wrote under the pseudonym of Jules Elysard and published in the *German Yearbook for the Arts and Sciences*, a publication of the young Hegelians. In English: Mikhail Bakunin, "The Reaction in Germany" in *Bakunin on Anarchy*, ed. and trans. S. Dolgoff (New York: Random House, 1972), 57.

50. "Since the beginning of the twentieth century, violence and destruction have been part of the basic signature of the modern. We find it used in capitalist as well as socialist economic systems, in the construction of nation-states, as well as in the dissolution and re-formation of empires." Lucian Hölscher, "Die Zukunft zerstört die Vergangenheit: Zerstörungspotentiale in den Zukunftswürfen des 20.Jahrhunderts," in *Aufbauen—Zerstören: Phänomene und Prozesse der Kunst* (Düsseldorf: Athena, 2007), 9.

mist Joseph Alois Schumpeter emigrated to the United States where he published his book *Capitalism, Socialism and Democracy* (1942).[51] The chapter of the book entitled "The Process of Creative Destruction" describes capitalism as an evolutionary system and, in that context, makes explicit reference to the arguments of Karl Marx. In Schumpeter's view, capitalism is an economic system that is permanently in motion and can neither be stopped at any point nor come to completion. "The fundamental impulse that sets and keeps the capitalist engine in motion," according to Schumpeter's assessment, does not come from outside through natural or social changes, but rather solely from within: It "comes from the new consumer goods, the new methods of production or transportation, the new markets, the new forms of industrial organization that capitalist enterprise creates" (83). For capitalism to create the new, it must constantly destroy its own structures, which is why Schumpeter also talks about a "history of revolutions" in this context; namely, capitalism takes advantage of continual advancements in new technologies and industries over old ones.

Schumpeter discovered that the capitalist system has an inherent tendency toward self-destruction.[52] As a consequence, however, this destruction gradually becomes less terrifying in that it constantly produces something new, mimicking the inherent logic of nature. In fact, the principle of creative destruction has something organic about it, which is also why he uses a metaphor of evolution in his description:

> . . . it illustrates the same process of industrial mutation . . . that incessantly revolutionizes the economic structure *from within*, incessantly destroying the old one, incessantly creating a new one. The process of Creative Destruction is the essential fact about capitalism. It is what

---

51. Joseph A. Schumpeter, *Capitalism, Socialism and Democracy* (London: Allen & Unwin, 1976).

52. "There is inherent in the capitalist system a tendency towards self-destruction. . . . The capitalist process not only destroys its own institutional framework but it also creates the conditions for another. Destruction may not be the right word after all. Perhaps I should have spoken of transformation" (Schumpeter, *Capitalism*, 162).

capitalism consists in and what every capitalist concern has got to live in (ibid., emphasis in original).

With this notion of "creative destruction" and its relation to evolutionary processes, Schumpeter develops the upbeat idea of a capitalism that constantly renews itself. He never lost his neoliberal faith in the progressive evolution of this economic system, even though he himself drove a bank to ruin during a time of great inflation and lost all his assets in the process.

As the example of Schumpeter shows, the idea of creative destruction not only applies to situations of political revolution, but it is also suited to capitalism and the bloodless dynamics of technological development. This principle has indeed always been relevant to the area of technology, as was pointed out by the American philosopher Emerson in the middle of the nineteenth century. He did not see the logic of obsolescence that characterizes linear technical evolution as "capitalism's own logic"; rather, it was the basic principle of cultural progress more generally. Emerson therefore recommended that the young industrial nation very consciously distance itself from the old Europe and its burdensome past, and then go on to emphasize its commitment to progress. As he clearly emphasizes in this context, new and old are necessarily dialectical notions, in which the one can make its mark and prevail only at the cost and with the assistance of the other. That is also why renewal inevitably entails forgetting and disposal. Emerson makes no secret of this, but rather speaks openly of "the inevitable pit which the creation of new thought opens for all that is old."[53] The use of the word "pit" here means something like "garbage heap" or "landfill." His examples of creative destruction relate to the linear process of replacing obsolete technologies that he describes as both nomological and irreversible:

New arts destroy the old. See the investment of capital in aqueducts made useless by hydraulics; fortifications, by gunpowder; roads and canals, by railways; sails, by steam, by electricity.

---

53. Ralph Waldo Emerson, "Circles" (1841), in *Selected Writings of R. W. Emerson*, ed. W. H. Gilman (New York: New American Library, 1965), 296.

This law of progress of the capitalist mode of production is today called "planned obsolescence" and, according to Emerson, applies equally well to culture as a whole. By this logic of progress, nothing is sacred; not even the works and values of Greek culture could take on a lasting exemplary function but had to be melted down to yield to the pressure of the new. Emerson was committed to focusing exclusively on the future and described himself as an "endless seeker with no past at my back" (304). This committed defender of the modern time regime, whose writing would exert strong influence on a young Nietzsche, wanted to replace "tradition" with "transformation" and point American culture wholly in the direction of a permanent renewal.

Let us finish up by taking a leap into the twentieth century, for Emerson's vision has been taken up in many Western societies. In the 1950s, it appeared in the form of the economic miracle in West Germany. Karl Jaspers, the philosopher, was in a position to observe this process of permanent renewal in German postwar society. However, he also saw the negative side of this phenomenon alongside the euphoric one: namely, the "increased consumption until everything permanent is annihilated."[54] Thus, Jaspers did not speak about "creative destruction," but instead analyzed a "constantly destructive mode of production":

> The process of production and consumption, now an end in itself, no longer builds a world in which human beings are at home and does not allow for goods to last. After the total destruction of 1945, this process could be resurrected quickly and efficiently through the work ethic and diligence of a people, as if nothing had happened (ibid.).

Under changed historical and cultural conditions, Jaspers sees the activity of such a renewal either as a frenzied eradication of the past or as an anesthetization of trauma and guilt by means of forgetting. The collective investment in economic rebuilding after 1945 allowed West German society to free itself from its own history by exclu-

---

54. Karl Jaspers, "Wahrheit, Freiheit, Friede," *Friedenspreise des Deutschen Buchhandels* acceptance speech, 1958, Börsenverein des Deutschen Buchhandels, 9; accessed August 29, 2018, http://www.existenz.us/volumes/Vol.9-2Jaspers.pdf.

sively focusing on the future, a dazzling example of which was provided by American "consumption."

The principle of creative destruction has not only arisen in revolutionary, technological, and economic contexts but in artistic contexts as well. Ernst Osterkamp has drawn attention to this aesthetic context in his exploration of the aesthetic work of Karl Philipp Moritz (1756–1793). In that work, he finds thinking and formulations attesting to the relevance of this principle for art theory. Osterkamp suggests that Moritz, a man of letters and founder of what the latter called an "empirical psychology," made use "of a nervous modern consciousness." The following statement comes from Moritz: "Is it not through the perpetual destruction of the individual that the species remains eternally young and beautiful?" He also speaks of the "destruction of the weak by the strong, of the imperfect by the perfect."[55] These comparisons suggest that Moritz is articulating an aesthetic logic of progress by drawing on the field of biological species' evolution and applying it to the field of artistic creation. As Osterkamp rightly points out, Moritz was not using the word "destruction" in the sense of an aesthetics of violence, but rather in the sense of a "violent aesthetic, that in its will to the perfect whole indissolubly binds artistic creation to the destruction of the imperfect, the resistant, the particular" (13). In this absolute will to artistic perfection, a new aspiration for a modern art appears—an art that is autonomous, newly sovereign, and responsible only for itself. Osterkamp, once again:

> The more highly developed the author's awareness is of modernity, the stronger the desire is to create an historical *tabula rasa* with their own work, so as to establish a connection between the absolute new beginning in art and the call for the absolute destruction of tradition (15).[56]

---

55. Ernst Osterkamp, "Kreative Zerstörung als ästhetisches Verfahren in Richard Wagners 'Meistersingern,'" in *Angst vor der Zerstörung: Der Meister Künste zwischen Archiv und Erinnern*, ed. R. Sollich et al., *Recherchen* 52 (Berlin: Theater der Zeit, 2008): 12.

56. However, we need to introduce some differentiations here that Osterkamp's essay, in its own way, revels in blurring. One important distinction should be made between a forgetting of tradition and a destruction of cultural material; another has to do with the range of incentives that motivate creative destruction.

Osterkamp takes the idea of "creative destruction" from Horst Bredekamp, who brings it—and this is another important area of application—into his account of the history of development of St. Peter's Square in Rome.[57] Of course, the principle of creative destruction governed not only the history of St. Peter's Square; it is also *the* paradigm of twentieth-century architecture. As an indication of its paradigmatic importance in the last century, reference could be made to a short radio feature that aired in Germany on May 30, 2009, as part of the "Denke ich an Deutschland" series, featuring the renowned architect Gottfried Böhm. Over the course of the program, Böhm reminisces about the postwar period and admits that he experienced it "not as a downfall, but as a beginning." He did not find the destruction around him disturbing; on the contrary, it held "appeal to make something out of what was still there." He supported the obsession with demolition that characterized the postwar period but admitted that, when viewed in hindsight, it had gone too far, though he had not noticed that at the time: "The old stuff was revolting to me." In a bit of a reversal, Böhm makes it clear that today he highly values much of what he had then categorically rejected and dismissed.

The obsession with demolition in West Germany had its counterpart in East Germany. Although during the Cold War the two Germanys were ideologically divided on all other issues, they were in full agreement on this particular point. In this sense, they shared the values and style of the so-called "postwar modernity." What the West called "demolition" and the East called "the removal of rubble" included the destruction of any remaining historical buildings. This systematic destruction was justified on both sides by notions

---

According to Moritz, this creative destruction is in no way directed toward the entirety of culture but is exclusively directed toward the sphere of art that celebrates the modern as a single totality. It is precisely this claim to an autonomous aesthetics that Richard Wagner is said to have reversed; his impulse of creative destruction applies to the new beginning of a totality of art, society, and politics that is diametrically opposed to Moritz's idea.

57. Since 2005, a research group at Humboldt University in Berlin called "Creative Destruction" has been exploring how social systems have undergone radical change throughout history.

of modern hygiene as well as contemporary ideas of society. Construction and reconstruction were characterized by the future and the principle of hope; as it so happened, "demolition" and "removing rubble" also made it possible for cities and peoples to be liberated from a contaminated historical legacy and to realize new social utopias. This particular time regime accepted the destruction of the old as the cost of making room for the new: whatever existed before was made obsolete in ever-faster cycles. We can speak quite neutrally of violence and destruction here, since these ideas never connote disaster and trauma in this context but rather are considered to be a "cleansing, exculpating preparation for a promising new beginning."[58]

The modern program of creative destruction has historical antecedents in European architecture. In his studies on the "past future," Lucian Hölscher has shown that in 1830 the European emergence into the future "became broadly accepted and so too was there an increased willingness to destroy what existed for the sake of the new."[59] Using the examples of the great urban centers of London and Paris, he shows that by the mid-nineteenth century at the latest, "the cultural process of self-destruction at the heart of modern societies had taken on a methodical form" (ibid.). Le Corbusier's new construction plans for Paris, Stockholm, and other major European cities involved the wholesale destruction of entire neighborhoods, to be replaced by uniform high-rises over large expanses of land. He first developed these plans after the First World War and then again after the Second World War. The greater the positive connotations of the new were, the easier it was to part with the old. This is how modern architecture carried out a temporal break and eliminated realms of experience in favor of ever-newer horizons of expectation.

In an essay entitled "Moderne als Wunsch: Krieg und Städtebau im 20. Jahrhundert" (Modernity as Desire: War and the Construction of Cities in the Twentieth Century), Albrecht Koschorke examines the "totalitarian side of modernity" (Rainer Zitelmann) in

---

58. Osterkamp, "Kreative Zerstörung," 26.
59. Hölscher, "Die Zukunft zerstört der Vergangenheit," 11.

relation to "theories of the modern."[60] In the essay, he inquires into the potential for violence in the twentieth century, violence that was unleashed in two world wars and, he contends, was then carried into the planning strategies of architects after both the First and Second World Wars. Koschorke's long-term approach to the twentieth century suggests that there is a consistent pattern of violence involved in severing realms of experience from horizons of expectation. Koschorke links this violence to a strong collective longing for "purification" implied by the modernization project. It consists, he writes, of "erasing the traces of the past with increasing rigor—be they of a personal or a collective nature" (35). In that context, he draws a surprising parallel between generals and architects who, he contends, implement the same program in their respective fields. Where generals are concerned, they longed for the First World War as an epochal break that should have achieved "the true and complete dissolution of the past" (27) in an "act of collective self-purification" (31). Using other means, Koschorke argues that architects pursued the politics of space under the banner of forgetting (36); they launched their "assault on the cities" (37) in the name of "bodily and moral health" (39). For both generals and architects, new visions could only be realized at the cost of what already existed. "All large planning," Koschorke summarizes, "involves the conscious and programmatic disregard for historical topography" (39). In architects' statements, the new architecture was represented as "a monstrous, high-speed, and brutal development" that had "torn away all bridges to the past" (ibid.). It is striking how the language of warfare aligns with that of city planning in these descriptions. Koschorke comments:

> What all radical planning programs of the twentieth century have in common is the awareness of a temporal break, that is, a now insurmountable opposition between historical traditions and current drives to innovation. They do not aim at reconciling the opposition, but rather try to stimulate it and make it even starker. That includes the libidinal and identificatory fulfillment of its destructive potential (41).

---

60. Albrecht Koschorke, "Moderne als Wunsch: Krieg und Städtebau im 20. Jahrhundert," *Leviathan: Zeitschrift für Sozialwissenschaft* 27, no. 1 (1999): 23–42.

Koschorke describes the principle of creative destruction as a "double-figure arising out of destructive and constructive tendencies" (31). At another point, he also talks about the "schizoid disposition of modernity" (33) and asks himself how it was possible to elevate traumata to the status of normative standards of activity.[61] In the dialectic of creative destruction, revolution is inseparable from ruins, as is utopia from trauma; the one is not to be had without the other. Notions like revolution and utopia symbolize an approach to history from the perspective of active planning and doing; notions like ruins and trauma, by contrast, are tied to the perspective of those who are passively subjected to history. The revolutionary power of the modern time regime consists precisely in its systematic ability to mask this ambivalence. As long as the gaze remains rigidly fixed on the success of revolutionary action to be expected in the future, it will only see the creative and constructive potential in the act of destruction. However, as soon as we consider the violent, destructive, and traumatizing side of this destruction, the revolutionary energy of the new begins to lose its magic.

Destroying and Preserving: The Invention of the Historical

> [M]oderns [are] cut off from a past that is maintained in a
> state of artificial survival due only to historicism.
>
> —*Bruno Latour*[62]

The word "historicism" is often used in two entirely different senses. In the first sense, it refers to the way in which a society draws on past eras of its own history when it is looking for aesthetic norms and historic precedents. In this sense, historicism is characterized by resuscitating and appropriating older styles and rediscovering he-

---

61. Koschorke closes his essay with the intention to further pursue the affect-economical dialectics of modernity and barbarism. "It is time to take stock of the 20th century and get beyond simple oppositions [like that of the oppositional pair modernity and barbarity—A. A.]" (42).

62. Latour, *We Have Never Been Modern*, 133.

roic figures, then by presenting these in compelling ways so that a society can imaginatively reflect on, and mythologize, itself. The demand that nations reinventing themselves get their bearings from their histories therefore goes hand in hand with the need to represent a middle class that had come into money throughout the course of industrialization. That is, this first sense of historicism becomes the natural enemy of modernity, which emphatically turned away from it in the wake of the First World War. In the eyes of the moderns, historicism became synonymous with regressive nostalgia and a lack of self-sufficiency, innovation, or creative energy.

Under the heading of "the invention of the historical," we are dealing with a second meaning of historicism that is an integral part of modernization. Ernst Schulin has vividly described how this is to be understood using the specific example of the French Revolution. As illustration, he uses a simple, everyday experience: when someone dies, a great deal of the personal effects from this lived life must be decluttered, aired out, removed, and destroyed. Everyone is familiar with this practical necessity: room must be made for the growth of new life. Following the frenzy of decluttering, though, according to Schulin, experience has shown that a countermovement often follows: As soon as one realizes that "too little remains, . . . the maintenance of tradition begins."[63] The past that had been perceived as an obstacle becomes precious when it starts to become scarce. Schulin's essay uses this everyday experience to explore a paradigmatic historical break: his theme is the birth of a new historicism from out of the spirit of the French Revolution. By "the rejection of the past," he means the great historical changes of direction that accompany a conscious break with tradition and the destruction of material culture. He sees modern historiography as a child of the Enlightenment; from the beginning, he writes, it is "the enemy of—existing, ruling—tradition. It is created to critically examine the dominant legacies of religion, society

---

63. Ernst Schulin, "Absage an und Wiederherstellung von Vergangenheit," in *Speicher des Gedächtnisses, Bibliotheken, Museen, Archive*, vol. 1: *Wiederherstellung von Vergangenheit, Kompensation von Geschichtsverlust*, ed. Peter Stachel and Moritz Csáky (Vienna: Passagen, 2000).

and state, and to recognize them in all their historical relativity" (24). Indeed, he adds:

> Though, these critical destructions are always and even increasingly associated with what I call "attempts at reconstruction." They are occasions for renewal: through preservation in archives and libraries, through being made available in new editions, through new history writing, and through new visualizations in artistic and publicly-engaging works (25).

The example of the French Revolution illustrates with particular clarity this double impulse of destruction/reconstruction. The radical break with traditions was carried out in public through symbolic acts of destruction, such as the public burning of the feudal archives of French aristocratic families on the Place Vendôme. The revolutionary impulse of destruction was also directed toward the dead, whose power over the present had to be broken. "In three days and nights during August 1793, 51 graves were destroyed" and with that, "as a monk commented, the work of twelve centuries was destroyed" (26). The wagonloads of smashed gravestones and sculptures arrived at a decommissioned cloister, which was then turned into a warehouse before gradually becoming a historical museum. The Musée des Monuments Français emerged in 1795 from out of the ruins and spoils. What had been pushed off pedestals and smashed to pieces in the morning was then collected in the afternoon and brought to the newly created institutions of the historical museum and the archive. As a stronghold of values and norms, these venerable traditions were *shattered*, but at the same time they were *preserved* as sites of historical knowledge. Alexandre Lenoir was given permission to reclaim these material remains as "monuments of art and education," on the condition that he assign them to an era that had been overcome and that he publicly disavow their relevance for the present. According to his apologetical argument, the statues still had a limited practical value, for future sculptors could continue to use them as standards in historical representations in order to depict clothing styles of the past all the more accurately.

In fact, historicism *does* have a great deal to do with obtaining the most accurate knowledge possible about past eras that are so far removed from us as to have become foreign. In Western modernity, historians would soon make this knowledge available in what was a new academic discipline, founded in the early nineteenth century. The new scientific ethos of this guild included a commitment of its members to base their research on a scholarly examination of verifiable primary sources. Certainly, historians since then have pursued knowledge along much the same lines, even when the knowledge produced was not only critical but also functioned as a means of political and ideological legitimation. But that does not change the fact that the ideal of critical history-writing belongs to the fundamentals of modernity and constitutes an important aspect of the modern temporal regime. Since that time, archivists, guardians, museum curators, historians, and other humanities scholars belong to the groups of professional specialists of the past, all of whom are now workers in the great vineyard of historicism.

Destroying and preserving are thus the two opposing impulses of modernization that were coupled together in a new way during the French Revolution. The impulse of destruction finds expression in the radical elimination of the monarchy, the aristocracy, and monasteries, together with their privileges, traditions, buildings, and material collections. These destructions took place violently, by means of the guillotine, burnings, acts of renaming, and, not least, the introduction of a new calendar—the quintessential symbol for a new beginning. The other impulse of preservation came hot on the heels of these acts of destruction and was expressed in the form of newly developed institutions: the historical archive, the modern museum, and historiography itself. For not everything that was brutally eliminated in the Revolution was thereby immediately and irreversibly destroyed. Some of it was put to the side and placed under the protection of institutions that gathered and preserved material remains, transforming them into objects of a growing body of historical knowledge. As such, what society had left behind and felt it no longer needed was not only conserved but also remained present in fragments and was eventually put on display for public viewing.

Modernity's drive for innovation brought out a new interest in the old in its coevolution with the new. That is why Koselleck speaks of the "history of progress and of historism [*sic*]."[64] Under these conditions, the historian would become the professional guardian, specialist, and defender of a past that otherwise no one would bother with. So, this "invention of the historical" presupposes a radical break of the present from the past.

Pure Past

Virginia Woolf once defined history as that "which is past the touch and control of the living."[65] Here Woolf is emphasizing the first and most important quality of the past: that is, its having passed, being past. The past is past by virtue of the irreversibility and the unchangeability of linear time, and this is precisely the precondition for its professional treatment by historians. They can begin their work only once the door separating us from the past has been definitively slammed shut. On this point, Rudolf Schlögl once again: "The greater the variety generated by a society's mode of differentiation, the more the temporal registers of past, present, and future have to be clearly distinguished from one another, and the more abstract the temporal concept has to be."[66] Especially important in this case is the distinction between the past and present, since historical scholarship depends so heavily on it. Drawing this line makes "the invention of the historical" possible in the first place so that it is, in effect, the foundational act of this "modern" discipline.

The central characteristic of the past, according to the modern time regime, is therefore that it *has* passed. Until now, no one had really thought much about this, the assumption being that the past just does this all on its own—entirely independent of what humans think, do, or will—and as a natural function of linear time. Historical research is based on this representation of a denaturalized and acculturated homogeneous time characterized as "flowing, direc-

---

64. Reinhart Koselleck, "History, Histories, and Formal Time Structures," in *Futures Past*, 103.
65. Virginia Woolf, *Orlando: A Biography* (UK: Harmondsworth, 1975), 225.
66. Schlögl, "Zeit und Ereignisse," 5.

tional, and irreversible."[67] This abstract but nonetheless meta-phorical notion of the "flow of time," timeline, or time's "arrow" is important for the constitution of academic history, because the historian must have some way of indicating that the past with which he or she is engaging really has past. For instance, the "past" in this sense can mean that the last witnesses have passed away and no longer have a say in the interpretation of the past. The provocative claim that the historical witness is the natural enemy of the historian[68] can be explained quite simply in terms of this basic temporal structure of academic history. For it is only once any interference caused by living experience and memory in the present is no longer biologically possible (after about a hundred years, say) that the still-present past turns into what Koselleck calls a "pure past." The historian's domain is precisely *not* the witnesses' polyphonic and un-avoidably cacophonic blending of multiple voices, but rather the disembodied and silent archive, in which voices are detached from their living carriers and are *objectified* as sources and documents. Koselleck has described this conversion of the present into the pure past—which happens automatically, owing to the irreversible flow of time—in the following way:

> The research criteria are becoming more austere, but they are—perhaps—also less vivid, less saturated with the empirical, even though they promise to recognize or appreciate more in their objectivity. The moral consternation, the disguised protective functions, the accusations and the designations of guilt by historiography—all these techniques of mastering the past lose their quality as existential political matters; they fade in favor of individual academic research and analyses controlled by hypotheses.[69]

---

67. Chris Lorenz, "Geschichte, Gegenwärtigkeit und Zeit," in *Phänomen Zeit: Dimensionen und Strukturen in Kultur und Wissenschaft*, ed. Dietmar Goltschigg (Tübingen: Stauffenburg, 2011), 128; see also Hodges, "Rethinking Time's Arrow."

68. This statement, originally made by Wolfgang Kraushaar, now circulates as a well-known saying.

69. Reinhart Koselleck, "Afterword to Charlotte Beradt's *The Third Reich of Dreams*," in *The Practice of Conceptual History: Timing History, Spacing Concepts*, trans. Todd Samuel Presner et al. (Stanford: Stanford University Press, 2002), 327.

In other words, historical research begins with the delimitation and definition of the "pure past" as its subject area.[70] Other disciplines are responsible for the present and have their own approaches and methodologies. For example, the social sciences (among them, psychology, sociology, and political science) are specialized to observe, describe, explain, conduct interviews, gather statistics, assess, and interpret what is true in the present. By contrast, historians keep themselves at a safe distance from the present. They do that not because they are reactionary or backward, but because their professional ethos demands it of them. At the same time, their ethos of impartiality is closely tied to the temporal distance the historians maintain with the present. Temporal distance from the subject of their research functions as nothing less than the guarantee of their objectivity. On this point, Chris Lorenz writes:

> The discipline of history has staked its fundamental claim to being a science—as well as its foundational ideas about objectivity and impartiality—on its temporal distance. In what follows, I would like to argue that academic history cannot call its conception of time into question without at the same time having its own scientific standard also called into question.[71]

That is why Rudolf Schlögl emphasizes that "since the eighteenth century, the task of a professionalized discipline of history has been to liberate the present . . . from the past."[72] As a result, at the same time it also pursued the reciprocal goal of systematically liberating the past from the present.

Several (creative) writers also belonged to this era's group of workers in the vineyard of historicism. But I'm not thinking here of the historical novel that, as in the case of Walter Scott's *Waverley*, retrieves a history by means of imagining an unchanged present that had vanished out of contemporary memory just sixty years earlier.

---

70. On the question of the historical emergence of contemporary history (*Zeitgeschichte*), see Konrad H. Jarausch and Martin Sabrow, eds., *Verletztes Gedächtnis: Erinnerungskultur und Zeitgeschichte im Konflikt* (Frankfurt am Main: Campus Verlag, 2002).
71. Lorenz, "Geschichte, Gegenwärtigkeit und Zeit," 128.
72. Schlögl, "Zeit und Ereignisse," 6.

Rather, I'm thinking about authors who made the experience of this irreversible historical change itself the subject of their writing. My two literary examples come from the middle of the nineteenth century. The first has to do not with the French Revolution, but instead with the Industrial Revolution. Steam engines, railways, and electricity introduced irreversible changes to the means of production, transportation, and the world of experience. By means of new technologies and the capitalist production of commodities, a great deal was suddenly outdated and devalued. However, this does not mean that everything automatically ended up in the great trash heap about which Emerson had written so approvingly. That is, another alternative was at hand: the archive of literature. The writer Annette von Droste-Hülshoff experienced this temporal transformation, which she too felt to be irreversible, with a great deal less enthusiasm than her American counterpart Emerson. Indeed, she develops a rather more nostalgic disposition, fostering a delicate sensibility for those rural areas that had not yet been touched by the momentum of change. Her reaction to industrial transformation led to a new type of literary project: she set to working on an ethnographic description of the rural areas of her homeland of Westfalen, Germany. Writing with a strong sense of the historical changes that were under way, she was convinced that what she was describing would, in the foreseeable future, vanish forever:

> That was the physiognomy of the land until today, and in forty years' time, it will be no longer. Population and self-indulgence are visibly growing and, along with them, needs and industry. The smaller picturesque heaths are being divided up. Cultures of slowly growing broadleaf are being neglected, so as to secure a faster yield with coniferous wood. And soon enough, the spruce forests and endless wheat fields will have transformed the character of the landscape, as its former inhabitants, with their ancient mores and customs, vanish more and more; we grasp therefore what now exists in its singularity, ere the slippery blanket that is gradually covering Europe also smothers this quiet corner of the world.[73]

---

73. Annette von Droste-Hülshoff, "Bilder aus Westfalen," in *Werke in einem Band*, ed. Clemens Hesselhaus (Munich: Hanser, 1984), 724ff. "Must we add that everything that we've said here only has to do with peasantry?—I think 'not,' city dwellers are indeed all the same no matter where they are, townsfolk and city folk

Droste-Hülshoff was convinced that, within the time frame of one or two generations, reality as she knew it could be changed to the point of becoming unrecognizable. In this context, she developed an acutely historical sense that not only concentrated on events and stories but also extended to everyday objects, traditions, and landscapes that were on the verge of disappearing. Similar to Baudelaire, her sense of the ephemeral and transitory character of the present had become sharper. But unlike that poet, rather than allowing herself to be delivered over to this change, she sought to capture the present-day Westphalian landscape—one that had already become historical—through her descriptions of it and thus, to save it in a literary archive.

At roughly the same time as Droste-Hülshoff, the American author Nathaniel Hawthorne was writing the short story "Main Street." The title concerns the central artery of a small town in America where the narrator had grown up. The narrative deals with a dramatic historical transformation that had occurred in this place over the last two centuries. In a historical-pictorial broadsheet designed in the style of a puppet theater with movable panels of panoramic scenery, Hawthorne brings the history of this place and the ghosts of its ancestors before the eyes of his readers. The first image in this imaginary panorama shows a thick forest on the site of today's main street, a forest that had seen no axe and in which no European had yet made their mark. On a narrow path walks an Indian "squaw" with a "red" chief by her side. The chief's midnight dancing and shrieking, the narrator remarks, terrified the white settlers who had come to the area. Yet, the narrator contends, the chief himself would be even more terrified if, during a necromancy, he could see the future as well as the feats the white man will achieve reflected in a pool of water. Namely, he would have a vision of a stately hall housing a historical museum "where, among countless

---

alike.—or, that this whole state of things will slow down and that perhaps things won't be so bad in forty years or so?—also unfortunately 'no,' that's how it is everywhere!" (760f). On this point, see also Marcus Wellmann, "Stille Winkel im Strom der Welt? Zur geohistorischen Imagination des 'Biedermeier," Inaugural lecture at the University of Konstanz, January 11, 2012.

curiosities of earth and sea, a few Indian arrow-heads shall be trea-sured up as memorials of a vanished race."[74]

In nineteenth-century museums of the kind Hawthorne was writ-ing about, some relics of the past do find refuge. They are the traces of a past world and of extinct races—evidence of an irreversibly closed chapter of American history. The narrative of Hawthorne's pictorial schema is clearly directed toward the future. It tells the history of a place from its original wildness to the marvels of white civilization. Modernity gained a foothold here, along with the arrival of white settlers. The new historical meaning connected to the place reconstructs the prehistory of this place that no longer bears any relation to the living present. The white settlements of the American wilderness and the industrialization of Westphalen have both cut the present off from the past, though in different ways; in one form or another, modernization accelerates historical transformation. However, what is cut off is not merely destroyed, but is actually semipreserved through traces, whether they be found in history writing, in literary archives, or in local museums. These institutions owe their existence to the historical conscious-ness that, as Arno Borst puts it so concisely, "recognizes differ-ences between eras."[75]

Acceleration

> We declare that the world's wonder has been enriched by
> a fresh beauty: the beauty of speed. . . . [A] roaring car
> that seems to be driving under shrapnel is more beautiful
> than the *Victory of Samothrace*.[76]

---

74. Nathaniel Hawthorne, "Main Street," in *Sketches and Tales*, ed. Roy H. Pearce (Cambridge, UK: Cambridge University Press, 1982), 1024.

75. Arno Borst, "Barbarossas Erwachen: Zur Geschichte der deutschen Iden-tität," in *Identität: Poetik und Hermeneutik*, vol. 8, ed. Odo Marquard and Karl-heinz Stierle (Munich: Fink, 1979), 19.

76. Marinetti, "The Foundation of Futurism," 244.

"Speed, that is the time that races."[77] The theme of acceleration figures so prominently in the discourse on time and modernity that, now and then, the modern time regime as a whole has been reduced to this single characteristic. Awareness of this phenomenon is in no way new; since the beginning of the nineteenth century, it has belonged to the established array of descriptions of modernization. Science, writes Thomas Macaulay in his famous 1837 essay on Francis Bacon, "has multiplied the power of human muscles; it has accelerated motion; it has annihilated distance."[78]

However, the dominance of this theme has its drawbacks because of how it commits us to a linear construction of time's arrow. Whoever researches time exclusively in terms of its increased tempo has only slowing down or standstill as possible counternotions.[79] To get out of this impasse, it is nevertheless important to conceive of the social and cultural problem of time not simply as a problem of different speeds on a linear time line but also as a qualitative coexistence of different temporalities. The discussion in chapter 1 of different "presents" in the context of different kinds of temporal experience helps to open our thinking to a multiplicity of such qualitative temporalities and can help us avoid the trap of a totalizing rhetoric of acceleration.

Wherever acceleration is at issue, we should therefore seriously consider whether, in using this catchword, we are dealing with a real finding, a thought-image or metaphor, or a somewhat alarmist reference to a trendy issue.[80] Acceleration always takes place on many levels that are not necessarily related to one another. Our analyses therefore gain precision when we distinguish between different kinds of acceleration: that of transportation, of communications technologies, of sociocultural transformation, and of the subjective experience of an increasingly fast pace.

---

77. Georg Elwert, "In Search of Time: Different Time-Experiences in Different Cultures," in *Maps of Time*, ed. Zmag Smitek and Borut Brumen (Ljubljana: Filozofaska fakulteta Ljubljana, 2001), 239. Elwert examines various cultural modalities of time, among others the status of waiting.
78. Macaulay, "Francis Bacon," 375.
79. Brose, "Kulturen der Ungleichzeitigkeit."
80. Raphael, "Ordnungsmuster der 'Hochmodern,'" 82.

We shall begin with the accelerated pace of transportation. There was already talk of it as early as the Industrial Revolution; the invention of the steam engine and the railway had caused a marked change in temporal experience. The first English stretch of railway was laid in 1825 between Stockton and Darlington, ten years before the first such stretch in Germany (the second followed five years later between Liverpool and Manchester). Henry David Thoreau, who had retreated into the solitude and "wilderness" of the New England woods in order to practice the American virtues of self-reliance and autonomy, remained connected to society by means of the railway. He was thus able to observe first-hand the new temporality introduced by railway travel, one that had everywhere accelerated the pulse of life, speech, and even thought:

> The startings and arrivals of the cars are now the epochs in the village day. They go and come with such regularity and precision, and their whistle can be heard so far, that the farmers set their clocks by them, and thus one well conducted institution regulates a whole country. Have not men improved somewhat in punctuality since the railroad was invented? Do they not talk and think faster in the depot than they did in the stage-office?[81]

The new temporal sensibility was less and less inclined to follow the natural rhythms of day and night or even the seasons; it was increasingly determined by the precision of clock-time that synchronized social time, say, in the form of schedules. By the end of the nineteenth century, the historian Frederick Jackson Turner was celebrating the advance of the railway into the wilderness and calling the expansion of railroad networks a great harbinger of progress. The wilderness, he writes, "has been interpenetrated by lines of civilization growing ever more numerous. It is like the steady growth of a complex nervous system for the originally simple, inert continent."[82] Heinrich Heine, who was present at the opening

---

81. Henry David Thoreau, "Sounds," in *Walden, or Life in the Woods* (Boston/New York: Houghton Mifflin, 1889), 184ff.

82. Frederick Jackson Turner, "The Significance of the Frontier," in *The Frontier in American History* (New York: Holt, Rinehart & Winston, 1962), 14ff.

of the lines from Paris to Orléans and to Rome, spoke of a new stage in world history that is destabilizing our ways of seeing and our ideas, even the most basic ones of time and space. Similar to how we respond to globalization today, and to those extensive networks of communication, transport, and commercial media that have caused the world to shrink to the size of a so-called "global village," Heine is responding to the new speeds of his own time that suddenly caused space itself to contract: "I seem to see the mountains and forests of every country coming to Paris. I smell the perfume of German lime-trees; the billows of the North Sea are bounding and roaring before my door."[83]

Whereas defenders of the new technology saw the potential for humans to increasingly dominate space and time, critics and doubters saw "the annihilation of space and time."[84] The first train passengers were ill-prepared for the new speeds. They experienced dizziness; from the perspective of those in the "flying salon," as Joseph von Eichendorff called railway cars, the contours of the fleeting landscape disintegrated. The literary author George Eliot, a contemporary of Annette von Droste-Hülshoff's, feared that ever-increasing speeds of transportation would lead to the impoverishment of sensory experience and storytelling. She contrasted the richness of perceptions, memories, and stories to be had during a tranquil excursion by stagecoach with a futuristic voyage in a high-speed shuttle, which takes not only one's breath away but one's experience, as well. According to Eliot, it is like being shot through the barrel of a gun: "The tube-journey can never lead to much fiction and narrative; it is as barren as an exclamatory O!"[85]

George Eliot's futuristic phantasy has only been partially realized in the age of jet planes and high-speed trains. On the one hand, avia-

83. Heinrich Heine, "Lutetia," in *The Works of Heinrich Heine*, vol. 18 (*French Affairs*, vol. 2), trans. C. G. Leland (Hans Breitmann) (London: William Heinemann, 1893), 369.

84. Wolfgang Schivelbusch, *The Railway Journey*, trans. A. Hollo (Berkeley: University of California Press, 1986), 130.

85. George Eliot, *Felix Holt, The Radical* (Oxford: Oxford University Press, 1998), 5.

tion technology has certainly delivered on the utopia of the nine-teenth century in the most radical way and has turned travel into a largely nonsensual experience, the spectacular views notwithstand-ing. On the other hand, though, it also compensates for what Eliot criticizes as a loss of experience by showing movies on board. How-ever, Eliot did anticipate an important development that is often dis-cussed in the literature on acceleration: the greater impoverishment of experience due to the increasingly technological and abstract conditions of our lives. As with the loss of sensory perceptions, the disappearance of the social art of storytelling concerns the accelera-tion of time, for the simple reason that noticing and recounting take time. Storytelling is also time-consuming—time that is, of course, in ever-shorter supply.

Acceleration, however, concerns not just the increasing speed of commerce and transportation, but also, and even more fundamen-tally, the way in which people experience sociocultural change. This change becomes a lived experience when new political realities, social institutions, or technological innovations suddenly and irre-vocably turn the previously lived present into an obsolete and termi-nated past. Once again, we are dealing with the aforementioned "constant temporal breaks of the new self-reproducing experience of hiatus,"[86] ones that not only make progress possible but also, and inevitably, result in the acceleration syndrome. This modern tendency produces a dynamic that increasingly shortens the present, because the past breaks from it ever more rapidly. The closer the past ap-proaches to the present, the shorter the present becomes. And when the past become synonymous with obsolescence, foreignness, and alterity, the separation from and confrontation with this "world of yesterday" become constant features of the modern experience of time. It is no longer simply a matter of divorcing oneself from the old world and the lives of older generations, but also increasingly from parts of one's own life and one's own self as well. This percep-tion of accelerated change results in a kind of vertigo that differs from that of the "flying salon" of the railway car. An experience of chronic overload tends to occur when:

---

86. Koselleck and Meier, "Fortschritt," 392.

Everything is changing faster than one could have expected up until that point, or than one had experienced before. It arises because of the shorter time spans of elements of the unknown in the everyday life of those who experience it, one that is in no way deducible from previous experience: this distinguishes the experience of acceleration.[87]

This experience of temporal acceleration has characterized every generation in modernity. It can be traced back not so much to particular historical events as to the constant changes precipitated by the scientific and technological developments in which Europe has wrapped itself like a "slippery blanket" since the mid-nineteenth century. This formulation, from Droste-Hülshoff, clearly conveys how temporal acceleration goes hand in hand with a weakening of traditions and customs, and how this in turn generates a loss of trust in the lived world.

In the twentieth century, the potential for technological change increased once again, yet this time the change was exponential. By 1926, the linguist and literature theorist I. A. Richards was already convinced that the world had fundamentally changed, partly by design and partly by accident, and that:

the fairly near future is likely to see an almost complete reorganization of our lives, in their intimate aspects as much as in their public. Man himself is changing, together with his circumstances; he has changed in the past, it is true, but never perhaps so swiftly.[88]

Later philosophers have questioned Richards' optimistic faith in the limitless capacity of human beings to adapt. The more all-encompassing the reorganization, the less that critics of acceleration have tended to believe that a person can adapt to those changes and keep up with the accelerated pace. Georg Simmel, Günther Anders, and Odo Marquard, to name only three, all shared the conviction that human beings are simply not capable of keeping pace with this

---

87. Reinhart Koselleck, "Gibt es eine Beschleunigung der Geschichte?," in *Zeitschriften: Studien zur Historik* (Frankfurt: Suhrkamp, 2000), 164.
88. I. A. Richards, "Science and Poetry" (1926), in *Poetry and Sciences* (New York: W. W. Norton, 1970), 15. Cited in Gumbrecht, *In 1926*, 390.

kind of accelerated change: Because of their embodied existences, they fall hopelessly behind fast-paced technological developments. Indeed, a dangerous gap opens up here between, on the one hand, the "obsolescence of human beings" and, on the other, their overly technologized world: we humans seem to have become a dinosaur in our own mechanized theme park.

As was discussed in the introduction, the basic meaning of the notion of "modern" boils down to a heightened awareness of time itself. Acceleration, in particular, produces just such an increased awareness of time, and it has itself been decisively pushed along by technological developments. What the inventions of the telescope and the microscope in the seventeenth and eighteenth centuries meant for the possibility of visualizing space, color photography and film at the beginning of the twentieth century meant for visualizing time. Hawthorne still had to make use of a pictorial broadsheet for his imaginary panorama to visualize the historical changes of his "Main Street" over the course of two centuries. In the meantime, however, film or digital images can now not only run forward and backward, but in addition they can be sped up or slowed down. Such technological feats suspend the established criteria of perception and can lead to breakthroughs that take us well beyond our ordinary sensory perception; they allow insights into other time-worlds and so serve to intensify and complicate the experience of temporal awareness.

Throughout the period of the Enlightenment, the introduction of the modern time regime was tied to an increased economization of time. So, during that era, a new lifestyle developed that turned time itself into a valuable asset, both for the economy and for the shaping of the self. In early capitalism, time was not only translatable into money; it was also relevant to personal salvation, dependent as the latter was on discipline and good time management. The seventeenth-century Protestant conviction that time was in short supply supports the new subjective experience of an increasingly fast pace of living. In the secularized world, this basic mood remains; it changes only in the sense that it now becomes a social concern rather than a religious one. "In light of the social status of actors, both the efficient use of time and the shortage of time appear as visible signs of one's significance and of one's belonging to the elite."[89]

We shall once again draw on literary examples from different historical eras to substantiate the phenomenon of the modern experience of accelerated time. In Goethe's 1809 novel *Elective Affinities*, modern temporal acceleration is already a topic of conversation—well before the invention of airplanes or railways or film. The critical experience that Goethe investigates is not therefore based on technological inventions but on how quickly bodies of knowledge become obsolete. In the relevant scene of his novel, the captain is asked by his hosts to clarify the broad range of meanings of the term "affinity," the concept in the book's title. He begins his explanation with a remarkable apology:

'I shall be very glad to,' the Captain replied, since it was to him that Charlotte had turned with her question, 'as well as I can, at least, from what I read about it some ten years ago. Whether people in the scientific world still think the same on the subject, whether it accords with the newer doctrines, I could not say.'

'It is a bad business,' Eduard cried, 'that we cannot nowadays learn anything that will last a lifetime. Our forefathers stuck to the teaching they were given when they were young, but we have to unlearn everything every five years if we are not to go completely out of fashion.'[90]

At roughly the same time as the publication of Goethe's novel, the University of Berlin (1810) was founded. Within the framework of the Prussian Educational Reforms, the production of knowledge underwent a fundamental modernization in accordance with the principles of the university's founder, Wilhelm von Humboldt. By virtue of this process, a body of knowledge was increasingly distanced from everyday understanding, becoming more scientific, more differentiated, and more specialized. Goethe's dialogue here makes pointed reference to this change currently under way in the

---

89. Wolfgang Kaschuba, *Die Überwindung der Distanz: Zeit und Raum in der europäischen Moderne* (Frankfurt: Fischer, 2004), 44.

90. J. W. Goethe, *Elective Affinities*, trans. D. Constantine (Oxford: Oxford University Press, 1994), 30.

world of knowledge. While the captain provides his knowledge in response, somewhat meekly adding an expiration date of about ten years, Eduard again reduces this cycle of knowledge-decay by half. Acceleration itself clearly has the tendency to increase—that is, to accelerate. Eduard fears the idea that "life-long learning" displaces "learning for life"; for him, this is something of a nightmare, not at all a positive development regarding education. The accelerated invalidation of knowledge takes away its dignity altogether, which is why he equates it with short-term fashion trends.[91]

Clearly, this exchange has a two-fold meaning. First, in the context of the modern production of knowledge that is systematically accelerated and institutionally reinforced, it illustrates the dangers of a body of knowledge that is constantly subject to rapid invalidation and displacement. Second, it suggests that when knowledge is relevant for shorter and shorter periods of time, important basic competences get lost. People become more and more dependent on experts and increasingly less confident in their own knowledge. As a consequence, foundational cultural values such as accumulated experience, maturity, and development must be constantly subjected to a rethinking. The philosopher Odo Marquard takes up this problem that *Elective Affinities* raises and articulates it more generally, using the ideas of "childishness" and "tachogenic unworldliness":

> Since, nowadays, what is familiar becomes obsolete at a faster and faster rate, and the future world will increasingly be different from the world which we have experienced so far, the world becomes foreign to us (as modern human beings), and we become unworldly. Modern grown-ups become childlike. Even when we go gray, we remain green.[92]

---

91. This brief episode from *Elective Affinities* by no means exhausts the relevance of Goethe for our topic. Indeed, one could quite easily write an entire book on Goethe's engagement with the time regime of modernity. Manfred Osten already comes very close to such a project in his *Alles "veloziferisch" oder Goethes Entdeckung der Langsamkeit: Zur Modernität eines Klassikers im 21. Jahrhundert* (Frankfurt am Main: Insel, 2003).

92. Odo Marquard, "The Age of Unworldliness? A Contribution to the Analysis of the Present," in *In Defence of the Accidental: Philosophical Studies*, trans. Robert M. Wallace (New York: Oxford University Press, 1991), 77.

In addition to what Goethe describes as the dynamics of fashion, the main context for the acceleration of time and change is the market economy and modern consumer behavior. A dialectics of innovation and obsolescence regulates the replacement cycles of technology as well as those of fashion, both of which are closely tied to the economic conditions of a capitalist market. In the time regime of the modern, fashion quickly forces what is new or novel to become old and outdated. New product lines are increasingly being marketed in terms of "latest generations," thus biologizing our attraction to the new. "The more short-lived a period," writes the philosopher and critic Walter Benjamin, "the more susceptible it is to fashion. . . . Fashion prescribes the ritual according to which the commodity fetish demands to be worshipped."[93] On the market, the production of new commodities attracts attention and unleashes desire, while at the same time it makes what is already known—the status quo—appear unattractive and obsolete.

Obsolescence is a subtle and unremarkable kind of forgetting that takes place by means of abrogation and inattention. The philosopher Siegfried Kracauer and the art theorist Adolf Loos participated in an interesting exchange about the issue of obsolescence in relation to the question of design and stylistic changes. In Loos's work *Ornament and Crime* (1908), he writes that "*[t]he evolution of culture is synonymous with the removal of ornamentation from objects of everyday use*" (167).[94] For Loos, the eradication of the ornament was a "timely" demand of progress in the name of an increasing abstraction that took aim at the cluttered over-adornment of historicism. Kracauer, by contrast, was also thinking about ornament, though in the context of the traditions of guild artistry and handiwork where they still retained a value in modern society. He could not support Loos's radical claim. For him, the complete rejection of the ornament in modern culture causes the "bridge to

---

93. Walter Benjamin, *The Arcades Project*, trans. Howard Eiland and Kevin McLaughlin (Cambridge, MA: Harvard University Press, 2003), 8, 80.

94. Adolf Loos, "Ornament and Crime," in *Ornament and Crime: Selected Essays*, ed. Adolf Opel, trans. Michael Mitchell (Riverside, CA: Ariadne Press, 1998), 167.

yesterday" to collapse, a bridge that, as he puts it, secures "a hold in time."[95] By contrast, Loos wants to replace the ornament—whose production was tedious, and which was technically as well as aesthetically obsolete—with modern design. Design had the opposite meaning and function as the ornament, for it does not cling to the past but rather stimulates a sense for the new. For Loos, design has extremely positive connotations as an accelerator of cultural change:

> A consumer who has furnishings he cannot stand after ten years . . . is better than one who buys something only when the old one becomes worn out with use. Industry needs that. The rapid changes in fashion provide employment for millions.[96]

Here Loos is demonstrating the close connection between the development of industry, the economy, and consumer society—one that characterizes life in the modern city and is geared toward temporal acceleration. In a technologically advanced society, after ten years, it is deemed high time to replace an article of daily use, even if it still works. Whoever does not participate in this rhythm of replacement endangers industry and compromises whatever degree of economic vitality the broader society has achieved.

Hermann Lübbe emphasizes the logic of progress, overhaul, or replacement at work here in a brilliant distinction between "old" and "outdated" tools: "Whereas one used to replace tools that had gotten 'old' with a new one of the same type, today, dependent as we are on a contraction of the present, 'outdated' tools are more and more often replaced with more advanced tools."[97] The idea of "the contraction of the present" also comes from Lübbe, whose important contributions to the modern time regime we shall now examine more closely.

---

95. Sigfried Kracauer, *Straßen in Berlin und anderswo* (Frankfurt am Main: Suhrkamp, 2009), 24. I am grateful to Magdalena Pagliarulo for this reference.
96. Loos, "Ornament and Crime," 172.
97. Hermann Lübbe, *Im Zug der Zeit: Verkürzter Aufenthalt in der Gegenwart* (Heidelberg: Springer, 1992), 15.

Increased commercial tempos, historical change, and a fast pace of living are aspects of modern acceleration that are closely related to one another. The phrase "the contraction of the present" confronts us once again with the question with which we introduced our reflections on the relation between time and modernity: how long does the present last? Of course, we can use something like an objective yardstick to determine the shrinking suitability or relevance of our knowledge, our clothing, our technological toys, or our furniture. As a consequence, many see a hallmark of the modern in the "faster pace of change in living conditions and forms of life that have been overcome more quickly than all previous historical experience."[98] This acceleration is the direct outcome of a pressure to innovate, which is itself propelled by consumer confidence and also by the assumption that every innovation represents an improvement. The flipside of this permanent innovation is, despite all, a general loss of trust: it serves to undermine the foundations of a supportive and familiar lived world in which the foundations of knowledge and the coordinates of taste are disrupted "every ten years" or "every five years." Regarding the problem of the contraction of the present, it is of course a question of a process with its own dynamic, one that is not easy to stop.

But what does it mean when the present contracts to the "now moment"? Hartmut Rosa, a sociologist and theorist of speed, summarizes this scenario in the surreal freeze-frame of an ultramodern time sensibility:

> It seems as if everything around us were constantly in motion, as if we stood on a kind of slope leading directly into the abyss; if you don't keep climbing—updating your knowledge, buying new clothing, installing the latest software, following the news, exercising and keeping fit, sustaining friendships—you'll lose ground and be buried beneath the time that just keeps rolling along.[99]

---

98. Lothar Gall, *Europa auf dem Weg in die Moderne 1850–1890* (Munich: Oldenbourg, 1993), 53. For a consideration of the other face of Europe that is continually being forgotten, see Israel Bartal, *Geschichte der Juden im östlichen Europa 1772–1881* (Göttingen: Vandenhoeck & Ruprecht, 2010).

99. Hartmut Rosa, "Kein Halt auf der Ebene der Geschwindigkeit," *Frankfurter Rundschau*, August 3, 2004, no. 178, 16; see also Rosa, *Beschleunigung*, and "Jedes Ding hat keine Zeit?"

At its extreme, the temporal experiences of an accelerated process bring to mind a variant of Baudelaire's discovery of the present as a now moment. His artistic experiment in aesthetic "ecstasy" has turned into a condition that another theorist of speed has aptly described as "polar inertia."[100]

---

100.   Paul Virilio, *Polar Inertia* (New York: Sage Publications, 2000).

4

Concepts of Time
in Late Modernity

"Polar inertia"—of course, it cannot go on like this. Not only have
we arrived at a temporal limit, it seems, but we have also arrived at
the absolute dead end of the modern time regime, in terms of both
its compatibility with the rhythms of human life and the logic internal to the dynamics it has unleashed. As the following chapter
will demonstrate, these problems and their implications have been
the subject of intensified philosophical reflection and debate since
the 1980s. The positions taken—I shall group them under the heading "Concepts of Time in Late Modernity"—all grapple with the
aporias, or inner contradictions, of the modern temporal regime
and its possible alternatives or compensations, without losing sight
of the epistemic presuppositions of this temporal ontology in the
process.

Compensation Theory

Of course, we welcome acceleration when it is a question of trains and planes getting us to our desired destinations on time, or when medicine develops a cure for serious health problems as quickly as possible. But we experience it as an annoyance and a threat when it erodes the foundations of lived experience, dismantles familiar spaces, or turns us into illiterates of the everyday world by constantly forcing us to adapt to a dizzying pace of change. Representatives of so-called "compensation theory" have taken up these problems resulting from the modern time regime and reflected deeply on them. In so doing, they have made important contributions to an awareness of the modern temporal regime, including having the merit of broaching its paradoxes and problems. While their examinations bring clarity to the complexity of this temporal regime, they simultaneously remain firmly anchored in this time regime as committed theorists of modernization.

Compensation theory emerged out of the school of the philosopher Joachim Ritter. Ritter held a graduate seminar (the Collegium Philosophicum) in Munich beginning in 1947, and many members of the "generation of 1945" who had begun their studies after the war took part. This liberal-conservative group kept its distance from utopian positions like that of Marxism, but also from the strongly held ethical positions of critical theory. In this respect, the group's members must be categorized as proponents of modernization theory and *not* of critical theory. The philosophers Hermann Lübbe and Odo Marquard, in particular, outlined the principles of this approach and powerfully defended them. Since their work defends a late stage of the modern time regime, I would like to identify them here as the "rear guard of modernization theory."[1] Their contribution to the modern reflection on time revolves around the

---

1. A certain irony consists in the fact that when Helmut Shelsky traced the youthful development of this generation of the so-called '45ers (born between 1926 and 1928), he called them the "advance guard of progress." The two are compatible, insofar as both attest to the sustained commitment of this generation to modernization theory. Helmut Shelsky, *Die skeptische Generation: Eine Soziologie der deutschen Jugend* (Düsseldorf: Diederichs, 1963), 50.

150   Chapter 4

following key pairs of opposites: acceleration and constancy, innovation and obsolescence, and renewal and preservation. Yet they no longer take these pairs—as was done in the time regime of high modernity—as antitheses, whereby the one asserts itself only at the expense of the other. Instead, as theorists of *deceleration*, they ask themselves *not* how the iron law of progress inscribed into the foundations of the modern time regime can be overcome, but how it can be made somewhat more bearable for the people who must continue to live under its sway. Their answer to the problem of constant acceleration is the idea of compensation, which they use to revise and modify the structure of the modern time regime without fundamentally calling it into question. On the contrary, they develop a late-modern theory of time in which the pairs of opposites they discuss can be brought into a relation of dialectical tension with one another.

The basic principle of compensation theory goes as follows: if we actively encourage people to slow down and create periods of downtime for themselves, the modern dynamics of acceleration become easier to bear.[2] This also implies that the dynamics of the modern time regime—one the modernization theorists take to be self-evident, having the objective logic of a natural law—can function all the more effectively when they are outmaneuvered from time to time and their effects cushioned. The representatives of compensation theory therefore *do not* ask: Are there blind spots, injustices, or dangerous asymmetries implicit to this temporal regime that exact costs at the levels of human life and material sustainability that are just too high? Instead, they ask the question as to how the modern time regime can better accommodate people's needs. So, for them, it is not a question of finding alternatives to this temporal regime or of changing it in any fundamental way, for they hold it to be an unassailable reality and the ontological foundation of the world in which we live.

Before I present the arguments of two prominent representatives of compensation theory, I would like first to introduce their principal ideas by means of two literary examples. First, *Ortsgespräch* (Local Call), based on the life of its author, Florian Illies (born in

---

2. Brose, "Kulturen der Ungleichzeitigkeit."

1971): like Annette von Droste-Hülshoff's ethnographic description of her Westphalian homeland, this literary work also involves a report from the province, this time from the small town of Schlitz in Fuldatal. As the jacket blurb suggests, this town has "an abandoned train station, a post office, a museum of local history, and the largest candle in the world. The church dates from 812 and the pizzeria from 1985."[3] This place, the jacket blurb continues,

> exemplifies the most beautiful of all places: home. That place that we might often want to fight against but are unable to: Our connection to it remains. *Ortsgespräch* tells of the love of rural life and of the breathtaking in-between space of the German province, of the memories of the meadow around the swimming pool and carnivals, of the stationery shop on the corner, and the apple harvest in the fall (ibid.).

Ortsgespräch was greeted by a flurry of critical reviews. One reviewer saw it as nothing more than an exercise in nostalgia and as a collection of clichés borrowed from a nineteenth-century ideal of rural life. He contended that the description of the hometown as a place untouched by global acceleration obfuscates actual developments like big-box stores and suburban sprawl.[4] Illies was therefore labeled by reviewers as a conservative idyllist (albeit of a fairly high-end variety). These reactions clearly show the extent to which the work was being measured against the normative standard of the modern time regime. The author is criticized for having a backward sense of time because he thinks it is still possible to portray a hometown in 2006 with no reference to globalization. This charge of escapism makes it abundantly clear how strongly influenced our everyday values and debates are by the normative pressure of the modern time regime: by virtue of its compulsory breaks, it keeps forcing us to choose between progressive and regressive, between good and bad. What interests me about Illies's text is something else entirely, namely, the brilliant way in which the author sheds light on the logic of compensation theory. This he does particularly well

---

3. Florian Illies, *Ortsgespräch* (Munich: Karl Blessing, 2006).
4. Kolja Mensing, *Die Tageszeitung*, August 23, 2006; accessed August 29, 2018, www.perlentaucher.de/buch/24936.html.

in a chapter that narrates his going into his childhood bedroom, one which he no longer occupies but still visits with some regularity, and which he describes as his "local museum":

> It costs nothing to visit my local museum. . . . The museum is my parents' house—and the houses of my aunts and the neighbors are its outposts. Of course, I could have gone to the real heritage museum up there in the castle. But there's stuff in there that I don't understand anymore. . . . In my museum, things are more routine, more banal. That's how it was at one time, everything there was obvious for me, boring, normal. They only become exhibits when I look back at them, because they're now props from a play that will never be performed again, or at most, twice a year, maybe three times, when aunt Do has her birthday or at Christmas, when I go home and visit the local museum and its outposts. Everyday things became something special, the kitchen and the bathroom became a kind of technical museum.[5]

"[P]rops from a play that will never be performed again"—that could just as well be an affecting description of what the Indian chief from Hawthorne's story "Main Street" discovers in his vision of the local heritage museum. After all, as is the case with a heritage museum in a small town, the author's private museum becomes a scene in which what was once present has irreversibly turned into the past. But the present has turned into the past not because people have moved away, and not because of renovations, additions, or other acts of revitalization, but rather because its relics are retained, preserved, exhibited, and available for viewing. As we have already seen emphasized in the work of Ernst Schulin, the value of the past increases at the very moment when we realize that too much of it has already been thrown away. After the past in the time regime of the modern has been devalued and discarded, it again becomes meaningful—as "a play that will never be performed again"—in the context of a shortage economy. This is not solely a matter of spinning wheels and threshing flails, but also involves new retro-cult objects like old lawnmowers, toasters, and computers that are put up for sale on eBay and go to the highest bidder.[6] Innovation can be inferred from

---

5. Illies, *Ortsgespräch*, 186ff.
6. Samuel Raphael, *The Theatres of Memory, Vol. I: Past and Present in Contemporary Culture* (London: Verso, 1994).

"antiquation"; likewise, the increasingly fast pace of our technological life-world can be inferred from a museum's "arrest." As
Lübbe insists, that is precisely the "basis of our pleasure in historical objects."[7] With the museum, acceleration becomes not only visible but also bearable—and that is precisely what the dialectic of
compensation consists of. Progress generates the nostalgic heritage
museum in the same way that the convex generates the concave; as
a site of temporal standstill that is cordoned off, the museum compensates for the loss of familiarity experienced in a rapidly changing life-world.

Seven Characteristics of the Modern Experience of Time (Hermann Lübbe)

Hermann Lübbe has developed his thinking about the modern understanding of time over the course of many books, all of which
are as relevant to the topic as they are brilliant. We cannot hope to
do justice to the full extent of Lübbe's thinking here; rather, we shall
focus our efforts on one essay in particular in which he sums up his
most important arguments on the topic in his customary barbed
style.[8] As with Niklas Luhmann, Lübbe's work also suggests that
the impulse of modernization theory is to begin with the discovery
of a vocabulary of *tabula rasa* to express ideas that are as concise
and technical as possible. Lübbe openly admits his preference for
"new ideas with artificial names" that are "semantically constructed
and association-free." In his essay, he compiles seven characteristics
that, he argues, constitute the modern experience of time. We shall
briefly introduce each of those characteristics here, a number of
which will overlap with some aspects of the modern time regime
that we have already examined. Lübbe's commitment to the modern
time regime is already made clear in the very first sentence of his

---

7. Hermann Lübbe, *Der Fortschritt und das Museum: Über den Grund unseres
Vergnügens an historischen Gegenständen* (London: Institute of Germanic Studies,
1982).

8. Hermann Lübbe, *Zeit-Erfahrungen: Sieben Begriffe zur Beschreibung moderner Zivilizationsdynamik, Abhandlungen der Geistes- und Sozialwissenschaftlichen Klasse 5* (Academy of Sciences and Literature, Mainz/Stuttgart: Steiner, 1996).

essay, which begins with a statement that unmistakably belongs to theorists of modernization: "The evolutionary dynamic of a scientific-technological civilization," he claims, "remains unbroken" (5).

The first idea Lübbe uses to characterize the modern time regime is his own new invention: *preception* [Präzeption]. One should not be thinking here of formulations such as "Praeceptor Germaniae" but rather, and more simply, in terms of "reception." Lübbe understands reception to be "the interest in appropriating the past." However, reception in this sense is only possible when, for starters, something has already been retained and put aside. With *preception*, by contrast, he is referring to the preliminary material work that goes into "the guarantee and provision of historical sources." Archives, museums, and libraries preserve a great deal of what is no longer useful in the present context but that has new meaning and value as the medium of "a historical past that is made present" (8). With this idea of preception, Lübbe is referring to the complex that I have been describing with the phrase "the invention of the historical." Just as historical museums are dependent on authentic artifacts, historiography depends on written sources. However, the written material used for this purpose has already undergone a radical functional transformation, for the "inventory of records" that emerges out of everyday contexts must, with the break of the past from the present, turn into the "archive of history."[9] According to Lübbe, securing and preserving inventory "involves nothing less than the determination, in the present, of the interests of those who come after regarding the past that our present will have become in the future" (11). To put it in simpler terms, archivists anticipate "the interests that future generations have in making the past present" (so, in effect, Lübbe could have simply replaced his bulky neologism of "preception" with the concept of the "archive").

We have just encountered Lübbe's second idea, *the shortage of the present*, in our discussion of acceleration theory. This idea is much more transparent than "preception" and has also entered into

---

9. Alongside the production and collection of bureaucratic records, many other archives exist: those of families, private collectors, companies, institutions, and artists, to name a few.

everyday speech. Lübbe illustrates what is specifically at stake in this idea by using the example of the diminishing half-life of literature in the natural sciences. While the number of published titles is constantly rising, at the same time, the period for which this literature remains valid is getting progressively shorter. Here is Lübbe's wonderfully concise way of putting it: "The very fact of the dynamics of intensified innovation shortens the chronological span of the past that is retained as still relevant" (14). So, the fundamental question Lübbe is posing here is the same as our own: How long does the present last? Given the short life span of scientific knowledge, publications dating back five years or more are no longer consulted: what concerned the captain and Eduard in Goethe's *Elective Affinities* two hundred years ago has become normalized in the natural sciences in our own day. In contrast to this normalization in the sciences, according to Lübbe, people experience the shortage of the present in everyday life as a permanent crisis of perception and experience. Because of how the human senses work, people are incapable of experiencing a moment "that would be nothing but a non-extended transfer of the past into the future" (16). With a view to this basic structure of human perception, therefore, every lived present requires a minimum duration.[10]

With the third idea, *the expansion of the future*, Lübbe is drawing attention to a qualitative change in the future. In short, the future takes up more space because it touches ever closer on the present. As a consequence, the future is also becoming more and more unpredictable. To the extent that everything is changing more radically and more quickly, the possibility of prognostication goes down. The gap between the realm of experience and the horizon of expectation is, for Lübbe, becoming a gap between the present and the future. The odds that the future will continue to resemble the present "goes down with an increasing dynamism of civilization" (17). According to Lübbe, there is unfortunately neither remedy nor compensation for this situation: "As a consequence, uncertainty about

---

10. It takes three seconds for a perceptual image to be generated, which is why one also speaks of a three-second window. Cf. Ernst Pöppel, *Grenzen des Bewusstseins: Über Wirklichkeit und Welterfahrung* (Stuttgart: DVA, 1988).

the future is the cost we must pay for the historically unprecedented benefits of the prosperity given by modern civilization." Instead of certainty regarding the future, a new and large-scale need arises for planning and coordination, one that at the same time exceeds human capacities. Lübbe's assessment brings to mind Koselleck's argument regarding how an increased sense of agency or power over history unleashes new forms of powerlessness. Here, too, we see the downsides of the future as pure potentiality. Even some compensation theorists take these downsides into account, especially those who consider the costs of the modern time regime, though they do tend to be more sanguine about such things. So, they do this by adopting an emphatically nonalarmist and, as we shall now see, occasionally downright stoic posture.

While on the one hand the future breaks away from the present because of increased complexity, on the other hand the past moves ever closer to it. With his fourth concept, *the growth of relics*, Lübbe is referring to how objects quickly become obsolete as use-objects because of the accelerated development of technology and can only be understood historically. As a result, they become a part of history exhibited in museums. Lübbe claims: "The degree of musealization present in our contemporary culture has no historical precedent" (20). The invention of the historical that is once again the topic of discussion has, according to Lübbe, turned into a generalized fascination and a kind of popular sport: museum visits now have the character of mass movements, whereby historical museums or museums of technology, in contrast to art museums, attract special attention. As retro-cultures (see Florian Illies), tendencies to historicize are now also spreading beyond the walls of differentiated subsystems like historiography or museums that were constructed for that express purpose: "This tendency to self-historicize has begun to exercise a huge influence on the atmosphere of our private lives" (21). Lübbe's suggestion here is interesting: the modern time regime does not just permanently jettison objects made obsolete by new technologies, but it also stimulates the desire "to retain these pasts in the present through their artifacts." Lübbe has worked out this dialectic of modernization and historicization in its many contemporary guises (24). However, he stops short of seeing the "attention we pay to the past of our civilization determined by ever-advancing progress" as a form of escapism (a criticism that reviewers had made of Florian Illies on the basis of his "reactionary notion of home"); rather, he sees it as an important attempt to compensate that consists of "transforming an increase in foreignness" into "a normative shape of 'having been other.'" Only on this basis, Lübbe suggests, is "modern civilization able to relate the past to the future, a relation that makes possible both identity and further development" (24ff).[11]

At this point in Lübbe's analysis, "identity" comes up in a sudden and somewhat awkward way. The notion of collective identity first arose in the 1980s and generally refers to a normative understanding of selfhood that is shared with others and is based on roots, family, ethnicity, or culture. It actually has no real place in the vocabulary of the compensation theorists, and Lübbe makes it clear that he is referring to something quite different: he is talking about the singularity and irreplaceability of a person or a collective. What a passport is for an individual, history is for the collective. This history, which Lübbe thinks about in terms of objective historiography, is useful for the official identification of a person—much like a passport is—but at the level of the collective. Therefore, Lübbe's concept of identity as an objective and stable entity has nothing whatsoever to do with the notion of identity understood by cultural theory as a fluid construction that functions through symbolic performances as a normative self-image.[12]

Lübbe's fifth concept is entirely obscure and somewhat meaningless: *evolutionary illaminarity*. The word "laminar" (from Lat. *lamina*, sheet or scale) refers to a uniform or streamlined current, so "illaminar" invokes the opposite, namely an inconsistent trend. A flow of water amid rocks in a surf would be an example of this

11. See also Hermann Lübbe, "Zur Identitätspräsentationsfunktion der Historie," in *Identität: Poetik und Hermeneutik VIII*, ed. Odo Marquard and Karlheize Stierle (Munich: Fink, 1979).

12. Lübbe has recently summarized his argument about this in the following way: "Identity is a descriptive inventory because, as a factual result of a history, everyone has one." Hermann Lübbe, *Vom Parteigenossen zum Bundesbürger: Über beschwiegene und historisierte Vergangenheiten* (Munich: Fink, 2007), 116ff.

inconsistency. Lübbe argues that there are also such abutments or obstacles in the temporal flow of modernity, meaning that it does not merely sweep everything along with it and make everything fade away but rather also has things countering that movement. In this context, Lübbe is thinking above all of artworks that are described as "classic" because they are protected from changes in taste and so have no expiration date: "[W]ith increasingly dynamic cultural and artistic processes," he writes, "cultural artifacts have an increasingly greater resistance to aging" (222). The special status of classical works of art leads Lübbe to consider not the cultural processes of selection and canonization, but simply the empirical character of their resistance to aging. As rocks in the "illaminary" time flow of modernity, according to his account, they are spontaneously immune to change. This immunity, or so goes the circular argument, provides so-called "classical" works and objects with a "sustained contemporaneity" (27).[13]

Baudelaire had already spoken about this phenomenon of the "simultaneity of the non-simultaneous" and the dialectic of the now-moment and continuity when he defined the modern as "the ephemeral, the fugitive, the contingent, the half of art whose other half is the eternal and the immutable." It is the merit of Lübbe's analysis to have introduced the counterclaim of classical art as an important aspect in the discussion regarding the modern time regime, since for most modernization theorists the phenomenon of the classic is nothing but an irritating annoyance. In the eyes of the '68ers, classics are not to be revered but deconstructed. They prefer to emphasize that the function of art was to break with the past by means of innovation. The self-evident fact is seldom mentioned that, in culture, not everything is put into play at once, and that every society has a large reserve of inventory at its disposal that is protected from historical

---

13.   Whereas Lübbe emphasizes the dialectic between movement and stasis in his notion of illaminarity, Koselleck emphasizes the heterogeneity of different "temporal layers" in his use of the figure of "the simultaneity of the non-simultaneous." On this point, see Helge Jordheim, "'Unzählbar viele Zeiten': Die Sattelzeit im Spiegel der Gleichzeitigkeit des Ungleichzeitigen," in *Begriffene Geschichte: Beiträge zu Werk Reinhart Kosellecks*, ed. Hans Joas and Peter Vogt (Frankfurt am Main: Suhrkamp, 2011), 449–80.

change. Canonized texts in the areas of religion, law, and art are only a few examples of time-resistant collections that are not automatically given over to decay and forgetting. The question of how such "boulders" resist time in the midst of its "flow"—that is, how resistance to time is itself created and maintained—is a central theme for theories of cultural memory.[14] Although such a theme is well within Lübbe's reach at this point, it is at the same time unthinkable: one may well get to a systems theory of society via the modern time regime, but there is no way to get to its culture.

By contrast, Lübbe's second-last notion, *network densification*, is lucid and transparent. However, he is thinking about "network" not in terms of the structure of digital communication with which the word is so commonly associated today, but rather as a more general set of "regionally and socially expanding interdependencies" in the transition from modernization to globalization. For the two, taken together, constitute the modern idea of a homogenous world time and a global society. By means of new transportation technologies and information transmission, networks have become much more extended and increasingly dense. The wilderness, to cite Frederick Jackson Turner once again, "has been interpenetrated by lines of civilization growing ever more numerous. It is like the steady growth of a complex nervous system for the originally simple, inert continent."[15] According to Lübbe, an important outcome of this network densification in the course of the world's global transformation is its "decentralizing effect."[16] For instance, the rural–urban divide that has influenced human ways of life for centuries is now being dismantled by means of ongoing network densification. The results are "cultural processes of homogenization," a trend that those who call on urban planners to protect unique and "longstanding architectural groupings of buildings" are currently resisting in a compensatory way. The impression of a "so-called unified civilization" [*Einheitszivilisation*] is therefore as superficial as it is deceptive, for here, too, the tried-and-true dynamics of modernization—

14. See Assmann, *Zeit und Tradition*.
15. Turner, "The Significance of the Frontier," 14 et. seq.
16. Lübbe, *Zeit Erfahrungen*, 30.

renewal and preservation—are at work. In the face of growing uniformity in technological advancements, the "consciously intensified desire to conserve our ancestral particularities" (32) is also on the rise. Even in the time of Annette von Droste-Hülshoff, it was already assumed that the world was becoming irrevocably more homogeneous, with increased technology. Therefore, the author is left with no choice but to safeguard the ancestral particularity of her homeland at the last minute in a literary archive, "ere the slippery blanket that is gradually covering Europe also smothers this quiet corner of the world."

Lübbe added *empirical apocalypticism*—the seventh and last, "last but not least," he says (!)—to his phenomenology of the modern experience of time (33). He could also have called it the "loss of utopia" or the "threat of the future." The notion of apocalypse stems, of course, from the arsenals of religious myth. End-time catastrophes, that at one time exercised a great fascination over religious fringe groups, have found sustained expression today in the mainstream entertainment business. For Lübbe, the apocalypse has been an empirical fact ever since it became possible for modern civilization to calculate its own end (to say nothing of its own chances of survival) with high degrees of accuracy, given current levels of resource depletion and pollutants. Having bid farewell to notions of utopia, visions of the future, and anticipation, the *telos* to which the modern time regime is now directed has become the endless planning for a calculable end-time catastrophe! Despite how shocking this view is, the compensation theorist keeps his or her pessimism within limits. Lübbe reassures us with his sanguine closing statement, by suggesting that the more empirically verifiable this apocalypse becomes, the more "one acts in a focused way to counter it." It therefore remains for us to hope that in this case the end-time vision "has the character of a self-destroying prophecy" (36). Lübbe also adds: "We will survive," admitting that not much time remains for us to secure the conditions for that survival.

So, that is the abridged version of Lübbe's seven basic ideas in which he sums up the dynamic temporal sensibility of late-modern civilization. In it, there is as little of the high modern spirit of optimism as there is the categorical imperative of rupture and getting over it. The importance of his perceptive and pointed analyses lies in how it draws out the paradoxes and the dialectical tensions of the late-modern temporal regime. Compensation theorists made it clear that, at the beginning of the 1980s, the modern time regime had lost much of its mobilizing power. The old slogans extolling the virtues of modern "storm and stress" do not hold much appeal nowadays; rather, it is more a matter of getting a grip on the undesirable side effects of this temporal orientation.

At this point, I would like to recap the most important premises of compensation theory.

1. Compensation theory is structured by a systematic *dialectic*. The dynamics of modernity and progress are no longer thought of in terms of a simple image of time's arrow, but rather in terms of a complex of oppositions that emerge from one another and remain in tension with each other. Every movement automatically includes its opposite here: innovation includes obsolescence; acceleration includes resistance to change; progress involves demolition; homogenization involves the emergence of difference; and so on. As a result, oppositions do not fall apart as contradictions would, but rather they accentuate how paradoxical the modern time regime is as it becomes increasingly flexible in its latest phase.

2. Modernization, in the sense of the deliberate coevolution of science, technology, and economy, tends to increasingly outstrip the human scale of things. Because the current of progress, only ever flowing in one direction, has proven itself unlivable for humans, abutments have been built into the temporal model of the modern dynamics of civilization that better allow people to accommodate themselves to this environment. What has proven to be increasingly problematic about the logic of accelerated progress must now be compensated for by means of people-friendly measures. Finally, "the evolutionary dynamics of scientific-technological civilization" is not therefore "unbroken," because according to compensation theory, it comes equipped with corresponding dampeners. Compensation theory focuses on this complex

functional connection, in accordance with which not only resistance movements but also the logic of technology, on the
one hand, and human needs and requirements, on the other,
must be balanced.

3.   Hermann Lübbe's analysis of the modern experience of time,
carried out in the mid-'90s, differs substantially from Ernst
Bloch's work in the mid-'60s. Thirty years earlier, the view
to the future was still borne on utopian hopes. Lübbe's *apocalypse* has replaced Bloch's notion of *utopia*. Compensation
theory does indeed still have "a lot of future on offer," but
in the interim, its thinking of progress has become more conservative. Every dynamic civilization, Lübbe writes, is "at
the same time a conservative civilization" (27). Actually, it
should have been called a "conserving" civilization, or something to that effect, though this difference between the two
words is clearly so minimal for him that it requires no further explanation. The way that compensation theorists think
about progress is no longer euphoric but rather ranges from
skepticism to pessimism; it increasingly identifies a danger
in the dynamics of acceleration as well as a potential end to
the world in the goal of progress. Given how pragmatic they
tend to be, however, fearmongering and alarmism are far
from their minds. To the contrary, for them it is a matter of
moderation and mitigating damage. In the end, one can
always protect oneself from an all-too-gloomy future by
seeking shelter in the charmed worlds of ancestry and heritage, where one can forget these worries and live more or
less indifferently to the movements of progress.

The Future Needs a Past (Odo Marquard)

Contrary to the foundational principle of modernization, namely, a
temporal break, the claims of compensation theory amount to an
interweaving of the future and the past. In light of the gap that opens
up between "rapid and unwanted change" on the one hand, and
"dependence on residual familiarities" on the other, both the need
and the attempt have arisen "to relate the past to the future, a

relation that makes identity and its further development possible."[17] Theorists of time in late modernity tend to focus with increasing concern on determining the point at which the horizon of expectation and the space of experience might come apart entirely, and are devoting attention to the possible ways in which the past and the future can still be held together somehow.

Although squarely situated on the terrain of modernization theory, compensation theorists take the problems associated with its temporal regime very seriously. In their analysis, they deploy the tools of dialectical interpretation, which they use in an entirely different way than theorists of modernity who interpret the modern project in terms of a "vacillation between utopias and apocalypses" (ibid.). Compensation theorists use dialectics not to emphasize the dark sides of modernity but to hold its problems in check. Odo Marquard, the second compensation theorist we will talk about here, has already been introduced with his ideas of "tachometric unworldliness" and "childishness."[18] These ideas capture the logic of a speed of innovation whereby, as everything ages more and more rapidly, we are less and less able to accumulate relevant experience and knowledge, and so must always learn everything over again. "Since, nowadays, what is familiar becomes obsolete at a faster and faster rate, and the future world will increasingly be different from the world which we have experienced so far, the world becomes foreign to us (as modern human beings), and we become unworldly. Modern grown-ups become childlike. Even when we become gray, we remain green" (77).

As a self-styled "traditionalist of modernity," Marquard focuses on the problem of modernization and becomes an advocate of deceleration. The modern temporal regime has pushed acceleration through breaks and divisions for long enough, he suggests; now it is time to shift to "compensatory continuities." Therefore, he emphasizes: "We must become increasingly attentive to these compensatory continuities, that is, to develop and to nurture a feel for continuities" (93). Here, Marquard is countering the fundamental

---

17. Lübbe, *Der Fortschritt und das Museum*, 25.
18. Odo Marquard, "The Age of Unworldliness?," 77.

principle of modern temporal rupture as he hauls the past—once so enthusiastically thrown overboard—bit by bit back into the boat. The 1960s highpoint of modernity, with its passion for "creative destruction," has been followed in the '80s and '90s not only by Lübbe's "dialectic of movement and stasis" but also by Marquard's gradual recuperation of the past. The aging modernization theorists have discovered that the past can function as compensation for the demands of modernization. For a volume of his collected essays that appeared on the occasion of his 75th birthday, Marquard chose the title *Zukunft braucht Herkunft* [*The Future Needs a Past*].[19] In the introduction to the book, he explains this choice and takes the opportunity to discredit several basic axioms of the modern time regime:

> Owing to the limitations of mortality, the brevity of our future binds us to what we already were. We cannot constantly start again from the very beginning. That is why we remain overwhelmingly bound to the past, and whoever wants to change it bears the burden of proof: the burden of justifying why changing in this particular case is a good idea. . . . To be sure, one might think that change is always an improvement, but that is simply not the case. That is why we need our past more than we do our future. The one who holds this position does not need to justify it; the one who wants to get rid of it does (8).

Theorists of late modernity no longer unconditionally adopt the premise of modernization theorists like I. A. Richards, that "[m]an himself is changing, together with his circumstances; he has changed in the past, it is true, but never perhaps so swiftly."[20] On the contrary, they are increasingly clear on the limits of the human ability to adapt to circumstances they have created for themselves. Given how central issues like rupture, division, and severing are to the modern time regime, it is significant that Marquard should articulate his more conservative and skeptical position using precisely such images. In the essay entitled "Zukunft braucht Herkunft.

---

19. Odo Marquard, "Zukunft braucht Herkunft: Philosophische Betrachtungen über Modernität und Menschlichkeit," in *Zukunft braucht Herkunft: Philosophische Essays* (Stuttgart: Reclam, 2003).

20. Richards, "Science and Poetry," 15. Cited in Gumbrecht, *In 1926*, 390.

Philosophische Betrachtungen über Modernität und Menschlichkeit" (The Future Needs a Past: Philosophical Observations on Modernity and Humanity), he argues that the surgeon must have very good reasons before he or she takes up the knife: "Lege artis, one operates only when one has to (that is, when there are compelling reasons to do so); otherwise one does not, and never on everything."[21] So, there is one thing that human beings cannot do, and that is to start all over again with no context or presuppositions. With this basic idea, the emphasis increasingly shifts from the future to past experience. In Marquard's work, the dialectic of "acceleration and deceleration," that characterizes compensation theory, amounts to a double orientation in time: "In the modern world, we must live both: Speed (future) and slowness (past)."[22]

In the essay, Marquard formulates his arguments regarding how to rectify the modern project. For him, modernity is not an incomplete project that awaits its completion, but one that must constantly adapt to a human scale. Therefore, he develops an anthropology that focuses on the limits of the modernization project. Like Koselleck, he dates the beginning of modernization to the middle of the eighteenth century—the epoch of the Enlightenment and its radical break with tradition: "Only at this time does the human future emphatically become the new, independent of the many linguistic, religious, cultural, and familial traditions of the past: The great power of modernization lies in its tendency to neutralize tradition" (235). Within the framework of the modernization project, "traditional realities" were replaced by four artificial and global "functional realities": the natural sciences, technology, the economy, and information technologies. In the arenas of politics and ethics, as well, modernization makes it possible to develop institutions that function independently of tradition: The secular state is one such institution, based on the principle of the division of powers, and human rights discourse is another, guaranteeing everyone the equal right to individuality and difference.

---

21. Marquard, "Zukunft braucht Herkunft," 8.
22. Ibid., 239.

While Marquard affirms these developments as true achievements, at the same time he questions their association with a necessarily accelerated pace of change. In the first instance, he discounts the modern fiction of beginning: "Humans are always late-comers. Wherever they begin is never really a beginning" (238). What results from this belatedness, he argues, is the definition of the human as a "hypoleptic" being; that is, a being that "comes after" and so is necessarily tied to traditions, habits, the past. So, he replaces the demand for constant rupture with a sense of continuity: "The new would not be possible without a great deal of the old."[23] What he calls "old" here concedes a place to the relatively slower pace of human development, in comparison to a world that changes much too quickly. To capture this human need for stability, he offers a surprising image: that of a teddy bear. Just as children carry around their teddy bears with them as comforts in an unfamiliar world, so too do adults carry around their teddy bears in the form of the classics, museums, or their families—completely atavistic quirks, to be sure, but ones that turn out to be utterly indispensable: in a world characterized by high speeds of innovation, what is already old has the virtue of being least "susceptible to aging."

However, in the 1970s, Marquard's teacher Joachim Ritter had come up with a completely different way of putting it, which was to articulate "the disharmony between what we come from and what is to come." At that time, philosophers and historians were focused on developing a theory of modernization in support of fundamental cultural values, such as secularity or a free and endlessly mobile subjectivity. Since the 1980s and '90s, other cultural values have emerged that modernization theory had overlooked or disregarded, such as personal connections to religion, nation, history, family, regional areas, or historical cityscapes. At a fundamental level, all these refer to past worlds, which is the reason why it once again became crucial to build bridges between the past and future in order to open up new possibilities for identity and direction. But here, it seems that we have already said too much. For there is no trace of these ideas in Marquard who, as a compensation

---

23. Marquard, "The Age of Unworldliness?," 81.

theorist, espouses a connection between the future and the past. They appear neither in the lexicon of theories of modernization nor in that of compensation theory. In other words, there is also no way to get from Marquard's work to a cultural or constructivist theory of identity. In the context of compensation theory, then, the past remains at the level of the teddy bear—an outdated quirk of predetermined size that is tolerated as a therapeutic necessity but offers no resources whatsoever for the construction of an identity. Rather, the past is to be used as a decelerator, an anthropological concession to human limitations: just the right amount of the past serves as a remedy to ease the pain of modernization—no more and no less.

The fine line between compensation theory and what, since the 1990s, has more and more frequently been referred to as "memory culture" has already been blurred for the outside world. Marquard's formula "the future needs a past" came into circulation and has since become standard fare in the rhetoric of politicians and official speakers, who make liberal use of it. A good example is the speech that Germany's former Federal President Horst Köhler gave in April 2008, on the occasion of the reopening of the Halberstadt Cathedral. That medieval cathedral's treasury is exceptional in that it has remained in the same location for its entire existence and is considered to be the only one of its kind in Europe. It consists of 650 artworks, including altarpieces and sculptures, manuscripts, furnishings, gold works, and world-renowned masterworks of textile work. The value of this cathedral treasury, according to Culture Minister Jan-Hendrik Olbertz, "could be increased if we succeeded in making it into a tourist attraction."[24] The arenas of politics, culture, and economy, so carefully kept separate in modernization theory, are suddenly brought closer together.

Addressing some 800 assembled guests, Köhler placed his speech under the watchword of "the future needs a past," for which he expressed his thanks to Odo Marquard. However, the use to which he puts Marquard's formula has less to do with compensation per se than with pride in tradition:

---

24. Accessed August 29, 2018, https://www.ekd.de/news_2008_04_11_3 _domschatz_halberstadt.htm, April 11, 2008.

The reopening of the cathedral treasury, here, in the venerable Halberstadt cathedral, sends a clear and unambiguous signal. It says that we are reconnecting with old traditions, we see ourselves in clear relation to a history that extends much farther back than the previous century and the devastation and destruction left behind by war and dictatorship in our country and in this city. If I understand correctly, for you in Halberstadt this day signals that you are not just looking to the future with confidence, collective spirit, and energy, but you are also securing your deep roots in history and in your heritage. . . . There is no future without a past. An essential aspect of identity is an awareness of one's own history. When the cathedral treasury is reopened today, an important lineage and heritage of this city and this region will once again become visible, that of Christian Europe during the medieval period, in which so much was discovered, rediscovered, or developed that continues to determine who we are today.[25]

Köhler is using the formula "the future needs a past" in order to make a very explicit offer to his audience: that of an identity. In presenting the residents of Halberstadt with their roots in a long historical trajectory, it is not a matter, for him, of acceleration or of deceleration. Instead, he is much more interested in making them an offer of a new pan-German identity that can draw on the long collective history of Christian Europe and can mitigate the effects of the dramatic break in that unity from 1945 to 1989. He very clearly does not see this offer as compensation for the demands of modernization and globalization. He is not offering stability in the context of accelerated change; rather, his focus is on identity and orientation as a response to the "devastation and destruction left behind by war and dictatorship in our country and in this city." Identity is not simply a stable reference point, or even a recognized feature that is constantly undergoing change, but first emerges in the present through a choice of affiliation: local, ethnic, cultural, national, transnational. So Köhler uses the term "past" not in the sense of a determinist lineage but in the sense of a new resource, an accessible and flexible set of possible sites and historical events that can be appropriated and become part of the identity. At the same

---

25. Address given by Horst Köhler on April 13, 2008, in Halberstadt, Government publication Bulletin 31–2; accessed August 29, 2018, https://www.bundes regierung.de/Content/DE/Bulletin/2008/04/31-2-bpr.html.

time, he also makes several other offers to the people of Halberstadt. Following the brief period of the German Democratic Republic (GDR) and a divided Germany, the cathedral treasury can help sketch out a new identity on the basis of a long history that reaches from the Christian medieval period to the nonviolent revolution, the end of the GDR, and into the present. With reference to another site of memory, the Gleimhaus, he invokes another tradition, this time a non-Christian one. Köhler explains: "Other roots of where we come from are also visible there: the German Enlightenment and German classicism. We also thrive on that legacy and are actively preserving it, because it is so very valuable to us" (ibid.).

The past that Marquard evidently has in mind—heritage [*Herkunft*]—is not exactly the same as what Köhler means by the notion of "legacy." As with words like "identity" and "orientation," one will also not find the word "legacy" in the vocabulary of modernization theorists. Whereas we are invariably influenced by our heritage—whether we like it or not—a legacy can be accepted, rejected, reinterpreted, and appropriated in one way or another. A legacy, once handed down, is nothing so long as it is not taken up. Following 1989, the futures of the two divided German states had withered and now had to be replaced by a new collective future; but this time, it was a question not only of adjusting to a new future but also of discovering and sketching out new pasts. At the same time, this experience of a historical break represented an opportunity to reflect on the constructive character of history and identity in the cultural sciences. Specifically, one could suddenly and concretely see how the premises of the development of an identity shift alongside historical, political, and cultural frameworks. For instance, during the Cold War, Halberstadt was entirely focused on other things: the Peasants' Wars were much more important at that time than the legacy of Christianity or the history of the liberal middle-class. As a result of this evident shift, it became obvious to everyone how selective, biased, and malleable we are as we choose our reference points in the past, and how they constitute us, according to our current requirements.

However, this perspective does not imply that identity constructions are therefore superficial, fictional, or manipulative. It only means that identities are chosen or taken on, responded to, and lived by people, and as a consequence are a central aspect of a broad set of cultural practices. These practices are then observed, considered, evaluated, and criticized at a meta-level. To conclude this brief excursus on identity: the past is therefore anything *but* a reliable expanse that, like a teddy bear, guarantees a foothold in a world undergoing change at an increasingly rapid pace. Neither does it refer to the stable substance of a valuable legacy, as in the case of the over-one-thousand-year-old Halberstadt Cathedral treasury. For, if one does not draw on such a legacy and it fails to take hold as an important reference point, it will remain inert. What ends up being invoked in history and how it is used depends on the needs, values, and interests of those who—like Horst Köhler in Halberstadt in 2008—appeal to it in a specific temporal context.

Compensation Theory and Memory Theory—Two Different Approaches to the Past

Within the framework of modernization theory, what we call "the past" is synonymous with what happened and, by virtue of its nomological understanding of temporal change, is irretrievably past. Modern culture, however, has created special enclaves in which the past remains present and is therefore subject to interpretation. These are the institutions of historical study in which the historian is at liberty to engage this past, once it is irretrievably past and detached from the present. In his novella *Disorder and Early Sorrow*, Thomas Mann sketches a literary portrait of a history professor, and in it he emphasizes the strict separation of the temporal orders of the past and the present that constitutes this science in the first place. "For the temper of timelessness, the temper of eternity—thus the scholar communes with himself when he takes his walk by the river before supper—that temper broods over the past; and it is a temper much better suited to the nervous system of a history professor than are the excesses of the present. The past is immortalized; that is to say, it is dead; and death is the root of all godliness and all abiding significance."[26] This past can calm one's nerves because it is dead and decisively over, because it rests in peace and is withdrawn from the changing grip of the present, and above all because it no longer makes demands on us, the living. It is this past, immobilized under glass and characterized by Koselleck as "pure past," that constitutes the object of historical study.

Compensation theorists have modified this picture of the past in certain ways. They have demonstrated that the past not only is distinct and irretrievable, but that it also extends into the present as "collections of relics" or as "heritage" and therefore has important deceleration effects. Something is still to be gained from the past in its presentation of how what has become obsolete nonetheless endures. It has more than entertainment value: it preserves a foothold and provides some measure of stability and reassurance in the context of an ever-changing modern time. But what is above all reassuring about the past is that it *is* past, and what is already dead does not die. As a consequence, what has already become timeless and eternal tends to be seen as particularly reliable and permanent.

These ways of accessing the past in the context of modernization theory are markedly different from those established in the context of memory theory, which establishes the relation between time, identity, and culture on an entirely different basis. As William Faulkner puts it in one of his plays: "The past is never dead, it's not even past."[27] Christa Wolf's novel *A Model Childhood* also begins with this proposition. Her version is as follows: "What is past is not dead; it is not even past. We cut ourselves off from it; we pretend to be strangers."[28] Within the framework of memory theory, the past is indeed anything but "dead." In cases of guilt and failure, it haunts the present or comes back into the present as a quicksilver material

26. Thomas Mann, *Disorder and Early Sorrow*, in *Stories of Three Decades*, trans. H. T. Lowe-Porter (New York: Modern Library, 1934), 506.

27. William Faulkner, *Requiem for a Nun*, in *Sanctuary and Requiem for a Nun* (New York: Signet Books, 1961), 229.

28. Christa Wolf, *A Model Childhood*, trans. U. Molinaro and H. Rappolt (New York: Farrar, Straus & Giroux, 1980), 3.

from which identities and meaning are made. In any case, it is precisely not a sedative: rather, the past demands a great deal of effort and is often the cause of arguments and controversies about remembering and forgetting. It also becomes the subject of claims and demands, confessions and accusations, appropriations and rejections. In brief: clearly much more is at stake in conjuring up the past than continuity, deceleration, and stability in the face of the rapid changes of modern time.

From the perspective of memory theory, the past is precisely *not* what always reliably stays the same and remains identical with itself. To the contrary, it constantly changes in accordance with the changing perspectives and needs of those in the present. The first premise of memory theory is therefore the *desubstantialization of the past*, which fundamentally calls into question its stability and solidity. Of course, some material relics do extend from the past into the present but, for all that, they do not actually embody some "past in itself," because even material relics depend on contemporary contexts, framings, and interpretations. In other words, there is no such thing as the past in itself; as bygone, vanished, and lost time, it can only ever be confirmed, made present, and preserved in objects, ideas, representations, and reenactments. From this constructivist perspective, Freud's insight regarding the "belatedness" of subjective reality becomes important, in that a reality has always already been explained before it can become an object in the subject's experience of reality. In this context, explanations are not to be confused with hermeneutics, for the past is certainly not a stable text in relation to which new interpretations arise. "Explanations" here refer not to the competence of an expert but to the primary, necessary, and unavoidable operation of the individual human mind. For people who must situate themselves in time, to explain and appropriate the past is a way of coping with existence. This intimate and symbiotic relation between the past and the present is therefore a constantly changing and open-ended process.

Breaks in historical continuity lead to more than just a "renunciation of the past," however. At the same time, they can also spark strong interest in the "reconstitution of the past" (and not only in the context of the historical sciences). As one book title has it, the collapse of the Soviet Union also led to the "reawakening" of history in eastern Europe.[29] Still, it was not history in the singular that was awoken, nor were histories awoken on their own: what emerged was a contest between different memories and different versions of history. In particular, the long-suppressed memory of Stalinist violence and the suffering brought on by experiences of flight and expulsion were brought once again into the public eye. So, following 1989, the past implies not so much distancing and historicization but the very opposite—memory and recovery, whereby the space of experience and the horizon of expectation become closely linked once again.

A third difference should be noted between memory theory and compensation theory, regarding the understanding of time. Whereas compensation theory squarely focuses on reclaiming positive traditions, memory theory engages with the dark, shameful, and traumatic chapters of one's own history. With this form of historical recovery, it cannot simply be a matter of stabilizing or legitimating one's own identity, precisely because it involves engaging with what one would rather have forgotten, or what calls into question one's positive self-image. For various reasons, modernization theorists as well as compensation theorists are silent on the issue of this debilitating and negative dimension of the past. Nonetheless, the idea that everything that happened is automatically settled simply because it is past is no longer widely shared, and neither is the assumption that the past is only of interest to historians. This is particularly true of traumatic histories that have not yet been dealt with; as a consequence, debilitating episodes "resurface" and come to haunt subsequent generations. Such episodes return in memory precisely when the moral sensibility of a society shifts in relation to its own historical wrongdoings. For survivors, such events have not retreated into the past but remain present in often uncontrollable and subterranean forms. And it is not only as a function of

---

29. Frank Schirrmacher, ed., *Im Osten erwacht die Geschichte: Essays zur Revolution in Mittel- und Osteuropa* (Stuttgart: Deutsche Verlags-Anstalt, 1990).

their pathological effects that they remain present, but also because of their ethical dimensions. Genocides like the Holocaust, the decimation of Indigenous peoples, the crime of slavery, and other flagrant atrocities against humanity are not resolved by virtue of the fact that they are "past": in recent times, they have demanded complex forms of belated symbolic treatment by means of memory, recognition, restitution, and ultimately the honoring of the dead.

5

Is Time out of Joint?

Nos sumus tempora—"We are the times," as Augustine puts it.[1] Humans beings do not exist solely in terms of natural cycles and predetermined processes but live consciously in time and must create rhythms and fixed coordinates for themselves. This holds equally true for the theories they leave behind. These theories have long been shaped by religious teachings and beliefs: those convinced that the gods regulate time or that God controls time must not overly concern themselves with the past and future of human existence. But those who, in the interests of secular and worldly authority, believe they can actively interfere with and thereby plan the future and make history themselves will adopt a different cultural time frame. Modernization has created a new temporal regime to support and legitimate this process of self-empowerment and worldly authority.

---

1. "Nos sumus Tempora: Quales sumus, talia sunt Tempora," Saint Augustine, Sermon 80:8.

This book tells the story of this temporal regime. It details its emergence, its history, its crisis. As is the case with all narratives, here, too, one can only get hold of something once one has gotten to know it in retrospect. For it is only when alternatives present themselves on the horizon that the shape of something first becomes visible; until then, it had appeared as the self-evident and natural environment of the way things are. Changes that happen to a temporal self-understanding do so gradually; they often go unnoticed for long periods. There is no visible break or demarcation of the kind that historicists might wish for, no formal farewell or common rupture, but instead only an increasing number of shifts in attitudes and perspectives. The argument of this book is that the modern time regime reached a crisis point by the 1980s. It took two decades— so, until around 2000—before the outlines of a new temporal orientation would emerge: one that has meanwhile been elaborated and discussed on a global scale. We might claim that this turning point represents the end of a central feature of the history of Western modernization. This history has thus entered a new phase in which it relinquishes some of its arrogance, develops a more receptive attitude toward other cultures, and develops guidelines for a fuller engagement with them. The Western historical myth of progress or the dynamics of linear development, leading to ever-greater degrees of differentiation and complexity, is no longer assumed to be either natural or inevitable. As a consequence, this temporal ontology has come to be increasingly understood as a cultural construct with a distinct history. At the same time, it itself also becomes historicized. In this context, historicization speaks to an impetus toward reflection, which can only be eliminated from the world through a great effort of "self-blinkering," to borrow a term from Odo Marquard. In this light, we stand not at the terminal end of the modern time regime but merely at the beginning of its renewal.

Before sketching out the main features of this renewal, we must first consider the disorientation and uncertainty that accompanies this temporal reorientation. Like Shakespeare's Hamlet at the beginning of the Renaissance four hundred years ago, we are today being confronted with a change of temporal ontology: Hamlet's cry "The time is out of joint!" is an alarming diagnosis that has been steadily intensifying since the beginning of the twenty-first century, and it has only become more and more deafening.

Total Recall—The Rhetoric of Catastrophe and the Broad Present

> When the future collapses, the past rushes in.
>
> —JOHN TORPEY[2]

> What serves no use becomes a heavy burden; the moment can use only what it itself creates.
>
> —GOETHE, FAUST I[3] (684–685)

"Alles kommt zurück" (Everything comes back)—or so says the chorus of a pop hit often played by Swiss Air during the landing of its aircraft. This chorus could serve equally well as the motto for the crisis of the modern time regime, for it contains the basic argument made by critics of the present temporal orientation: in their eyes, it has largely turned into a foggy *dis*orientation with no value whatsoever for the purposes of truth, experience, or direction. Among these critics of time, we shall focus on the distinct voices of François Hartog, Hans Ulrich Gumbrecht, and John Torpey.

Crises of temporality have often occurred. Nietzsche discusses one of these crises in the second of his *Untimely Meditations* when he confronts the historicism of the late-nineteenth century. In that work, he rails against the architectural styles of the period—for instance, that mishmash of styles that was standard for the home decor and facade work of middle-class homes: Gothic, Renaissance, Baroque, and classicist styles were, with the help of the little prefix "neo," retrieved in the present and carelessly pieced together. Nietzsche castigated these merely decorative elements imported

---

2. John Torpey, "The Pursuit of the Past: A Polemical Perspective," in *Theorizing Historical Consciousness*, ed. Peter Seixas (Toronto: University of Toronto Press, 2004), 242.
3. Goethe, *Faust I and II*, lines 684–85; 20.

from other eras as false and superficial, as deceitful and infertile in contrast to "genuine" culture, which "can grow and flourish only out of life."[4] He draws on moral (in terms of deceit) and biological (infertile) values in his critique. The continued effectiveness of his polemic cannot be overestimated: his analysis provided subsequent generations with the values and arguments they needed to justify the destruction of historicist buildings—or, at least, to knock down their ornaments and facades—under the banner of a purity of taste.

Of course, Nietzsche's critique of historicism was not limited to matters of style or architecture; its primary target was a new form of knowledge production that had recently been established in the university's new disciplines for the human sciences. The relation to the past of these disciplines was predicated on renouncing a relation to the present: only in that way could a "pure past" be entirely divorced from the present. For Nietzsche, historicism's pure past entailed a levelling of all events of the past. These now became pure objects of scientific study and thereby lost all relations to the present in the form of selective or self-affirming appropriations. For historical research, everything was equally interesting. Nietzsche experienced this broadening of historical interest as a hollowing-out of memory in terms of how the past supports various functions in the present, such as choice, values, meaning, and identity. Using apocalyptical imagery, he describes historicism as "the madly thoughtless shattering and dismantling of all foundations, their dissolution into a continual evolving that flows ceaselessly away, the tireless unspinning and historicizing of all there has ever been by modern man, the great cross-spider at the node of the cosmic web" (108).

Nietzsche's rhetoric of crisis and catastrophe has exerted a lasting influence on our thinking and our evaluations. At the center of this rhetoric, the imagery of sickness and impotence, as well as of flooding, disorientation, and total powerlessness, stands out particularly strongly:

---

4. Nietzsche, "On the Uses and Disadvantages of History for Life," 117.

But it is sick, this unchained life, and needs to be cured. It is sick with many illnesses and . . . is suffering from the malady of history. Excess of history has attacked life's plastic powers, it no longer knows how to employ the past as a nourishing food (120).

At that time, his central argument is that "knowledge of the past has at all times been desired only in the service of the future and the present and not for the weakening of the present or for depriving a vigorous future of its roots" (77). According to Nietzsche, this knowledge of the past, cut off from the present, is mushrooming out of control with all the force of a tsunami:

[N]ow all the frontiers have been torn down and all that has ever been rushes upon mankind. . . . Historical knowledge streams in unceasingly from inexhaustible wells, the strange and incoherent forces its way forward, memory opens all its gates and yet is not open wide enough (78).

Contemporary critics of the new historicism have undoubtedly taken inspiration from this description. Their critique is not aimed at a professional historical scholarship that threatens the vitality of the present, however, but at a culture of remembrance that has since become a serious contender for this very scholarship. This new temporal crisis did not, in fact, come about as a consequence of an explosion of irrelevant knowledge cut off from the present and saved in academic archives; according to these critics, rather, the present itself has become addicted to the past, and any power of discrimination that might have arisen from being cut off from the past has been sacrificed.

In this chapter, we shall undertake a detailed examination of three authors whose work is representative of approaches taken in the field: the literary scholar Hans Ulrich Gumbrecht, the French ethnologist and professor of historiography François Hartog, and the American political scientist John Torpey. Despite coming from different disciplines, perspectives, and cultural contexts, all three have engaged deeply with problems arising out of the *re*ordering and *dis*ordering of past, present, and future.

Following an early work on the idea of "the modern" in the 1970s, Hans Ulrich Gumbrecht again took up the theme of temporality toward the end of the twentieth century. His first in-depth study of time, *In 1926: Living at the Edge of Time*, appeared in 1997.[5] In the book, Gumbrecht has no desire to constitute 1926 as an epoch-making year, let alone a suspiciously celebratory one; rather, he is arguing for the recovery of a historicized past as "present"— practically a Proustian undertaking, though here it is carried out not through involuntary memory, but through an empathic reliving of the past. In his 2010 book *Our Broad Present*, he elaborates on his thinking about transformations in our temporal ordering that had been presented in a more general way in the earlier work.[6] *After 1945: Latency as Origin of the Present* came out in 2012, and combines autobiography, analyses of time, and a notion of latency.[7] Looking back, he writes that these works grew out of the impulse "to explain and refine my idea about the emergence of a new chronotope." My own ideas, considerations, and study concerning the theme of time can also be traced back to the turn of the last century and have increasingly focused on the reconstruction of our cultural order of time.[8] In retrospect, it has become clear to me that despite how my own work developed in isolation, it was nonetheless anything but a lonely foray: others were also quietly working away at a problem that was becoming increasingly urgent. Much of that work has now been published, and dialogue is beginning to take place in various forms.

In Gumbrecht's most recent book, I encountered a passage I would like to invoke at this point—freed from the worry of an erratic solo effort!—as a concise and relevant summary of my own thinking. In that work, he concludes by arguing that the dimensions of past, present, and future have fundamentally and irreversibly

---

5. Gumbrecht, *In 1926*.

6. Hans Ulrich Gumbrecht, *Our Broad Present: Time and Contemporary Culture*, trans. Henry Erik Butler (New York: Columbia University Press, 2014).

7. Hans Ulrich Gumbrecht, *After 1945: Latency as Origin of the Present*, trans. Leland Stanford Junior University (Stanford: Stanford University Press, 2013). In addition to this book written for the general public, another book soon appeared on the theme of latency that was the result of academic collaboration: Hans Ulrich Gumbrecht and Florian Klinger, eds., *Latenz: Blinde Passagiere in den Geisteswissenschaften* (Göttingen: Vindenhoeck & Ruprecht, 2011).

8. A. Assmann, *Zeit und Tradition*.

changed and that the chronotope of "historical time" has reached its limit. Three fundamental conditions of our temporal understanding, long assumed to be inviolable, are no longer dominant: "leaving the past behind, going through a present of mere transition, and entering the future as a horizon of possibilities." According to Gumbrecht, previous generations had taken these assumptions for granted to such an extent that

[T]hey confused this specific topology with "time itself" or "History" *per se*. Because the previous generation took these conditions to be metahistorical, transcultural, and therefore inevitable, there was no way to think that something about "time" had begun to change.[9]

While I wholeheartedly agree with this assessment, my own position differs from Gumbrecht's in responding to the following question: What caused this turn and how should it be assessed? Gumbrecht articulates the crisis of the new historicism by using the phrase "broad present," a notion we have already encountered in an earlier chapter of this book. This broad present is for him the opposite of "presence," an idea that—with certain displacements and qualifications—picks up on Nietzsche's notion of "life." While Nietzsche finds this ideal embodied in Greek antiquity, Gumbrecht finds it in the culture of mass spectator sports. Gumbrecht's small-scale understanding of presence and Nietzsche's large-scale understanding of life both celebrate the image of a "fulfilled present"; both attempt to articulate an experience that grounds the subject in space and time, limits the visual field, produces a horizon, and, finally, generates the intensity of a total experience capable of dissolving the dreary boundaries between inside and outside, body and spirit, surface and depth, human subject and object-world.

Gumbrecht develops his theory of presence against the backdrop of a gloomy diagnosis of the present that has resulted from the loss of historical time. Within the chronotope of historical time, people were accustomed to moving freely through temporal spaces and "[leaving] the past behind; the distance afforded by the present

---

9. Gumbrecht, *After 1945*, 200ff.

moment depreciated the value of past experiences as points of orientation," whereas the "the future [presented] itself as an open horizon of possibilities."[10] According to his analysis, two key developments now separate us from this temporal orientation. First, "the future no longer presents itself as an open horizon of possibilities; instead, it is a dimension increasingly closed to all prognoses—and which, at the same time, seems to draw near as a menace" (xiii). And second,

> [W]e are no longer able to bequeath anything to posterity. Instead of providing points of orientation, pasts flood our present; automated, electronic systems of memory play a central role in the process. Between the pasts that engulf us and the menacing future, the present has turned into a dimension of expanding simultaneities. All the pasts of recent memory form part of this spreading present; it is increasingly difficult for us to exclude any kind of fashion or music that originated in recent decades from the time now (xiii).

Here, Gumbrecht is vividly describing what it might mean to "destroy the past to an adequate extent" (Rudolf Schlögl) once the paradigm of progress has lost its power. The loss of the ability to forget, which Nietzsche attributed to a hypertrophied historical research, Gumbrecht chalks up to the immense storage capacities of our electronic media. Between a threatening future and an overwhelming past, the present expands as a temporal milieu characterized by simultaneity, stasis, and stagnation. The present, which in the modern time regime was merely the tipping point and transitional "now moment," has become, according to Gumbrecht, a kind of waiting room of world history, but not even remotely a waiting for an end time: "When nothing can be left behind, each recent past is imposed, in the present, on previously existing and stored pasts, and in this ever-broadening present of the new chronotope there will be a diminished sense of what each 'now'—each present—really 'is.'"[11]

Gumbrecht dates this change at the end of the 1980s and associates it with the transition to a digital world. With "the unprece-

---

10. Gumbrecht, *Our Broad Present*, xii.
11. Gumbrecht, *After 1945*, 199.

dented storage capacity of electronic media compounds," a zeal for preservation and collection arose that now bring pasts into the present in a haphazard way, with no need for attention or judgment: "Today the computer has made knowledge accessible at levels previously unimaginable in scope and density—at the same time, however, its use raises a question: What is this knowledge good for?" As was previously the case for Nietzsche, for Gumbrecht the new chronotope of the "broad present" is based on a crisis of forgetting. Since we can no longer leave any aspect whatsoever of the past behind, "it is impossible to forget anything" in this broadening present. Gumbrecht expresses this inability—as did Nietzsche—using the language of implosion, stagnation, and the proliferation of information. His verdict is that, along with its loss of a future-orientation, Western society has also lost its capacity to select and assess information. Using keywords like "forgetting," "unlimited access," and "hypercommunication," Gumbrecht adopts Nietzsche's rhetoric of flooding and overloaded knowledge-storage systems. Those who use this vocabulary risk falling into a depressive state, Gumbrecht suggests; the only remedy that we have left at our disposal is to yearn for and seek out moments of presence in the *waste land* of the broad present.

François Hartog also registers a fundamental change in our ordering of time after 1989—and the picture he paints is even more dire. He speaks not only of a "broad present" but also of a new "presentism." The end of the Cold War saw a collapse of the future and, simultaneously, of our linear understanding of history. Both the future and the past have gotten lost in this new omnipresent: "'Presentism' pretends to be its own horizon and it tries to shape both the future and the past according to its own image, so to speak, as a-temporal replicas of itself."[12] Hartog argues that the current presentism has abolished the past and replaced it with its fictitious reconstruction in the present. Like Gumbrecht, Hartog also attributes this current temporal pathology to the destruction of clear divisions between past, present, and future. In turn, this leads

---

12. Cited in Chris Lorenz, "Unstuck in Time: Or, the Sudden Presence of the Past," in *Performing the Past: Memory, History, and Identity in Modern Europe*, ed. Karin Tilmans et al. (Amsterdam: Amsterdam University Press, 2010), 88.

both of them to consider the growing influence of memory culture. Gumbrecht sees little of value in the turn to memory:

> German intellectuals, in particular, are of [*sic*] fond of celebrating this displacement as a turn to a nebulous "something better," which they call *Memoria-Kultur*. However, the problematic consequences of pasts flooding the present cannot be foreseen. Maybe, as Niklas Luhmann once remarked, it really isn't necessary to declare every factory chimney in eastern Westphalia a national monument to be preserved at any cost.[13]

In the nineteenth century, Annette von Droste-Hülshoff was still trying to save the East Westphalian landscape—which was being threatened by factory chimneys during the Industrial Revolution—in her literary archive. The Zollverein Coal Mine Industrial Complex in Bochum, with its winding towers, has been a UNESCO World Heritage Site since 2001. The industrial monument has been converted into a theme park and is today the attraction and centerpiece of the whole region. Like Hermann Lübbe, Gumbrecht associates "memorial culture" less with a historical burden (one thinks of the chimneys of the crematoria at Auschwitz-Birkenau, which were also made a World Heritage Site in 2001) than with the history of technology. Surprisingly enough, neither Gumbrecht nor Hartog has anything to say about pasts that are not "past," about wounds or traumas, about claims or recognition—simply put: the dominant themes of the 1980s and '90s. For Hartog, the form of memory dominating our contemporary present is that of heritage (*patrimoine*). He sees in this idea of heritage a relation to the past that has no historical substance whatsoever: as pure construction, it is, he argues, wholly a reflection of the present.

> Heritage associations demonstrate the construction of a memory that is not a given, and therefore has not been lost. They work towards the construction of a symbolic universe. Heritage has nothing to do with the past but only with the present, as a category of action in the present that concerns only the present.[14]

---

13. Gumbrecht, *Our Broad Present*, 31.
14. Glevarec and Saez, cited in François Hartog, "Time and Heritage," 14. Translation modified.

The claim that memory can only be produced in the present—that all aspects of the past are reconstructed in accordance with the changing paradigms of the present—has by now become commonplace. However, Hartog's claim that a memory, insofar as it is selected, reinterpreted, and appropriated, has "nothing to do with the past" seems grossly exaggerated. It derives its stridency from the need to draw as clear a line as possible between the legitimate treatments of the past found in historical scholarship on the one side, and those treatments emerging out of other social contexts and institutions on the other. This line separates a "pure past," which derives its objectivity from its clear distance from the present, from memory's "usable past," which is brought back into the present. For Hartog, there is no legitimate way to use the past: any appropriation of the past is automatically a misuse. It follows, then, that his view of new cultures of memory must necessarily be wholly negative, and that interest in cultural heritage and questions of memory has gotten out of control. It means:

> . . . that we will soon reach the point where we call everything "heritage." As memories are increasingly reclaimed or demanded, everything could be considered heritage or is liable to become heritage. The same inflation seems to reign in both areas: In that way, "the cult of heritage" and "musealization" are approaching ever closer to the present (12).

Hartog explains this obsessive engagement with memory and cultural heritage in terms of a search for collective identity:

> Heritage thus becomes an invitation for collective anamnesis. The "ardent obligation" of heritage, with its requirements for conservation, renovation, and commemoration, is added to the "duty" of memory, with its recent public translation of repentance (10).

Hartog is conflating two quite different forms of interest in the past here: the threat to cultural memorials and their protection, on the one hand, and the acknowledgment of historical guilt, on the other. He denounces both these forms of investment or involvement in the past as wrong-headed. In fact, for Hartog, the obsessive engagement with memory and heritage has much more to do with tourism, consumption, and the economy than it does with the past itself. Therefore, he sees memory and heritage as nothing more than the sign of "a massive, overwhelming, omnipresent present, that has no horizon other than itself, daily creating the past and the future that, day after day, it needs" (14).

Like Gumbrecht, Hartog, too, sees the current present in a dystopian light, as the result of an alarming departure from the norm. Yet, differing from the rather melancholic mood Gumbrecht develops in response to it, Hartog the historian sees this new development as a direct threat to his own profession. In a polemical style, he once again pits good "history" against bad "memory." He thus distinguishes the terminology of the (good) "monument" of professional history-writing from the (bad) "memorial" of contemporary identity politics. While the "monument" stands for the unambiguously objective inventory of history that reaches out from the past into the present, the bad "memorial" refers to the particular interests of social actors who formulate their own aims in the present as standards for the future. "The memorial takes precedence over the monument or the latter turns into a memorial. The past attracts more than history; the presence of the past, the evocation and the emotions win out over keeping a distance and mediation" (16). And who is to blame for this development? In the struggle over the past, Hartog claims that memory activists have prevailed against the nation-state and historical scholarship. What he finds particularly egregious is the sudden proliferation of those actors who, with their claims to identity, democratize, popularize, and pluralize the past. Indeed, alongside the work of historians, it is certainly true that a large number of memory projects are meanwhile being developed that bring the past back at specific sites and appropriate it into contemporary consciousness. There is no denying that these new ways of using the past can also be subject to abuse, ones that must be critically evaluated and judged. For Hartog, though, there is a single black-and-white line to be drawn between memory-culture and historical scholarship. The alarmist tone of his assessment reflects a fear that the new memorial activities endanger the continued existence of historians in universities, archives, and museums. In the same way that the melancholic Gumbrecht sees the broad present in terms of the generalized phenomenon of decadence, Hartog sees the heritage industry as the demise of history.

Unlike the more skeptical compensation theorists who still see ways out of the problems associated with the modern temporal regime, according to Gumbrecht and Hartog, the end of modern time is already nigh: the time is, indeed, hopelessly out of joint. In response, the rhetoric they use to describe the shortcomings of the new chronotope takes on alarmist Nietzschean overtones. Whereas Gumbrecht is more or less resigned to this change, Hartog vehemently and categorically denounces its associated dangers and undesirable developments as departures from the (implicit) norm of modern temporality.

This "clash" in conceptions of time becomes particularly clear in light of the incompatibility of certain key ideas. For Hartog, the notion of "collective identity" is as illegitimate as the idea that the past is constructed in the present and must be safeguarded for the future. Both Gumbrecht and Hartog attribute different symptoms to the demise of our culture; for Gumbrecht, the key problem is digitalization, which fully realizes the mind/body dualism so characteristic of modernity; for Hartog, it is the heritage industry, which has infiltrated the domain of historians and endangered it with the mass appeal of theme parks and historical tourism. The one envisions the past as completely stored and fully retrievable at the push of a button—the other, as fully commercialized. Both describe the "broad present" exactly as Nietzsche once described historicism—as a culture of "total recall" that has forgotten how to forget. When memory becomes hypertrophic, it topples into forgetting, and the culture of memorialization turns out to be organized amnesia.[15]

---

15. This idea of "organized amnesia" also permeates George Steiner's description of "after-culture." This is his term for the ongoing deterioration of high-culture, a term the cultural critic uses to describe, among other things, the global charge of (youth) culture: "The catastrophic decline of memorization in our own modern education and adult resources is one of the crucial, though as yet little understood, symptoms of an after-culture." Steiner, *In Bluebeard's Castle*, 107. Almost fifty years later, his assessment of the dangers of the increasing capacity of computers is at once prophetic and archaic.

Whereas Gumbrecht and Hartog associate the flooding of the present by the past with waves in retroculture and heritage culture, John Torpey sees a danger in how an overpowering past can escalate conflicts over past occurrences of historical violence. It must be said that he himself has made significant contributions to the conceptualization and analysis of the processes that nation-states adopt as they transition from dictatorship to democracy.[16] In that work, he has done a wonderful job of showing how crucial these critical self-examinations are on the part of transitional states as they grapple with their violent pasts for processes of political transformation. As a consequence of doing that work, however, Torpey became disillusioned. In light of increasing pressure from victims' groups in the United States, as well as the social and political consequences associated with it, he became an avowed opponent of this kind of politics of history. The more relevant and topical the pasts of victims' groups become, he suggests, the more rapidly does the idea of a nationwide collective future fall apart. These findings led Torpey to reverse the direction of his research in quite radical ways. He no longer made the case for memory—its recognition, or "working through"—and deplored both the change in perspective from the future to the past and the collapse of the old temporal order. Torpey speaks for many intellectuals, scholars, journalists, and politicians tired of the ever-broadening past in the present. They no longer want to hear anything about the "veritable tidal wave of 'memory,' 'historical consciousness,' 'coming to terms with the past.'"[17] Their prescription is simple enough: all that has to be done is to turn away from the past and toward the future. Torpey seems concerned about the "prevailing sense of catastrophe" among elites in the Euro-Atlantic world: through its one-sided focus on violence, crime, and guilt, "Europe—once thought of as the homeland of the Enlightenment—replaces Africa as the *dark continent*" (250). He fiercely polemizes against overvaluing the past insofar as it leads to a weakened orientation toward the future: "These future-

---

16. John Torpey, *Politics and the Past: On Repairing Historical Injustices* (New York: Rowman & Littlefield, 2003).
17. Torpey, "The Pursuit of the Past," 251.

oriented projects have been widely replaced across the intellectual and political landscape by concerns about coming to terms with the past that have extensively supplanted more utopian preoccupations."[18] He sums up the collapse of the modern temporal regime in the following way: "We might call this the *involution* of the progressive impulse that has animated much of modern history—the deflection of what was once regarded as the forward march of progress and its turning inward upon itself."[19]

Torpey gives a simple explanation for his resistance to the backward-looking orientation: "We should be aware that this preoccupation is in substantial part a replacement for paradises lost" (252). Torpey's position here is well-suited to compensation theory, in which a dialectical explanation exposes the unreasonable demands of the modernization process at the same time as it addresses the need for compensation as replacement for the losses that accompany accelerating historical change. All the same, it has to be said that Torpey's stark opposition between the "paradises lost" of the past and the "promised land" of the future once again conjures up the narrative of modernization in its particularly American version, in order to resurrect with brute force the good old days of the modern temporal regime.

Connections between the Past, Present, and Future

Hartog, Gumbrecht, and Torpey each use the normative standard of the modern temporal regime as the backdrop for their analyses—a standard whose loss they either melancholically or bitterly regret. All three ascribe the resulting temporal chaos, lamented as a dominant feature of the current disorientation, to a new memorial culture without elaborating on either the origin of that culture or its presuppositions. They are convinced that this memorial culture (having perhaps fallen from the sky or having beset people with a

---

18. John Torpey, *Making Whole What Has Been Smashed* (Harvard: Harvard University Press, 2006), 8ff.

19. Torpey, "The Pursuit of the Past," 252.

kind of cultural disease) is completely blurring the otherwise clear boundaries of the temporal order and has destroyed culture in the process. The present, as Hartog, Gumbrecht, and Torpey all describe it, has become divorced from both the past and the future, and this has led to a chaotic and haphazard temporal disorder.

We could easily extend our list of examples: Voices speaking out about new insecurities and confusions in interactions with time are steadily increasing in number. The talk here is not about the proper use of one's time, nor does it involve concrete questions about temporal planning; rather, it concerns a widespread temporal disorientation and an inability to locate oneself in the dimensions of past, present, and future. Hartog speaks of a deep "perplexity" and creates surreal images of our temporal sensibility: "The past is knocking at the door, the future at the window and the present discovers that it has no floor to stand on."[20] Andreas Huyssen has also observed that the clear lines dividing the past, present, and future have been blurred. In language similar to Torpey, he speaks of an "*an attack of the past on the rest of time*, especially on some as yet unarticulated vision of an alternative future." His perspective on contemporary culture is similar to Gumbrecht's: he states that in the context of the Internet, Facebook, and Twitter, a voracious present "cannibalizes all manner of pasts and pulls them into the orbit of the present. Ultimately this not only destroys the temporal difference that is preserved, despite all fragility, in public and private memory, but it makes historical consciousness itself obsolete."[21]

Such diagnoses confirm that the loss of the modern temporal regime also entails the loss of many fundamental securities. In a concrete sense, Hamlet's old claim that "the time is out of joint" today means that something indeed seems to be wrong in the relation between the temporal registers of past, present, and future; it is becoming increasingly unclear how they mesh and how they diverge. We are experiencing a truly tectonic shift in the structure of these "timezones," and the meaning and arrangement of these different

---

20. Hartog, "Time, History, and the Writing of History," 110.

21. Andreas Huyssen, "The Crisis of Success: What Next in Memory Studies?," *Memory Studies* 5, no. 2 (2012): 228.

temporal levels are no longer self-evident. This experience is reflected in a dense critical discourse. Following the demise of the modern temporal regime, a serious uneasiness has spread regarding the new chronotope, the logic of which is not at all clear. First and foremost, no real consensus has emerged regarding the root cause of this unwelcome change or who should be considered the guilty party. Torpey accuses the West's elite of Euro-Atlantic nations that have focused exclusively on their violent histories rather than developing utopian perspectives for their future. Hartog, by contrast, identifies the custodians of the heritage industry as the guilty ones; Gumbrecht sees the new forms of media technology as the trigger for these deep disturbances of our temporal orientation; and Huyssen makes the culture industry, together with mass media, responsible for our problems with time. So, is there any way to get beyond this ambiguous and alarmist discourse?

To gain a new perspective on our time here, an approach involving historicization might be helpful. To develop this approach, we can draw on Hartog's exploration of how the various chronotopes have changed over time. He distinguishes between three "temporal regimes of history writing" in the various phases of Western culture, each of which has emphasized a different temporal register of the past, present, and future as their central reference point. He equates the *temporal regime of the past* with the period from antiquity to the Enlightenment and describes it as a backward-oriented form in which the past regulates the future. According to this paradigm, the past offers examples in accordance with which the present models itself.

The *temporal regime of the future* is said to have originated at the end of the eighteenth century, together with a new goal-oriented historical plan. Hartog speaks of a "modern temporal regime of history-writing" and suggests that its benchmark years were 1789–1989, giving it a duration of two centuries. Hartog argues that this new form of history writing emphasized the future: when seen in hindsight, the past and the present then become stages along the way to an as-yet unattained goal.[22] Over the last twenty-five years,

---

22. As for the perspective of historians, Hartog's pointed claim about the importance of the future for the modern *régime d'hisoricité* sounds somewhat paradoxical

he writes, we have "experienced a deep and rapid change in our relationship to time" (110). This temporal regime of the future is said
to have lasted past the end of the Second World War: Hartog identifies the 1960s, the '70s and, at other times, the '80s of the twentieth
century as its end point. The effective end of the modern future-
oriented ideology, he asserts, came in 1989. Following that, the
new *temporal regime of the present* is said to have taken hold, which
he equates with a permanent cultural crisis. In this phase, the focus
has been entirely displaced onto the present. According to Hartog,
this displacement entails the loss of the past as well as of the future,
and he very much doubts whether the old engine of the modern
temporal regime can be started up again. Since the modern temporal regime was created in Europe, he assumes that the next one
will come from somewhere else (110).

What is it about the "temporal regime of the present" and the
descriptions given of it by the cultural critics we have named here?
They agree on the following point: the entire temporal crisis is generated by the fact that we can no longer clearly distinguish between
the temporal registers of present, past, and future. What historians
view as an utterly necessary condition for their work—namely, the
separation of these temporal registers—has since given way to their
complete entanglement with one another. As a result, the past and
the future are said to have lost their functions; they no longer represent the virtually sacred dimensions of the objective real (the past),
or the expected not-yet (the future), but rather something created in,
and suited to, the (actual) present. This description is now so widely
accepted by cultural critics that it no longer raises any eyebrows. In
response, certain critics have now begun to differ from one another
in their diagnosis of our present: others respond by further en-
trenching their commitment to the withering modern temporal regime, while others (among whom I include myself) see this crisis as
an opportunity to engage in auto-critique, update theoretical paradigms, and further develop our understanding of this time regime.

---

for, despite all their enthusiasm for the future, the historian's focus is still undoubtedly
on the past. Hartog's claim evidently combines historical scholarship with the philosophy of history.

The ways we are formulating the changes undergone by our temporal order frequently resonate with the terms of Hartog's historical assessment. Yet, despite some surprising parallels at the level of conceptualization and modes of questioning, we are assuming fundamentally different presuppositions and, accordingly, we arrive at very different conclusions. Using the exact same ideas and concepts, the problem of time that interests both of us can be depicted differently. To make our disagreement clearer, I will return once again to Hartog's intriguing notion of the historical sequence of different temporal regimes, distinguished on the basis of their relative privileging of a particular temporal register. These observations could easily be generalized further: For example, the traditional temporal regime that privileges the past is arranged, in Hartog's vivid description, so that the light of the past shines onto the present and future (101). Traditional societies tend to locate the foundations of their values in the *past*, and that is how those values elude the definitive grasp of the present. As a result, certain episodes of the past become bound to a mythical time, become sacred, and so come to form a lasting foundation and a stable reference point for the present. But beyond sacred or mythological forms, such as those found in traditional societies, the past is also valued as a precious resource for any society that searches its own history for foundational values and that—"illaminarily" (Lübbe)—"rescues" specific people or events out of the flow of time so that they can function in the present as authoritative examples. This approach, that of *historia magistra vitae*, repeatedly explores history (and not only primordial mythical time) in search of heroes that can be rediscovered in the present and thus emulated. This is what Nietzsche calls "monumental history."

By comparison, cultures that privilege the *future* on its own are more recent. They are also the exception. That is, the future on its own has often had a bad reputation in many cultures: as a complete unknown, it could not possibly serve as a ground for society's values. In fact, many ancient cultures, such as in China or Mesopotamia, developed complex arts of avoiding the future. That is why these ancient cultures are said to have "mastered the future" (Stefan Maul): by means of sophisticated divination practices, this persistent element of the future's uncertainty could be effectively mitigated, and the culture's temporal system freed from it. Only after notions such as Messianism, apocalypse, and other forms of metaphysical hope for salvation arose in monotheistic religions like Judaism and Christianity, did Western cultures begin establishing positive, even hyperbolic, expectations for the future. Starting with the Enlightenment, people became more optimistic about the possibilities for improvement in their lives and started to think about the future in positive ways. As a consequence, the idea of progress and looking toward the future with hope started to seem realistic; that orientation successfully became the norm in both social institutions and the system of cultural values governing them. This modern temporal regime was endorsed, strengthened, and systematically developed not only by the Enlightenment, but also by ideologies like communism or the economic system of capitalism.

The third and final option regarding the logic of historical succession is an emphasis on the *present*. To add to the remarks made above, here we must ask the following question: what does the "present" mean in this context? According to Hartog, those who retreat into the present have been cut off from the past and no longer trust the future enough to orient themselves in accordance with it. One might describe this posture as self-centered escapism or as temporal parochialism but, regardless, even though it might actually exist, such a claim does little to illuminate the state of our present. The desire here is doubtless to affirm the present, divorced from the influence of the past as well as from the long-term planning for the future and commitments to it. However, as has been argued earlier in this book, focusing on a completely liberated present in such a way that life itself boils down to a vague and sensual moment cut off from everything else can, at the very most, be the ambition of a few artists, philosophers, and other "virtuosos of life." The desire to align oneself wholly with the present often goes along with a hedonistic way of life, which looks for moments of gratification and short-term fulfillment, though it can also be a form of self-denial and resignation. The cutting edge of the present is far too thin for it to be able to offer an entire society a solid foundation for cultural existence. Hovering on the thin edge of a liminal temporal "outside" between past and future may be an outstanding state of exception, yet it goes against everything that anthropology teaches us about cultural life. Without some kind of perspective on the future, people are not motivated and become aimless. And, lacking memories of some kind, they accumulate no experience and form no connections or identity. Viewed socially or culturally, then, the present is always already a prolonged *now* of varying duration. Without such a socially constructed duration, it would be impossible for anything at all to be experienced, communicated, acted, or even remembered.

Most of all, though, what is decisive about the present is that it is, and remains, the privileged site at which humans expand their present by creating their own future and past. This constructivist perspective is opposed to an essentialized understanding of the registers of past, present, and future as fixed, neutral, and objective temporal realms. For what comes to be understood and evaluated as the past or future does not follow a natural logic; it only takes on shape and meaning in the context of specific cultural frameworks. The important discovery first made in the 1980s, when the modern temporal regime was losing its hold, involved precisely the cultural status of time. It turns out that Augustine was doubly right: we *are* the times we construct for ourselves, and the only time we have at our disposal for this work is the present. Insofar as the past and the future either are "no longer" or are "not yet," they have no ontological basis. Human beings have the incredible ability to imagine what is temporally absent by virtue of remembering and anticipating; that is, they can conjure up or call forth what is no longer there, or what is not yet there. "There are three times," writes Augustine, "past, present, and future." And he continues: "a present of things past, a present of things present, a present of things to come."[23] As such, we precisely *never* limit ourselves to the ephemeral transitional stage of the present, but instead make use of both the past and the future to extend and stabilize such fragile and precarious things as our realms of experience and horizons of expectation.

This constructive and anthropological description forms the basis for theories of cultural memory. Such theories understand cultures

---

23. Saint Augustine, *Confessions*, trans. H. Chadwick (Oxford: Oxford University Press, 1992), XI.xx, p. 235.

to be varying modes of producing particular time frames and re-gard cultural memory as the "control mechanism" for maneuvering within any given temporal frame. In marked opposition to Hartog, who repeats the act of temporal rupture with his succession of the three modalities of past, future, and present, the framework of cultural memory emphasizes the ineluctable entanglement of these modalities. Hartog's succession of temporal modalities undoubtedly makes clear the important shifts in emphasis that have taken place between orientations toward the past and those toward the future. Yet a culture that is wholly focused on the present and makes no distinctions among different kinds of time—lost or stolen time, mythical or historical time, even sacred time—is simply tedious. The tedium of the present that Gumbrecht and Hartog describe sounds less like a description of everyday experience than a description of a fictional borderline state of "standby"—what myths sometimes call "limbo."

In the 1970s, two Russian semioticians, Yuri Lotman and Boris Uspenskij, were already describing the interweaving of temporal registers in highly detailed ways. The guiding premise of their work was that all cultures establish a temporal horizon for themselves. By their definition, time, culture, and memory are closely interconnected: "The culture that relates to its past through memory not only creates its future but also its past; in this sense, it forms a mechanism that acts against natural time."[24]

These Russian semioticians say it explicitly: cultural time is the very opposite of natural time! However, despite appearances, there is nothing particularly scandalous about this claim, but rather something quite self-evident. Hartog describes the same state of affairs but evaluates it very differently against the normative backdrop of the modern temporal regime: "We have been inhabiting a hypertrophied present which pretends to be its own horizon: no past, no future, or it generates its own past and its own future."[25] What is shocking to Hartog about contemporary memorial culture

---

24. Lotman and Uspenskij, cited in Lachmann, "Mnemonische Konzepte," 134ff.

25. Hartog, "Time, History, and the Writing of History," 108.

is that it creates its own past and future. But do historians not do this as well? That is, do historians not write their books in the present, and do they not draw on current standards of knowledge and current interpretative frameworks? What would a future or a past look like that was entirely independent of cultural institutions in the present? The insight of the constructivism of the 1980s—that "the past as such" does not exist—was an important one. Notions like "the past" or "history" can easily lend themselves to the sense that we are dealing with a substance, an ontological reality, that can then be taken as a clearly delineated object of historical scholarship. But the past only arises to the extent that it is focused on, thematized, constructed, and reconstructed in a present, which is after all the sole dimension of human perception, negotiation, thinking, and evaluating.

Of course, for the past to be investigated, something of it must remain and extend into the present. That is why traces and relics from other, now-inaccessible times are saved and interpreted. But then again, even these continual activities of collecting and storing, saving and securing away, opening up and explaining, are activities that take place in the present. The objective ideal of modern historiography has, alongside its image of itself as a neutral observer, created the notion of the past as a "period." As a consequence, it has expunged everything that pertains to the constructive character of its own modes of investigation and representation. This realization is in no way a dangerous postmodern heresy threatening to undermine the standards of objective historical study. Rather, it is an argument drawn from *common sense* [in English in the original—trans.], one that allows—indeed, this has already taken place—for the cultural foundations of the historical vocation to be more strongly implicated and reflected in the work of history itself.

The framework of a theory of cultural memory reveals new perspectives that can help us to better understand the crisis of the modern temporal regime by integrating it into broader contexts. Against this backdrop, the "crisis" looks less like a scandalous deviation from the modern temporal regime—less like a dangerous disease of time—and more like a return and rediscovery of those aspects of time that the modern temporal regime had dogmatically excluded.

The pendulum has swung back; the forgetting of the past and the obsession with the future that were built into the modern time regime are being dismantled in light of new ways of reactivating the past. The unreasonable demands of this temporal regime, which had little regard for anthropological necessities and sensitivities, are also being dismantled. In turn, critics of the new chronotope have responded by enumerating the problems and unreasonable demands of this new cultural order of time.

One of the problems they identify regarding the new chronotope has to do with how it multiplies entry points into the past. Yet the sense that the past is totally past, or that it is settled once and for all has, in fact, been gradually waning since the 1980s: in the interim, it has become increasingly obvious not only that the past is something that experts study but that it is also important to politics and society as well as to personal life. As a consequence, the primary meaning of historiography, now and in the future—its undoubted validity as a distinct and differentiated system of knowledge in modern Western culture—is not in question. But what *is* being called into question is simply the historians' claim that their method of accessing the past is the only legitimate one, and that they have exclusive rights to the past over all other individual and social interests. Since the 1980s, during the course of the debate regarding the cultural dimension of historical knowledge, new concepts have arisen that have noticeably changed our view of the human being as it was developed by theories of modernization. So, for instance, we have learned that the process of history does not necessarily lead to the autonomous individual, freed from all constraints. Of course, this form of life continues to be recognized and legally defended as a possible cultural option. But room has also been made for many other forms of life that can no longer be judged by this one standard as regressive or progressive. In this sense, the notion of "collective identity," a key term in the 1980s, broke with the ideas of modernization theory and exploded the cultural framework of the modern time regime. Since that decade, collective identities have become part of the basic inventory of cultural studies and our everyday experience: They are based on historical connections and on the principle of freely chosen belonging. Affiliation with such collective identities must by no means entail the rejection of free individuality. However, the anthropological understanding that human beings live in social, religious, ethnic, and cultural collectives does imply that they make use of their pasts for the construction of their identities in the present and future. Identities arise—and here the theory of (cultural) memory comes into play once again—through the shared remembering of significant moments and experiences that serve to differentiate this group from any other. As we now know, the postulate of the modern temporal regime—to separate the past out from the present and relegate it to the historians' domain—had the effect of deliberately hindering identity formation. But no person, and no group, exists exclusively in the present. One's own identity is always based on the awareness of a particular history. Historians might criticize the selective use of the past for the purposes of constituting identity in the present, but the truth is that such activity functions like something of a fundamental human law in many cultures. That is how new avenues to the past are opened up; they themselves break with the categorical imperative of "temporal break" and once again closely connect the past, the present, and the future. What people actually expect from history is precisely what professional historians have nothing whatever to say about: "the appropriation of the past, memory, the assurance of identity, and from time to time even entertainment."[26]

Although the historians' monopoly over the past has been broken, what has in no way been challenged is the authority that methodical historical work possesses to establish the truth of what happened. The "invention of the historical," in the sense of an independent, source-based, and demonstrable historiography, is and will remain a milestone of Western culture. Furthermore, we need the cultural competency of historical scholarship today, more than ever, as a groundwork for and corrective to constructions of historical memory. For this reason, it is counterproductive to play out historical study against the claims of memory, as Hartog does with his general invective against memorial culture and the heritage industry. His panic would definitely be justified in the context of a totalitarian

---

26. Kocka, "Historische Socialwissenschaft heute," 18.

regime, but in Western societies, his aggressive consternation over whether or not historians will continue to exist seems outlandish and misplaced. After all, the expertise of their autonomous domain of knowledge lays the groundwork for a democratic memory culture.

The temporal order of modernity, one that called for and enforced a strict separation of temporal registers, has evidently come to an end. As a consequence, our temporal orientation has become deeply confusing. This dis-orientation has a great deal to do with the large-scale recuperation of the past and with the ways that are being developed to engage with those reclaimed pasts for the construction of identities. Wherever we look, the gulf separating the realm of experience and the horizon of expectation is being bridged, and the past and present are again becoming more tightly bound to one another. My claim in this book is that this development is not so much about scandal or crisis as it is about restoring a degree of normalcy. The modern time regime has not completely lost its authority; rather, as more and more avenues for accessing the past have opened up, it has been placed within certain limits. It is often the case that the process of finding a new norm raises issues and problems. Instead of dismissing the new time regime wholesale and throwing ourselves into a battle of words between historians and memorialists, it would be much more productive for us to focus on those problems that all of us must now confront.

6

The Past Is Not Past; or, On Repairing the Modern Time Regime

"Modernity" is conceived both as a concept,
as a problem, and as a period.[1]
The failure of the modernization project has left us
with responsibilities, ones which
remain in the de-modernization project.

—*Bruno Latour*[2]

The clock of modernization strikes a chime when the desire to break from the past becomes overpowering. This determining factor is not a fundamental law of culture, however, but takes effect under very particular historical conditions. It applies to the French Revolution,

---

1. This is a description of a new academic journal called "History, Culture and Modernity" (HCM; www.history-culture-modernity.org), which was launched in 2013.
2. Bruno Latour, "The Recall of Modernity: Anthropological Approaches," trans. S. Muecke, *Cultural Studies Review* 13, no. 1 (2007): 25.

as well as, for example—but under very different circumstances—
the Federal Republic of Germany after the Second World War and
the Holocaust. Following 1945, this modernizing impulse once
again allowed for a radically new beginning, replacing the totalitarian National Socialist ideology with a democratic focus on the
division of powers, equality, and human rights. Subsequent to this
complete break from the past, the expectations of German postwar
society were squarely focused on the future.

The same was true of the generation of modernization theorists
who, understandably enough, embraced the opportunity for a new
beginning with particular enthusiasm. Following the period of economic recovery and political consolidation, they had great success
in creating the conditions for a fresh intellectual start. However, just
one generation later, it became clear that this stance had certain limitations; these theorists clearly wanted to know nothing about
"culture," its media, and its symbolic systems, or about the significance of "memory" as a form of personal, social, political, and cultural self-expression, which had been gaining in significance—and
not only in Germany—since the 1980s and 1990s. And, conve-
niently enough, the theoretical guidelines of the modern time regime prevented the issue of biographical experience from being
taken into consideration.

So, the time regime of the modern needed repairing. A first attempt at such repair came from the compensation theorists. Being
skeptical dialecticians, these theorists became the defenders of
human desires and sensitivities that had been mostly overlooked or
bracketed by the framework of modernization. Since people cannot tolerate a great deal of arbitrary innovation, they cushioned the
separation of the space of experience from the horizon of expectation and emphasized that the new is not possible without also ac-
commodating a great deal of the old. With their formula "the future
needs a past," they were pointing to a dialectic of modernization
that, alongside necessary innovations, must also invest in institutions of preservation as compensation:

> The historical sense is specifically modern: conservation activities, the
> museum, scholarly memory and historical orientation, generally speaking,

the humanities. Precisely because the modern culture of liberation even jettisons histories, it forces the education of this culture of conservation as—according to Ritter—"the organ of its spiritual compensation."[3]

With this analysis, compensation theorists systematically shifted onto the terrain of modernization theory. Saving the past by means of a "culture of preservation" is itself a central part of Western modernization and, as we have seen, can be traced back to the "invention of the historical." As expressions of this historical sense, Odo Marquard cites "conservation activities, the museum, scholarly memory and historical orientation, so generally speaking, the humanities." In this sense, for him, history continues to fall under the exclusive purview of professional archivists, curators, and historians, who are now increasingly called on to present it to an interested public. However, there is as yet no straight line leading from this compensatory culture of preservation to the entire spectrum of practices, problems, and controversies we now associate with the new catchphrase "cultures of memory." Under the paradigm of cultural memory, the past in particular is no longer the exclusive domain of the historian, nor can the use made of it be reduced to the function of a comforting medium of deceleration. The new entanglement of the past with the future—of the space of experience with the horizon of expectation—that characterizes the present time regime has implications, requirements, and effects that are much more far-reaching. It is increasingly true not only that the past guides the present and the future in a positive way, as we saw in the example of the speech about the Halberstadt Cathedral treasury, but also that the past is newly evaluated in light of the present's knowledge and demands. In that regard, new perspectives on and interests in the past—themselves tied to collective identities, major historical events, and traumatic experiences—have important roles to play.

The modern time regime therefore needs not only compensation, but also repair. The French ethnologist and anthropologist Bruno Latour writes: "If it is true that it was the Europeans who invented

---

3. Odo Marquard, "Zukunft und Herkunft," in *Skepsis und Zustimmung: Philosophische Studien* (Stuttgart: Reclam, 1994), 22.

modernity, it is important that they are able, if I dare say, to 'uninvent' it, or more precisely, to 'recall' it, just as industries recall defective products."[4] In this particular case, however, repairing the defective product of modernity involves transforming the whole business. Latour understands his critique of the modernization paradigm as a measure undertaken for the purposes of constructive repair:

> An industry only undertakes this painful operation in order to push itself even further ahead. Recalling modernity for Europeans cannot mean that they will abandon ambition, but, on the contrary, that they will finally become aware of their responsibility (29).

His call to reinvention is a call for self-awareness, which should lead to a more critical self-image and allow for new types of activity and interaction.

For Latour, the occasion for such a self-critique is the dawn of a new world-historical era. In this period of globalization, cultures like China or India possess an intensified spirit of optimism, now that Europe and the West are losing their prestige as the standard bearers of progress: "The idea of the West has set just like the occidental setting sun it is named after" (19). Throughout the course of this shift, modernization has been uncoupled from the West. While the West has dissolved into smaller units—"Europeans, North Americans, French, Japanese etc., each searching for a new basis, a footing or a site in order to become themselves once more"—today, modernization can occur wherever three qualities are present: "(technical) efficiency, (economic) profitability and (scientific) objectivity" (22).

Latour's overhaul of the fundamental convictions implicit to modernity requires a critique of the modern time regime, including "the obsession with time, novelty, innovation and progress" (21). In the course of this critique, Latour points out the contradiction between the idea of a continuous and homogenous temporal flow, on the one hand, and the drive to produce permanent breaks,

---

4. Latour, "The Recall of Modernity," 20.

caesuras, and incisions, on the other. He describes revolutions as a way of breaking with time and turning it into the past. However, this resource of revolution, which has always pushed us into the future, has recently been subject to a devaluation:

> Every new call to revolution, any epistemological break, any Coperni-can upheaval, any claim that certain practices have become outdated for-ever, will be deemed dangerous, or—what is still worse in the eyes of the moderns—outdated![5]

As an anthropologist, Latour also takes aim at the notion of a uni-form temporal flow, which has entrenched the contrast between "progressive" and "stagnating" cultures on the global stage. Whereas the face of modernity was always steadily pointed in the direction of the future, today it has turned in the other direction and now looks, panic-stricken, backward. These two extremes must be fol-lowed by a more realistic relationship with time, which Latour describes as "walking on egg shells," "in which each step is given careful precautionary consideration."[6]

Latour's demodernization project begins with the insight "We have never been modern!" That is, the modern project has been a largely utopian construct characterized by stark and abstract slo-gans, most of which were not taken up in everyday life because, as the compensation theorists clearly showed, they quickly came up against the anthropological limits of what is humanly possible (to say nothing about its violent impositions). According to Latour, even the moderns themselves who invented and enforced the new guide-lines could not live by them. While they preached the separation of nature and society or of past and future, they perforce lived through their blending. For this reason, it follows for Latour that we can and must rehabilitate and consciously accept much of what the modern cordoned off and excluded from its own sense of itself but has nevertheless unconsciously lived. Following the acts of separa-tion, differentiation, and rupture that were entirely in keeping with the pristine thinking of the modern, it is now time for interweaving,

---

5. Latour, *We Have Never Been Modern*, 141.
6. Marquard, "Zukunft braucht Herkunft," 28.

mixing, and devising new forms of expression.[7] Demodernization confirms the sense that the historical phase of European or "Western" dominance—along with its arrogance—has come to an end. According to Latour, a phase of global responsibility follows the phase of imperial power. He characterizes this new phase as an era of diplomacy, which requires a dramatic change in political style. The new political virtues are primarily civility, forbearance, and modesty. In diplomacy, there is negotiation: one speaks with a soft voice and, listening to others, one hopes to survive together with others.

Three New Categories: Culture, Identity, Memory

Since the 1980s, the reconfiguration of the Western understanding of time has been accompanied by the introduction of three terms that had no place in modernization theory but have subsequently advanced to become key ideas for our historical orientation and understanding of the world: culture, identity, and memory. These three notions form part of a new paradigm in cultural studies that first becomes possible, as Hobsbawm puts it, once "structure goes downhill and culture uphill."[8]

The term *culture* had no special status within the framework of modernization theory. When it was needed, it was used in a highly specific way: as a kind of synonym for artistic creations that exist in one social subsystem alongside others. The new idea of culture that has revolutionized the humanities since the 1980s has also radically changed the scope and meaning of the word. Since then, "culture" has become the common horizon encompassing developments amid multiple social subsystems. The equivalence of "Western culture" with "modernization," one that had enjoyed unquestioned

---

7. The acts of division that Latour is thinking about include the very structure of modern thought itself, one that generates a number of fundamental binary distinctions, such as nature/culture, unity/multiplicity, shell/kernel, surface/depth, but also the transcendental belief in a science that has masked and then forgotten its own context.

8. Conrad, cited in "Die Dynamik der Wenden," 136.

validity until quite recently, has thereby been loosened. At the same time, this loosening allows for a more precise examination of their relation. As we have seen, modernization is also another word for the modern myth of history, by which is meant a process that uniformly and naturally unfolds according to an established logic of differentiation and increasing levels of complexity within social structures. By contrast, cultures exist only in the plural as specific options and constructions that arise in relation to certain historical conditions, and that define those goals and values that respond to the specific needs of the society or its primary political classes. In this view, culture is no longer subordinate to an all-encompassing modernization; instead, modernization emerges as one specific form of Western culture. At the same time, this opens up the possibility of reflecting on the range of options and subsystems available in one's own culture, in addition to evaluating or expanding it in new ways. This possibility of renewal, however, differs from that of the modern temporal regime, in that the former does not aim at another radical break with the past. Rather, it takes place both in the interests of a self-critical anamnesis, or recollection, of certain agendas in the history of Western culture and in the interests of developing a sense of the necessity of particular changes in direction.

But what does culture *mean* in the new paradigm of cultural studies? At this point we must return once more to the concept of culture developed by Yuri Lotman and Boris Uspenskij in post-Stalinist Tartu, which represents an alternative to the presuppositions of modernization and compensation theory. Their theory of "culture as memory" is essentially supported by two suppositions:

1. The past is not automatically past.
2. The future and the past are constructed in the present.

The following important theoretical formulation should once again be submitted for discussion:

> It is the essence of culture that, in contrast to the natural course of things, the past does not pass; that is, the past does not simply disappear. Fixed in the memory of the culture, it achieves . . . duration. The memory of a

culture is designed not only to be a repository of texts, but it also has a certain generative mechanism. A culture connected to its past through its memory not only generates its future, but it generates its past as well. In this sense, it is a mechanism that goes against natural time.[9]

According to this theory, culture does not exist in the empty time of physics, which, though it does specify the tempo, does not specify either the meaning of time or its organizational structure. Rather, the task of culture is to establish temporal frames in which what is present remains effective in the future and what is past is retained in the present or can be brought back into the present. What is at issue here is the cultural capacity for memory, which is the fundamental prerequisite for a culture's ability to reproduce itself. That is how a culture can transform a temporal flow into guidelines for action, meaning, and direction—all of which transcend the brief lifespan of the individual and first make it possible for those who come later to communicate with those who came before. Because of their cultural environments, humans must not begin daily anew but can, by standing "on the shoulders of giants," deploy the spiritual potential of earlier generations. Through studying other cultures, one can move beyond the limitations of the modern view. From a comparative perspective, it immediately becomes clear that there is no culture that does *not* reproduce itself through forms of recollection—however these might be constituted. Only from this comparative perspective can a sense arise of the radically distinct trajectory of Western modernization, which sought to rid itself of any recourse to the past or merely tolerated it within the narrow confines of historical scholarship. No wonder, then, that modernization theorists such as François Hartog experience the confusing and varied realities of the new memory culture—complete with its practices, problems, and controversies—as a kind of culture shock. Against the background of cultural scholarship, this turn appears more as a corrective to and a release from an overly restrictive focus on innovation and the future.

---

9. Lotman/Ušpenskij, cited in Lachmann, "Mnemonische Konzepte," 134ff.

The construction of such a cultural time frame is markedly different from quantitative linear time, which dissolves at the very moment of its actualization. It also functions as protection against the forgetfulness of individuals. No cultural transmission can be established on their own spontaneous memory: "We consciously perceive very little. We store even less in short-term memory. Still less turns into long-term memory, hardly anything is remembered as biographically significant over an entire lifetime."[10] To supplement the frailty of individual memory, these cultural time frames create possibilities for reconsidering the past as well as prerequisites for reconnecting with ideas and experiences, creations and artifacts. These things do not exist in a timeless eternity, but are socially constructed and historically evolved reference points that hold together the present with the past and the future. Canonized texts, classical works of art, and normative historical dates are examples that show how not everything that has become past automatically ends up in the trash heap of what has been forgotten. Cultural practices and performances can repeatedly "bend" the linear flow of time into cultural strategies for actualizing and reappropriating the past.

Another idea that is missing from the vocabulary of the modernization theorists (or that is rejected on the grounds of its association with the memory paradigm) is that of *collective identities*. Paul Ricœur has shown that the concept of identity points in two different directions.[11] On the one hand, it can be related to the Latin word *idem* and can indicate individuality. This is the case, for example, when what is at issue is the material identity of historical structures, or the habits, customs, and preferences that remain the same despite all kinds of transitions. This form of identity appeals to compensation theorists as well, and Marquard gives it the image of a "teddy bear."[12] Just as children carry their teddy bears

10. Jan Philipp Reemtsma, "Wozu Gedenkstätten?," *Aus Politik und Zeitgeschichte* 25–26 (2010): 3ff.

11. Paul Ricœur, *Oneself as Another*, trans. Kathleen Blamey (Chicago: University of Chicago Press, 1995), 113–39.

12. Odo Marquard, "Innovationskultur als Kontinuitätskultur," in *Skepsis in der Moderne: Philosophische Studien* (Stuttgart: Reclam, 1994), 91.

around with them, so too should adults arm themselves against the overwhelming innovations of their surroundings with this kind of identity.

While this first meaning of the concept concerns objects and procedures, the second relates to subjects and their reflections. In this second meaning, the concept of identity is related to the Latin *ipse* and is relevant to both people and their self-images. In marked distinction from an "identity" that remains the same throughout time, the second meaning points to individuality as a dynamic process that takes place in time and that emphasizes the active, reflective, and constructive aspects of the individual's psychological development or the cultural formation of the person.

Within the paradigm of cultural studies, a third meaning of the term arose, "collective identity," by which is meant imagined self-images out of which smaller or larger groups, right up to nations and states, are constructed. These collective self-images are usually based on a narrative as well as on chosen key events, significant places, and cultural artifacts and practices that offer the group, together with a particular image of history, both a sense of their uniqueness and a historical orientation. To focus on this concept of collective identity more precisely, I want to cite Jürgen Kocka once again who, in 1996, admitted that the "winds had changed" and that the language of modernization theory had started to sound foreign to many. In retrospect, he explains the awakening of his generation as an attempt "to practice history as enlightenment and to learn from history. Meanwhile," he continues, "we have come to strongly demand other things from history: appropriation of the past, memory, guarantees, and a secure sense of identity, at times even entertainment."[13]

As we have seen, "learning from history" was never part of the paradigm of modernization theory. The formulation of *historia magistra vitae* was invoked time and again to demonstrate the impossibility of such learning. The generation to which Reinhart Koselleck, Jürgen Kocka, and Hans-Ulrich Wehler belong obviously *did*

---

13. Kocka, "Historische Sozialwissenschaft heute," 6, 18.

learn from history, albeit not through appropriation but instead by a type of conversion—that is, by turning away and freeing themselves as radically as possible from the period of National Socialism. To be sure, many intellectuals, artists, scholars, and politicians of that generation have made it their life's work to help lay and secure the cultural and intellectual foundations for West German democracy. The work of "owning" this negative past, with all its difficult problems of symbolization and commemoration, however, is something entirely different. This was a task they would pass on to the next generation, one to which I feel I belong.

The third idea that acquired an entirely new meaning within the paradigm of cultural studies is *memory*. This idea has been taken up in abstract labels like "cultural memory" and "memory culture" and meanwhile refers not only to the internal or psychological processes of the individual but also to a broad spectrum of cultural practices, such as conserving historical traces, archiving documents, collecting art and relics, and reactivating these by means of media or pedagogy. Here, it is not only a matter of what Marquard calls "preservation culture"; it actually involves all the possible forms that the social use of the past can take, which have again become an important and current topic in our cultural awareness once the dominance of the modern temporal regime had waned. Specifically, cultural memory is not simply a passive "storage memory," but also includes the aspect of reactivating the past and making it possible to appropriate it into an active "functional memory." The close connection between memory and identity requires that cultural memory create possibilities for identification and structures of participation that enable individuals as well as collectives to make the past their own. One cannot deal with these structures of participation and belonging—which in a democracy are only an offering and not an obligation imposed from the outside—by means of a static argument, which is what Jan Philipp Reemtsma, for instance, does. Like many other modernists, Reemtsma understands "talk in the first-person plural" to be metaphorical because "they don't even claim majorities anymore. . . . Also memorial sites—why they were built, what should become of them—is of interest only to a minority. But this minority has pushed its interest through as if it were that of the majority, who really only let it happen."[14]

When viewed through the lens of a theory of cultural memory, the past is not only an object of knowledge that can be filed in the archives, but is also a dimension of human experiences, memories, feelings, and questions of identity—all important and legitimate ties that intimately link the past with the present *and* the future. Despite the many examples of how history has been subject to political abuse, it remains the case that historical events are highly significant for individuals and groups. In his essay, Reemtsma makes a convincing case for why this might be so: "It is a question," he writes, "of historical interpretation for the purposes of self-interpretation: We want to take from history who we are and what we can hope for" (7).[15]

The Past Is Not Past: Historical Wounds and the Idea of Reversible Time

The "crisis" of the modern time regime arises not only from the fact that the future no longer holds the promise it once did and has itself become a problem. Along with the future, the past has also undergone a fundamental qualitative change. It is decidedly no longer the site where emotions are automatically neutralized and experiences effaced, as the modern temporal regime would have it. Alongside what historians define as a "pure" past, there are also "impure" forms of the past that are not easily separated from human experience, behavior, and understanding. The growing conviction is that the past is an inseparable part of culture, human existence, per-

---

14. Reemtsma, "Wozu Gedenkstätten?," 9. Reemtsma's formulations call to mind Ulrike Jureit's claim that the so-called '68ers were the self-empowered minority who turned society and posterity into the victims of their own personal memory obsession.

15. This same idea was expressed in simpler terms by a young woman who was invited to the Stuttgart Legislative Assembly on January 27, 2012, as a "Youth Guide": "It is simply about what kind of person one wants to be," she said.

sonal self-understanding, and collective identity. This is certainly true of events that are viewed as positive or heroic and that become part of traditional historical narratives. Such narratives appeal to pride (or humiliation, in the case of defeats) and justify a collective self-awareness that functions to mobilize the political masses. But a completely new development suggests that this trend is becoming increasingly true of negative experiences involving individual and collective suffering, whether characterized by trauma or guilt. These issues were simply not approachable for the longest time, because no adequate cultural narratives were available and because the descendants of those responsible for the suffering did not admit their own responsibility. As part of a new ethics of historical responsibility, these negative historical events are today becoming the focus of belated treatment. As long as the focus was exclusively on the future and on modernization, the suffering and trauma of those who had to bear a significant share of the costs of this story of progress were systematically shielded from view. What immediately comes to mind here is the example, mentioned earlier, of African Americans, whose own history of slavery and systemic racial discrimination did not fit into the official narrative of American history.

Collective memories like these can be understood using the historian and archaeologist Dipesh Chakrabarty's notion of "historical wounds," which he understands to be "a mix of history and memory."[16] He emphasizes that this notion of the historical wound did *not* originate from within Western historiography but rather from outside it—in fact, from a multicultural politics of recognition. An increased global awareness of the ethics of human rights—both in the abstract and in concrete political contexts—has played an important role in this politics of recognition: whereas academic historiography carefully avoids anything that might look like involvement or partisanship, the politics of recognition is based on the rightful existence of ethnic identities and the recognition of their historical experiences. Since their voices are often not found in historical

---

16. Dipesh Chakrabarty, "History and the Politics of Recognition," in *Manifestos for History*, ed. Keith Jenkins et al. (London/New York: Routledge, 2007), 78.

archives, the evidence of oral testimonials has taken on a new significance in this process.

These politics of recognition are an absolute first in history. They counter a centuries-old practice of *misrecognition* in which cultural "others" were denied the dignity accorded to human beings. This practice involved one group categorizing another as "inferior" in order to justify their oppression. Over time, this cultural differential would become fixed as a permanent and absolute marker, creating a permanent "state of exception." Yet this state is markedly different from the one that political theorist and law professor Carl Schmitt describes: whereas Schmitt's state of exception names a temporary suspension of the normative political order, the permanent state of exception I am describing is one in which the maltreatment of others through power structures, cultural stereotypes, and deeply entrenched social habits no longer requires justification.

This centuries-old—indeed, millennia-old—history of violence toward cultural others hit a breaking-point in the 1980s, at a time when various political orders, historical epistemologies, and cultural ontologies had started to lose legitimacy. This epochal turn did not happen through revolution or war, but instead through a transformation in consciousness that happened in many fields at the same time. Their medium was a cultural revolution of sorts, though not like the cultural revolutions of Stalin or Mao that maniacally sought to enforce "the new." To the contrary, this peaceful revolution was driven by a critical assessment of history and Western culture, and by an increased understanding of the imperial basis of the spread of Christianity, colonialism, anti-Semitism, and racism.

The awareness of "historical wounds" and new cultural practices of a politics of recognition arose in this critical environment. Such historical wounds are to be found among Indigenous peoples under colonial power, among victims of slavery and their descendants, but also among the survivors of Hitler's and Stalin's forced-labor camps, in situations of flight and displacement caused by ethnic cleansing, as well as in societies enforcing racial segregation, apartheid, or strict caste segregation. In the context of this long and horrifying history and the historical wounds it has created, the Holocaust appears not as an absolutely unique case but much more as the unsurpassable intensification of all these destructive tendencies.

It is undeniable that these new practices of memory are related to the transformation of our cultural temporal regime. However, as the following example shows, the connection between them is usually explained within the framework of compensation theory:

> There is also a rather vague sense that the preoccupation with memory is part of the changed structures of temporality at the end of the twentieth century and the beginning of the twenty-first. Against the "acceleration" of time through technical progress, the elimination of distance and the general blurring of territorial and spatial coordinates in an age of globalization, the recovery of "memory" aims at a temporal re-anchoring and even the much-talked-about "recovery of the real". Rather than a simple exhaustion of utopian energies, memory might signify a resistance to the new utopia of globalization and to teleological notions of history. . . . If one cannot change the future, one can at least preserve the past.[17]

According to this explanation, the modern temporal regime was responsible for an accelerated pace of change as well as for uprooting people from the local, which is why a culture of preservation arose to counter these trends. Theorists of historiography went beyond the viewpoint of compensation theory, however. Motivated by how explicit the changes in cultural attitudes toward time were becoming, they began to look more closely at the theoretical foundations of their own profession. In April 2011, Chris Lorenz and Berber Bevernage organized a conference on the topic of "Breaking Up Time: Negotiating the Borders between Present, Past, and Future," which proposed to put up for discussion the hitherto rarely questioned notion of the past that informs history writing. In the Call for Papers for the conference, they write the following:

> [T]aking a certain definition of "the past" for granted seems folly, if we consider that throughout history different cultures and societies have

---

17. Jan-Werner Müller, ed., *Memory and Power in Post-War Europe: Studies in the Presence of the Past* (Cambridge, UK: Cambridge University Press, 2002), 15ff. Cited by Lorenz, "Unstuck in Time," 101, fn81.

conceived of "the past" and the boundaries between "past," "present" and "future" in very different ways. We have only to look at the various conceptions of time that are used in law (legal time), history (historical time) and religion (religious time) to see how the Western notion of "the past" changes depending on the context in which it is being talked about.[18]

Lorenz is interested in the anomalies of the historical time regime. He coined the term "hot history" to describe anomalies such as the experience of traumatic pasts that do not simply pass—as one might expect them to—because of how they continue to make demands on the present for years, sometimes decades, afterward. Because of their connection to "historical wounds," such pasts resist the general tendency to automatically "cool off."

Bevernage has suggested the idea of "reversible time" to describe the temporal anomalies that historians have recently had to confront. Alongside episodes from the past that we retrieve because they are useful, there are also those we cannot control because they pursue us, become latent, and then at some point catch up to us again. A past that is associated with trauma and guilt continues to make demands on the present: it calls for recognition and the acceptance of responsibility. This "return" of traumatic memories is also connected to a new sensibility among historians, because history is now increasingly being told from the perspective of the victim. While the future-oriented modern temporal regime silently passed over the victims of history, the temporal regime of the new memory culture has brought these voices back into the present. As Bevernage emphasizes, examples of such a reversal in the direction of time's arrow can be seen in the fields of law, ethics, and psychotherapy. The lifting of the statute of limitations in cases of human rights violations is a clear sign of a rejection of the notion of linear time. It represents a powerful refusal to pass on or forget a past that still needs to be addressed in the present.

---

18. CFP–FRIAS workshop "Breaking Up Time: Settling the Borders between the Present, the Past, and the Future," Freiburg Institute for Advanced Studies, School of History, Albert-Ludwigs-Universität, Freiburg: 7–9 (April 2011); accessed April 6, 2018, http://www.frias.uni-freiburg.de/de/das-institut/archiv-frias/school-of-history/veranstaltungen/presentpastfuture07-090411.pdf/at_download/file.

"The idea that a hot present can automatically become a cold history," says Chris Lorenz, "is the temporal structure preferred by those who want to let bygones be bygone. Usually they are the ones who fear a court verdict."[19] Lorenz is suggesting that what has, up till now, been regarded as a fairly neutral temporal frame is, in fact, a very specific "politics of time."[20] Time does not flow in only one direction in the arenas of morality, psychotherapy, or law; the recognition of historical wounds and how they are handled in the present have also changed the premises of historiography. We have broken away from the idea that the past, as the sphere of what no longer exists, is fundamentally immune to change or to further human influence. What we are so used to thinking about as irretrievably dispensed with or finished can, in certain cases, become relevant and active again in the present. Orientation toward the future prompts us humans to be active, whereas orientation toward the past confronts us with the unforeseen consequences of our actions and holds us accountable.

Identity Politics—Intersections between History and Memory

The notion of collective identity puts us squarely in the political arena, which is also why many modernization theorists have fought so vehemently against expanding the concept of identity from individuals to collectives. Lutz Niethammer has summarized their misgivings, some of which are very serious, at times justifiably so.[21] For the new premises of cultural studies and identity politics seemed to open the floodgates on the manipulation of history: if, from now on, it is understood that all identities are "constructed" in the present, then according to what standard can self-images grounded in history be distinguished from those grounded in mythical

---

19. Lorenz, "Geschichte, Gegenwärtigkeit und Zeit," 134.
20. Bevernage, *History, Memory, and State-Sponsored Violence*, 15.
21. Lutz Niethammer, *Kollektive Identität: Heimliche Quellen einer unheimlichen Konjunktur* (Reinbeck: Rowohlt, 2000).

fiction? As an example of this complexity, we need only look at the example referred to in the introduction to this work: the change in collective identity that took place in Russia. Following the collapse of the Soviet Union, the key events of the nation's history were changed. In 2005, the deeply ingrained memorial day commemorating the October Revolution of 1917 was struck down by parliamentary decision and replaced by a hitherto unknown event (the 4th of November) from out of the distant past (invoking the expulsion of the Poles after their occupation of the Kremlin in 1612). This date reactivated a deep-seated fear of an enemy invasion, a move that was not bound to improve relations with Polish neighbors. At the same time, reference to a violent history vanished along with that old date—a reference that had created deep wounds in Europe as well as in the biographies of prominent Russians. By carefully circumventing this complex of violence under Stalinist rule, a positive image of Stalin could emerge that was belatedly polished up so that he could become a hero who had emerged victorious over Hitler. This intensely selective and self-congratulating evasion leads to a historical picture and a self-image that further serve to prevent both the recognition of Russia's own political victims and its rapprochement with other states that were part of this traumatic history.

The Russian historians who gave this new shape to Russia's historical picture are certainly not the first in history to take on the role of stooges to an authoritarian power politics. For centuries, all around the globe, positive self-images of the nation have everywhere been decreed from above. Such one-sided political interventions call for another type of historian who can work without commitments to identity or tradition and can critically distance him- or herself from the political myths of the nation. According to their own understanding, modern historians meet this demand by freeing themselves as much as possible from any obligations involving national identity and endeavoring to investigate historical events as objectively as possible.[22] For this reason the achievement of modern

---

22. Although all historians are situated within particular contexts, currently there is something like a global expansion of knowledge and consciousness on the

historical scholarship remains an invaluable resource of Western culture, particularly in contexts where the past is used for political purposes. In this respect, the ways in which history and memory coexist and intersect with one another, and how they mutually correct one another—that is, the construction of memory by history, on the one hand, and historical consciousness by memory, on the other—are crucially important. We can therefore not speak of the interweaving of the realm of experience and the horizon of expectation without also including the intersection of "memory" and "history."

Whatever is revisited and newly evaluated from within the framework of cultural memory—be they important events and achievements, or past shocks and traumas—is not the result of a supression of modern historiography, as Hartog suggests it is; rather all such reevaluations happen in light of it. In the 1990s, a discourse first emerged that polarized the notions of "history" and "memory" in such a way that they came to be seen as irreconcilable. From the perspective of modernization theory, what we call "history" therefore had to be protected from the onslaught of what we term "memory." From the perspective of the new paradigm of memory, "memory" was clearly marked off from "history." In the interim, almost no one doubts that *both* forms of relating to the past are legitimate and necessary. They belong together, to be sure, yet they must also remain clearly distinct from one another so that they can each be fully effective in terms of their function and their responsibilities. The new culture of memory has multiplied the possible modes of accessing the past, which has in turn led to a lifting of the monopoly that professional historians once had on the past. But this has not reduced the significance of their work in any way. On the contrary, the more that memory activists bustle about in this area, the more important it becomes to connect their presentations of the past and the resulting constructions of memory to the results of scholarly research. Memory culture is *legitimate*, even though it uses varying

---

grounds of an internationally recognized methodology that requires historians to focus on primary sources and truth and to hold to the guidelines of an international community of scholars.

media and ways to present the past (such as personal memories, films, exhibitions, and memorial ceremonies); it becomes *illegitimate* when it is put to the service of justifying "sovereign" greatness or power and, by dismissing historical knowledge, when it ignores or denies the claims of other histories. The movements of memories can certainly break from the procedures and norms of historiography, though they cannot cut ties with the universe of historical knowledge altogether. Nowadays, it is generally accepted that history and memory rely on each other as mutual correctives;[23] in essence, this recognition is a continuation of a consensus reached in recent years that goes as follows: *A memory culture without historical scholarship is blind, and historical scholarship with no reference to memory is empty.*

Two Trends in the Politics of History

In the current politics of history, two trends are incompatible with one another. The first can be designated as *a politics of self-assertion.* It involves an investment developed in the nineteenth century in the construction of positive national self-images, focusing initially on heroic honor and then later on the heroics of collective suffering. According to this paradigm, the sole task of a politics of history is to sustain and celebrate a national identity. The prism of national memory tends to narrow in on acceptable segments of history and to elevate these to the level of myth. In the context of a traumatic past, there are only three roles that a national memory can adopt: that of the victor who overcame evil, that of the resistance fighter and martyr who fought against evil, or that of the victim who passively suffered the evil. Whatever lies beyond these positions and perspectives cannot, or only with great difficulty can, become part of an accepted narrative; it is for this reason that they are either "forgotten" or often denied at an official level.

---

23. Jay Winter, "Introduction—The Performance of the Past: Memory, History, Identity," in *Performing the Past: Memory, History, and Identity in Modern Europe*, ed. Karin Tilmans et al. (Amsterdam: Amsterdam University Press, 2010).

The other trend can be summarized using the phrase *a politics of regret*. Here it is a matter of constructing national memories that allow for a perpetrator's perspective and, by recognizing guilt, that make it possible for a general public to accept responsibility and integrate negative episodes into the national memory. This recognition of the (other) victims of one's own history is an absolute first in history. To the same extent that it used to be self-evident to complain about the victims of one's own politics of "othering," what has now come to the fore is a readiness to mourn and to regret the victims of one's own politics.

The past has always been subject to political use and abuse. At the end of the twentieth century, however, another innovation occurred: That is, memory research itself, alongside which a critical discourse has developed that analyzes past and current practices of national memory construction. Political decisions regarding history are thus no longer made solely in the context of political motivations but have recently become the focus of observers and commentators, both internal and external. Because of this critical public scrutiny taking place at a transnational level, the politics of history have fundamentally shifted, even if—viewed globally—they have not changed nearly enough.

The differences between the two trends can be quickly illustrated by means of an example. The politics of self-assertion is based on a construction of memory that builds up a narrative of *continuity*. In that respect, only episodes of history are selected that, even amid evidence to the contrary, prove the present greatness, significance, and continuity of a nation. In cases of a politics of regret, by contrast, the construction of memory is not based on continuity but rather on *rupture and change*. In this respect, a symbolic self-distancing from the crimes of the past takes place, making it possible both to recognize the crimes and, at the same time, to break from them. There are those who worry that as a consequence of these politics, a permanent shadow will fall on the collective self-image and that it will be permanently damaged by the admission of various wrongdoings and crimes. Yet this worry can be overcome through the new ethical conviction that, in the case of documented historical crimes, it is not by means of silence and denial but solely by means of expressions of regret and the recognition of victims that a positive self-image can be restored.

This attitude has become more prevalent in the last few decades in the context of societies transitioning from dictatorship to democracy. But it can also lead to changes in national self-images without changes to the political system, as we increasingly see in the growing number of examples of a politics of regret in the former colonial states. By contrast, for victorious nations like Russia and the United States, which because of their positions of strength do not have to bend to pressure, they have no reason to change their historical self-images of strength and self-assertion. Here, a fear remains that national pride will be damaged, and that this will result in a loss of face and diminished power. But for notorious victim nations like Lithuania—and, in a different sense, also Poland—the exclusive focus on their own suffering seems to create barriers that prevent them from developing an empathic relation to other victims: namely, those of their own making. Both throughout Europe and all over the world, examples abound of both kinds of politics of history, and there are also minorities within the individual states that campaign for the opposite position. In states that have made themselves known for a politics of regret, pressure can mount to move in the direction of renationalizing the political in the name of pride and honor, whereas states with a strong nationalistic outlook often adopt transnational perspectives on that history that work to recognize the victims as well as protect minorities. In Russia, for example, some voices are being raised for a politics of self-assertion, as well as those for a politics of regret, as the following two excerpts show:

(1)

History is a form of social self-awareness. Using an anthropological metaphor, one might say that history is the memory of society. History connects individuals to a nation. The self-awareness of a person cannot be negative. When it becomes negative, frustration and psychological disturbances follow. In extreme cases, a person will need therapeutic and psychiatric help. The same is true for a society; its self-image cannot be negative. For this reason, school education must give a positive image and give the students a positive image of their country. When we build up a negative relationship to the history of our fatherland and portray the past as a black hole by reducing it to a collection of crimes and misdeeds, we make a whole young generation neurotic.

(2)

Our history was heroic at times and horrifying at times; it was beautiful as well as ugly—but when all is said and done, it is our history. The authors of our textbooks have used this point of departure as the foundation of their work, and they will continue to work in this spirit for the love of their land.[24]

These descriptions reflect the various memory constructions of, on the one hand, self-assertion and, on the other, regret. In the final instance, the question of which faction will ultimately prevail will be a question of power and political will, to be sure—but it will also be a question of social education.

---

24. (1): Aleksandr Filippov and Aleksandr Danilov, authors of the new teaching aids for the subject of history, Independent Newspaper (NG) from September 17, 2008. (2): Dmitry Volodikhin, coauthor of the textbook *Russian History, 1900–1945* (2008), statement from September 9, 2008. I thank Kevin M. F. Platt for this reference; for him, this latter statement contains an important feature of Russian culture—the subordination of the one to the many. Kevin M. F. Platt, "History, Social Discipline, and Trauma in Russia" (lecture given to the History, Memory, Politics Seminar, the Helsinki Collegium for Advanced Studies, Finland, 2011).

CONCLUSION

Too Much Past and Too Little Future

In the summer of 1920, two friends shared a room in a Russian sanatorium. Following a time of revolution, war, and cultural-revolutionary praxis, they were both preoccupied with the serious question of how to think about time. They developed very different solutions to this basic cultural problem that, for their own amusement and mutual enlightenment, they sent back and forth to each other in the form of letters. Their conflict was later published as "Correspondence Across a Room" and it has had an ongoing impact.[1] M. O. Gershenzon, later an essayist and scholar, was one of the interlocutors, and he took on the role of the futurist in this locking of horns. In his defense of forgetting in the name of the future, he again introduces all the arguments against the weight of the past.

---

1. Lachmann, "Mnemonische Konzepte," 132–35.

He compared it to a "heavy yoke . . . a too-heavy, too-warm piece of clothing" and longed for the happiness of a complete renewal: "What a great happiness it would be to slip into the river Lethe, and wash away without a trace the memory of all religions and philosophical systems, of all knowledges, arts, poetry, and to set foot on the shore naked, like the first human being." He could no longer identify with a heritage, for "it was not I who acquired this knowledge through lived experience: It is a general and foreign knowledge, coming from forefathers and ancestors." Rather than preparing him for life, he found that this cultural inheritance hindered him: "Countless knowledges have tethered me like millions of unbreakable threads, the whole lot of them impersonal, unalterable, horrifyingly unavoidable" (ibid.).

His correspondent was Vyacheslav Ivanov, a symbolist writer and classical philologist, who, from his side of the room, took on the role of defense for the past, culture, and memory. He opposed the healing power that Gershenzon saw in the *tabula rasa* to that of the *thesaurus*. He resisted a notion of the past that sees it as dead and mummified, emphasizing that it also contains sacred bounties (he piously speaks of the "holy orders of the fathers") as well as the seeds of renewal. For him, culture is the very condition for a transgenerational and existential connection between the living and the dead. As such, it is an inheritance to be taken up, not rejected, and that is why he defines culture as

> . . . a living and everlasting memory, one that never dies in those who partake of its blessings! For these are given by the forefathers to our remotest descendants and not one iota of what was new at one time, the tablets impressed with the characters of the human spirit, will die away (134).

For Ivanov, though, this only applies to select traditions: the idea that the entire past has a hold on the present is one that he sees as purely chimerical. On the contrary, what is important for him is the selection of what will demand strong interest and will. The majority of the past is and remains past, dead, and atrophied; it lies before us like the "countless altars . . . and idols . . . of a monumental culture" that we carelessly and curiously walk by like strangers.

But there are also "forgotten . . . sites" at which we "stop at will and offer up a sacrifice, when we catch sight of unwitherable flowers invisible to humans that have sprouted up from ancient tombs" (ibid.). In this way, Ivanov opposes the "dead past" of his adversary with a "vitalizing memory": "Memory is a dynamic principle, forgetting is fatigue and an interruption of movement" (ibid.). Ivanov is very close to the modernist Ezra Pound here, who also overcame the stark opposition between "old" and "new" by focusing on a constructive engagement with tradition. At the same time, Pound summed up his own his artistic project with the imperative "Make It New!"[2]

In their very opposition, these two positions again reflect the polarization of future and past that, as we have seen, is specific to the modern time regime. Odo Marquard summarizes this distinctively modern temporal orientation in his usual pithy way: the modern world "begins where the human emerges out of their traditions: where its future is liberated from its background. Since the middle of the eighteenth century, this process has penetrated the language of philosophy, science, literature, and politics. . . . The human future was at that time, and only at that time, emphatically the new, in that it became independent of the different linguistic, religious, cultural, family heritages: The great powers of modernization [such as the natural sciences, technology, and the economy] work the trend toward neutralizing tradition."[3]

This description is exceedingly important and still highly relevant: the great powers of modernization do function *independently of tradition*. They are indifferent to culture. That is precisely where the difference lies between the natural sciences, on the one hand, and the human (or cultural) sciences, on the other. The time regime of the modern has lost neither its fascination nor its relevance in the natural sciences, technology, and the economy, for it is inseparable from them. Through that regime, the complexity of our world has been raised to a whole new level, yet people are also less and less

---

2. Ezra Pound, *Make It New: Essays by Ezra Pound* (New Haven: Yale University Press), 1935.
3. Marquard, *Zukunft braucht Herkunft*, 235.

prepared to make the norms of time that apply in these areas—and that undeniably continue to do so—into a generally binding measure of their lifestyles and cultural orientations. This has led to a backward swing of our temporal pendulum from the pole of the future to the pole of the past. Culture and modernity have been decoupled in the process.

Do we have too much past and too little future? The question has been posed again and again in light of the sheer number of violent pasts to be worked though and the booming heritage industry, as well as the ever-increasing numbers of museums, monuments, memorials, films, websites, and books with historical content. John Torpey has therefore warned: "We need to be aware, as we seek to mend the damage from the past, that a politics of the past may crowd out or replace a vision of progress."[4] Konrad Jarausch has also sounded this clarion in his assessment of sixty-five years of European memory. He sees a strong predominance of negative memories in Europe and finds positive values lacking:

> The impressive catalogue of human rights included in the document has therefore derived its significance more from a general realization of past evils that needed to be avoided than from a specific delineation of common values that would bind the community together in the present. . . . This failure is regrettable, because it tends to lock thinking about Europe into a negative mode. Europe has become a kind of insurance policy against the repetition of prior problems rather than a positive goal, based upon a shared vision for the future.

We should, however, guard against continuing to think about the future and the past in the mode of the modern temporal regime as an irreconcilable opposition, as Jarausch does here. His distinction between negative lessons, on the one hand, and positive values, on the other, is also problematic, since the future-oriented values that he embraces were distilled precisely out of Europe's history of violence. This kind of remembering does not limit itself—as was the case in earlier times and is still widely done today—to heroism or indeed one's own suffering. Insofar as memory can take up issues

---

4. Torpey, *Politics and the Past*, 26.

of shared culpability on the basis of an empathy for the suffering of others, the negative weight of history can be transformed into future-oriented values. The foundation of and responsibility for civil society emerged out of the collapse of civilization. Since the value of human dignity was won out of the most extreme destruction of human dignity, the positive value of this dignity remains tied to its negative genesis.[5] The meaning of a renewed confrontation with a past history of violence can, by means of a new principle, border on hope. The hope is that memory might release a painful experience from out of its sequestering and, by integrating it into the present, help to overcome emotional blockages that continue to weigh on a society's future. This form of memory is to be understood as an important investment in the future, not as a regressive backward glance. Although beset with problems and disappointments, this task of transforming the past of violent dictatorship into a possibly collective democratic future belongs to some of the most important future-oriented projects of the present time.

> The time is out of joint—O cursèd spite,
> That ever I was born to set it right!
>
> (Shakespeare, *Hamlet*, act I, sc. v, 188–89)

Hamlet makes this statement at the end of the first act of the eponymous play after he has met his father's ghost, heard his history, and had the task of revenge imposed upon him. This experience categorically separates him from the other characters in the play; he demands complete silence about this secret from his friend and escort on the terrace. He alone must bear the burden of the knowledge that "the time is out of joint," and he takes on the task of sorting it out. This scene resonates with our present moment: in our own time, the past has returned in many ways, and we have seen the extent to which this has caused the temporal registers to become

---

5. On this point, see Hans Joas, *Gewalt und Menschenwürde: Wie aus Erfahrungen Rechte werden* (ms. 2009), as well as Jay Winter, "Foreword: Remembrance as a Human Right," in *Memory and Political Change*, ed. Aleida Assmann et al. (Basingstoke, UK: Palgrave Macmillan, 2011), vii–xi.

disorganized. In this context we may observe a broad spectrum of possibilities, ranging from a nostalgic repetition of the past up to unwanted intrusions of a traumatic past. In our own time as well, these returns of the past raise the issue of how best to straighten things out or to realign them, how best to make judgments and promote recognition, to find balance, and to heal. In Hamlet's soliloquy, the rhyme of the words "spite" and "right" foreshadow that the powers of vengeance and justice, of curse and healing, will remain unresolved in the play. That tragic outlook has lost its hold on us in our current cultures of memory, yet at the same time it can provide us with the ethical touchstone we need to make judgments regarding malignant forms of the politics of history.

One thing does seem impossible, however, and that is that the modern temporal regime—which is now "out of joint"—could be reset once again, much as one does with a dislocated shoulder. The temporal structure of past, present, and future has collapsed and cannot simply be reproduced, but rather must be newly joined together. A new and substantial determination of the notions of past, present, and future belongs to that task, which is not the task of individual theorists of time but of society as a whole. A great deal has already been said in this book about the notion of the present; therefore, I would like to close by concentrating on the notions of the past and the future.

The notion of the past has dramatically increased in its range of meanings. The expression *tempi passata*, or "times long gone," makes clear what the past chiefly meant in the modern temporal regime: it referred to whatever had definitively lost its claim to practical use and general interest. In the interim, however, we can no longer speak of this clear connotation, because today we no longer have universal grounds for exclusion at our disposal that would serve to distinguish the present from the past in a generalized or normative way. Therefore, today, we can no longer be as certain as we used to be that a past has been laid to rest once and for all. As we see from books, films, exhibitions, and debates, the dead of past times are reawakening—are in fact, like Hamlet's father, knocking at the door of the present and insisting on being granted entry. Along

with that comes greatly increased expenditures in terms of attention, consideration, engagement, and reliving—expenditures which
only an economically stable democracy can afford. Such a democracy is willing and able to pay the price of confronting traumatic
pasts, because it is convinced that civil society will be stabilized as
a consequence. The return of the past in the present must therefore
be experienced not as a permanent deluge that makes the world disorienting and that causes people who feel as if they can no longer
leave anything behind to become apathetic. No one doubts that the
world has indeed become disorienting, especially in contrast to
the state of the world in the time of the Cold War. Still, there is no
evidence to support the claim that the hitherto pent-up (over both
the short term and the long term) confrontation with past violence
has made people incapable of facing the future, since the willful silence of perpetrators and the forced silence of victims are of a fundamentally different quality—one that generates psycho-historical
pressure in the long term and that demands to be recognized and
settled.

The notion of the future has also increased in its range of meanings. Up until recently, its meaning focused on the unexpected, on
what lies ahead, in either a positive or a negative sense. Further notions that are closely related to it are utopia, imagination, or the
new—all of which are related to this meaning of the future. This
meaning was in fact the engine of the modernization program,
whose possibilities meanwhile have been confronted with certain
limits. The prospect of permanent renewal and progress has become
an empty promise. This future per se no longer has the power today
to promise a continual improvement in quality of life. In no way
does that imply, however, that people could renounce the resource
of the future as an open horizon of expectation. Every new generation, every young person, has a claim to their own, self-determined
life, to the possibility of reshaping and co-shaping the world according to their own ideals. Certainly, many of the "huge utopian events
in the world," of which the philosopher Ernst Bloch spoke in his
Peace Prize speech, are now in ruins and have left behind ugly sink-
holes in their place. But others grow again and the "not-yet-known,
the not-yet-developed, the new, the objectively-real possible" remains

an irreplaceable resource for each new generation.[6] These sources of desire and motivation—as fantasy, as perspective, as projection, as project, as orientation and meaning—are indispensable sources of vitality, for there is nothing more genuinely human than the hope for new life and the desire to write oneself into the future.

Another meaning of the future understands it not as the unknown or the new, but rather as the continuation of the present and past that we already have or know, and that we hope continues to live or, at least, to exist. With this meaning, we are using entirely different ideas of the future than utopia or the new: they are, among others, immortality, legacy, afterlife, or sustainability. What is decisive about this second meaning of the future is that it does not presuppose a break from the present and the past. Instead of a break in time and clearing everything away for a *tabula rasa*, an affective connection can be affirmed to what exists and what is past that one does not want to ignore, neglect, or lose—much less destroy—but rather seeks to safeguard. This special connection requires attention and care; it is demanding and therefore only pertains to select cultural objects and practices. Alongside the ecological, today it is obvious that we must also consider a cultural form of sustainability. The kind of attention paid to specific collections, and the responsibility of leaving important cultural monuments intact for successive generations, in no way suspends the fundamental law of forgetting and destruction. The latter continues to be determined by the technological basis of modern society, predicated as it is on disposability and accelerated economic cycles in spite of certain countertrends. Even retro-trends rely on a scarcity economy, which is why the image of total recall and of a present that is completely saturated with the past belongs in a museum of speculative fiction.

The relation between the past, the present, and the future is a three-fold relationship in which one dimension cannot exist for long—as François Hartog suggests it can—without the others. Ordering this three-fold temporal structure anew and bringing the three dimensions into a balanced relation continues to be an open adventure. To be sure, it is also the greatest challenge posed by the

---

6. Bloch, "Widerstand und Friede."

demise of the modern time regime. Culture generates not only its past but also its future. Armed with the knowledge of the natural sciences and technology, humans are continually destroying the future through irreversible disturbances in ecological equilibria, but they are also generating the future by means of new notions of sustainability. In the same way, dealing with violent pasts can just as easily be understood as a kind of political and cultural sustainability. The quality of the past has changed—but the future is also no longer what it used to be! The decisive question therefore is no longer exclusively "What do we want from the past and the future?" More and more often, it is also "What do the past and the future want from us?"

WORKS CITED

Adorno, Theodor W., and Max Horkheimer. *Dialectic of Enlightenment*. Edited by Gunzelin Schmid Noerr. Translated by E. Jephcott. Stanford: Stanford University Press, 2002.

Antin, Mary. *The Promised Land*. Edited by Oscar Handlin. Princeton: Princeton University Press, 1969.

Assmann, Aleida. *Geschichte im Gedächtnis*. Munich: Beck, 2007.

——. *Zeit und Tradition: Kulturelle Strategien der Dauer*. Cologne: Böhlau, 1999.

Assmann, Aleida, and Linda Shortt, eds. *Memory and Political Change*. Basingstoke, UK: Palgrave Macmillan, 2011.

Assmann, Jan. *Thomas Mann und Ägypte: Mythos und Monotheisumus in den Josephsromanen*. Munich: Beck, 2006.

Auerbach, Erich. "Figura." *Archivium Romanicum* 22 (1938): 436–89.

Augustine, Saint. *Confessions*. Translated by H. Chadwick. Oxford: Oxford University Press, 1992.

Bachelard, Gaston. *The Formation of the Scientific Mind*. Manchester: Clinamen Press, 2006.

Bakhtin, Mikhail. *The Dialogic Imagination: Four Essays by M. M. Bakthin*. Translated by Caryl Emerson and Michael Holquist. Austin: University of Texas Press, 1981.

Bakunin, Mikhail. "The Reaction in Germany." In *Bakunin on Anarchy*, edited by S. Dolgoff. Translated by S. Dolgoff. New York: Random House, 1972.

Baldwin, James. "The American Dream and the American Negro." In *Collected Essays*, edited by Toni Morrison, 714–19. New York: Penguin, 1998.

——. "Many Thousands Gone." In *Collected Essays*, edited by Toni Morrison, 19–34. New York: Penguin Books, 1998.

Bartal, Israel. *Geschichte der Juden im östlichen Europa 1772–1881*. Göttingen: Vandenhoeck & Ruprecht, 2010.

Baudelaire, Charles. "The Painter of Modern Life." In *The Painter of Modern Life and Other Essays*, translated by Jonathan Mayne. London: Phaidon Press, 1964.

Bauman, Zygmunt. *Modernity and the Holocaust*. Cambridge, UK: Polity Press, 1989.

Bavaj, Riccardo. "'Modernisierung, Modernität und Moderne.' Ein wissenschaftlicher Diskurs und seine Bedeutung für die historische Einordnung des 'Dritten Reiches.'" *Historisches Jahrbuch* 125 (2005): 413–51.

Benjamin, Walter. *The Arcades Project*. Translated by Howard Eiland and Kevin McLaughlin. Cambridge, MA: Harvard University Press, 2003.

——. "Theses on the Philosophy of History." In *Illuminations*, edited by Hannah Arendt. Translated by Harry Zohn, 253–96. New York: Schocken, 1968.

Bergmann, Ina. "'To You, Perceptive Reader, I Bequeath My History': Die Renaissance des historischen Romans im 21. Jahrhundert." In *Amerikaniches Erzählen nach 2000*, edited by Sebastian Domsch. Munich: Text & Kritik, 2008.

Bevernage, Berber. *History, Memory, and State-Sponsored Violence: Time and Justice*. New York: Routledge, 2011.

Bevernage, Berber, and Chris Lorenz, eds. *Breaking Up Time: Negotiating the Borders Between Present, Past, and Future*. Göttingen: Vandenhoeck & Ruprecht, 2013.

Bloch, Ernst. "Widerstand und Friede." In *Friedenspreisrede des deutschen Buchhandels 1967*: 10–16.

Blum, André. *Potentiale des Vergessens*. Würzburg: Königshausen & Neumann, 2012.

Bollas, Christopher. *Being a Character: Psychoanalysis and Self Experience*. New York: Hill & Wang, 1992.

Borst, Arno. "Barbarossas Erwachen: Zur Geschichte der deutschen Identität." In *Identität: Poetik und Hermeneutik*, vol. 8, edited by Odo Marquard and Karlheinz Stierle, 17–60. Munich: Fink, 1979.

Böll, Heinrich. "Georg Büchners Gegenwärtigkeit." In *Georg Büchner und die Moderne: Texte, Analysen, Kommentar, Bd. 2: 1945–1980*, 375–79. Berlin: Erich Schmidt, 2002.

Brose, Hanns-Georg. "Kulturen der Ungleichzeitigkeit—jenseits der Alternativen von Kurzfristigkeit und Langfristigkeit bzw. Langsamkeit und Beschleunigung." Working paper 19 (January 2002) of the Cultural Studies Research Consortium *Norm und Symbol* (Konstanz University).

Brumm, Ursula. *American Thought and Religious Typology*. Translated by J. Hooglund. New Brunswick, NJ: Rutgers University Press, 1970.

Brunner, Otto, Werner Conze, and Reinhart Koselleck, eds. *Geschichtliche Grundbegriffe: Historisches Lexikon zur politisch-sozialen Sprache in Deutschland*, vol. 4. Stuttgart: Metzler, 1978.

Cancik, Hubert. *Antik. Modern: Beiträge zur römischen und deutschen Kulturgeschichte*. Edited by R. Faber, B. von Reibnitz, and J. Rüpke. Stuttgart: Metzler, 1998.

CFP—FRIAS Workshop. "Breaking up Time: Settling the Borders between the Present, the Past, and the Future." Freiburg Institute for Advanced Studies, School of History, Albert-Ludwigs-Universität, Freiburg, Germany: 7–9 (April 2011).

Chakrabarty, Dipesh. "History and the Politics of Recognition." In *Manifestos for History*, edited by Keith Jenkins and Sue Morgan, 77–87. London: Routledge, 2007.

Conrad, Christoph. "Die Dynamik der Wenden: Von der neuen Sozialgeschichte zum *cultural turn*." *Geschichte und Gesellschaft*, vol. 22: *Wege der Gesellschaftsgeschichte* (2006): 133–60.

Detmers, Ines, and Birte Heidemann, eds. *"From Popular Goethe to Global Pop": Suchen nach dem Westen zwischen Erinnerung, Ermächtigung und Entmachtung*. Amersterdam: Rodopi, 2013.

Druste-Hülsoff, Annette von. "Bilder aus Westfahlen." In *Werke in einem Band*, edited by Clemens Hesselhaus. Munich: Hanser, 1984.

Dux, Günter. "Das historische Bewusstsein der Zeuzeit: Anthropologie als Grundlagenwissenschaft." *Saeculum* 39 (1988): 82–95.

Eisenstadt, Shmuel N. *Tradition, Change, Modernity*. New York: Wiley, 1973.

Eliot, George. *Felix Holt, The Radical* (1866). Oxford: Oxford University Press, 1998.

Ellison, Ralph W. "Twentieth Century Fiction and the Black Mask of Humanity." In *Shadow and Act*, 24–44. New York: Random House, 1953.

Elwert, George. "In Search of Time: Different Time-Experiences in Different Cultures." In *Maps of Time*, edited by Zmag Smitek and Borut Brumen, 233–43. Ljubljana: Filozofaska fakulteta Ljubljana, 2001.

Emerson, Ralph Waldo. "The American Scholar" (1837). In *Selected Writings of R. W. Emerson*, edited by W. H. Gilman, 225–45. New York: New American Library, 1965.

——. "Circles" (1841). In *Selected Writings of R. W. Emerson*, edited by W. H. Gilman, 312–24. New York: New American Library, 1965.

Fabian, Johannes. *Time and the Other: How Anthropology Makes Its Object*. New York: Columbia University Press, 1983.

Faulkner, William. "Requiem for a Nun" (1950). In *Sanctuary and Requiem for a Nun*. New York: Signet Books, 1961.

Fiedler, Leslie. "Cross the Border—Close the Gap." In *Cross the Border—Close the Gap*, 61–85. New York: Stein & Day, 1971.

Frank, Michael, and Gabriele Rippl, eds. *Arbeit am Gedächtnis*. Munich: Fink, 2007.

Fuchs, Lawrence H. "Thinking about Immigration and Ethnicity in the United States." In *Immigrants in Two Democracies: French and American Experience*, edited by D. L. Horowitz and G. Noiriel. New York: New York University Press, 1992.

Gall, Lothar. *Europa auf dem Weg in die Moderne 1850–1890*. Munich: Oldenbourg, 1993.

Glevarec, Hervé, and Guy Saez. *La patrimonie saisi par les associations*. Paris: Documentation Français, 2002. Cited in François Hartog. "Time and Heritage." *Museum International 57*, no. 3 (2005): 7–18.

Goethe, J. W. *Elective Affinities*. Translated by D. Constantine. Oxford: Oxford University Press, 1994.

——. *Faust I and II*. Translated by S. Atkins. Boston: Suhrkamp/Insel, 1984.

Goettsche, Dirk. *Zeit im Roman: Literarische Zeitreflexion und die Geschichte des Zeitromans im späten 18. und 19. Jahrhundert*. Munich: Fink, 2001.

Gumbrecht, Hans Ulrich. *After 1945: Latency as Origin of the Present*. Translated by Leland Stanford Junior University. Stanford: Stanford University Press, 2013.

——. *In 1926: Living at the Edge of Time*. Cambridge, MA: Harvard University Press, 1997.

——. "Modern, Modernität, Moderne." In *Geschichtliche Grundbegriffe. Historisches Lexikon zur politisch-sozialen Sprache in Deutschland*, vol. 4, edited by Otto Brunner, Werner Conze, and Reinhart Koselleck. Stuttgart: Metzler 1978.

——. *Our Broad Present: Time and Contemporary Culture*. Translated by Henry Erik Butler. New York: Columbia University Press, 2014.

Gumbrecht, Hans Ulrich, and Florian Klinger, eds. *Latenz: Blinde Passagiere in den Geisteswissenschaften*. Göttingen: Vindenhoeck & Ruprecht, 2011.

Gumbrecht, Hans Ulrich, and Ursula Link-Heer, eds. *Epochenschwellen und Epochenstrukturen im Diskurs der Literature- und Sprachhistorie*. Frankfurt am Main: Suhrkamp, 1985.

Habermas, Jürgen. *Moral Consciousness and Communicative Action*. Translated by C. Lenhart and S. Weber Nicholsen. Cambridge, MA: MIT Press, 1990.

"Halberstädter Dom öffnet am Sonntag neue Räume für seinen Schatz." EKD. April 11, 2008. https://www.ekd.de/news_2008_04_11_3_domschatz_halberstadt.htm.

Handlin, Oscar. "Preface" to Mary Antin, *The Promised Land*. Edited by Oscar Handlin. Princeton, NJ: Princeton University Press, 1969.

Hartog, François. "Time and Heritage." *Museum International 57*, no. 3 (September 2005): 7–18.

——. "Time, History, and the Writing of History: The Order of Time." *History Making: The Intellectual and Social Formation of a Discipline*, edited by Rolf Torstendahl and Irmline Veit-Brause, 95–113. Stockholm: Almvqvist and Wiksell, 1996.

Hawthorne, Nathaniel. "Main Street" (1849). In *Sketches and Tales*, edited by Roy H. Pearce, 1023–50. Cambridge, UK: Cambridge University Press, 1982.

Hegel, G. W. F. *Introduction to the Philosophy of History*. Translated by Leo Rauch. Indianapolis: Hackett, 1988.

——. *The Philosophy of History*. Translated by J. Sibree. New York: Dover, 1956.

Heine, Heinrich. "Lutetia." In *The Works of Heinrich Heine*, vol. 18 (*French Affairs*, vol. 2). Translated by C. G. Leland (Hans Breitmann). London: William Heinemann, 1893.

Helsper, Werner, ed. *Jugend zwischen Moderne und Postmoderne*. Opladen, Germany: Leske und Budrich, 1991.

Hesse, Hermann. "Stages." In *The Glass Bead Game*. Translated by R. Winston and C. Winston. New York: Holt, Rinehart & Winston, 1969.

Hessel, Franz. *Walking in Berlin: A Flaneur in the Capital*. Translated by Amanda DeMarco. Cambridge, MA: MIT Press, 2017.

Heubach, Andrea. *Generationengerechtigkeit—Herausforderungen für die zeitgenössische Ethik*. Gottingen: Vandenhoek & Ruprecht, 2008.

Hodges, Matt. "Rethinking Time's Arrow. Bergson, Deleuze and the Anthropology of Time." *Anthropological Theory* 8, no. 4 (2008): 399–429.

Hölscher, Lucian. *Die Entdeckung der Zukunft*. Frankfurt: Fischer, 1999.

——. "Die Zukunft zerstört die Vergangenheit: Zerstörungspotentiale in den Zukunftsentwürfen des 20. Jahrhunderts." In *Aufbauen—Zerstören: Phänomene und Prozesse der Kunst*. Düsseldorf: Athena, 2007.

Huyssen, Andreas. "The Crisis of Success: What Next in Memory Studies?" *Memory Studies* 5, no. 2 (2012): 226–28.

——. "Present Pasts: Media, Politics, Amnesia." *Public Culture* 12, no. 1 (Winter 2000): 21–38.

Ilies, Florian. *1913. Der Sommer des Jarhhunderts*. Frankfurt: Fischer 2012.

——. *Ortsgespräch*. Munich: Karl Blessing, 2006.

Ingold, Felix, Philipp. *Der große Bruch*. Munich: C. H. Beck, 2000.

Jaraush, Konrad H. "Nightmares or Daydreams? A Postscript on the Europeanization of Memories." In *A European Memory? Contested Histories and Politics of Remembrance*, edited by Malgorzata Pakier and Bo Strath, 309–20. Oxford: Berghahn Books, 2010.

Jarausch, Konrad H., and Martin Sabrow, eds. *Verletztes Gedächtnis: Erinnerungskultur und Zeitgeschichte im Konflikt*. Frankfurt: Campus Verlag, 2002.

Jaspers, Karl. "Wahrheit, Freiheit, Friede." Speech, Reception of the Friedenspreis des Deutschen Buchhandels, 1958.

Jauß, Hans-Robert. "1912: Threshold to an Epoch. Apollinaire's Zone and Lundi Rue Christine." Translated by Roger Blood. *Yale French Studies* 74 (1988): 39–66.

——. *Zeit und Erinnerung in Marcel Prousts "A la Recherche du Temps Perdu": Ein Beitrag zur Theorie des Romans*. Heidelberg: Winter Verlag, 1955.

Jeftič, Karolina. *Literatur und modern Bilderfahrung: Zur Cézanne-Rezeption der Bloomsbury Group*. Munich: Fink, 2011.

Joas, Hans, and Peter Vogt, eds. *Begriffene Geschichte: Beiträge zu Werk Reinhart Kosellecks*. Frankfurt: Suhrkamp 2011.

Jordheim, Helge. "'Unzählbar viele Zeiten': Die Sattelzeit im Spiegel der Gleichzeitigkeit des Ungleichzeitigen." In *Begriffene Geschichte: Beiträge zu Werk Reinhart Kosellecks*, edited by Hans Joas and Peter Vogt, 449–80. Frankfurt: Suhrkamp, 2011.

Kaschuba, Wolfgang. *Die Überwindung der Distanz: Zeit und Raum in der europäischen Moderne*. Frankfurt: Fischer, 2004.

King, Vera. *Die Entstehung des Neuen in der Adoleszenz: Individuation, Generativität und Geschlecht in modernisierten Gesellschaften*. Wiesbaden: Verlag für Sozialwissenschaften, 2002.

Kittsteiner, Heinz D. *Wir werden gelebt. Formprobleme der Moderne*. Hamburg: Philo & Philo, 2006.

Koch, Gertrud. *Bruchlinien: Tendenzen der Holocaust Forschung*. Vienna: Böhlau, 1999.

Kocka, Jürgen. "Historische Sozialwissenschaft heute." In *Perspektiven der Gesellschaftsgeschichte*, edited by Manfred Hettling, Paul Nolte, et al., 5–24. Munich: Beck, 2002.

Köhler, Horst. "Zur Wiedereröffnung des Halberstädter Domschatzes." Speech, Halberstadt, April 13, 2008. Publications of the Government of the Federal Republic of Germany, Bulletin 31.2. https://www.bundesregierung.de/Content/DE/Bulletin/2008/04/31-2 bpr.html

Koschorke, Albrecht. "Moderne als Wunsch: Krieg und Städtebau im 20. Jahrhundert." *Leviathan: Zeitschift für Sozialwissenschaft* 27, no. 1 (1999): 23–42.

———. "On Epistemological Smugglers (Defoe, Descartes)." Lecture, POLNET Summer School at Konstanz University, 116, August 2004.

———. *Wahrheit und Erfindung: Grundzüge einer Allgemeinen Erzähltheorie*. Frankfurt: Fischer, 2012.

Koschorke, Albrecht, et al., eds. *Der fictive Staat: Konstruktionen des politischen Körpers in der Geschichte Europas*. Frankfurt am Main: Fischer, 2007.

Koselleck, Reinhart. "Afterword to Charlotte Beradt's *The Third Reigh of Dreams*." In *The Practice of Conceptual History: Timing History, Spacing Concepts*, translated by Todd Samuel Presner et al., 327–40. Stanford: Stanford University Press, 2002.

———. *Futures Past: On the Semantics of Historical Time*. Translated by Keith Tribe. New York: Columbia University Press, 2004.

———. "Geschichte/Historie." In *Geschichtliche Grundbegriffe: Historisches Lexicon zur politisch-sozialen Sprache in Deutschland, Bd. 4*, edited by Otto Brunner, Werner Conze, and Reinhart Koselleck, 593–717. Stuttgart: Klett-Cotta, 1975.

———. "Gibt es eine Beschleunigung der Geschichte?" In *Zeitschriften: Studien zur Historik*, 150–76. Frankfurt: Suhrkamp, 2000.

——. "Wie neu ist die Neuzeit?" In *Zeitgeschichten. Studien zur Historik*, 225–39. Frankfurt: Suhrkamp, 2003.

Koselleck, Reinhart, and Christian Meier. "Fortschritt." In *Geschichtliche Grundbegriffe: Historisches Lexicon zur politisch-sozialen Sprache in Deutschland, Bd. 2*, edited by Otto Brunner, Werner Conze, and Reinhart Koselleck, 351–423. Stuttgart: Klett-Cotta, 1975.

Kracauer, Siegfried. Quoted by David Frisby. "Siegfried Kracauer." In *Fragments of Modernity: Theories of Modernity in the Work of Simmel, Kracauer and Benjamin*, 109–186. Cambridge, UK: Polity Press, 1985.

——. *Straßen in Berlin und anderswo*. Frankfurt: Suhrkamp, 2009.

Lachmann, Renate. "Mnemonische Konzepte." In *Arbeit am Gedächtnis*, edited by Michael Frank and Gabriele Rippl, 131–45. Munich: Fink, 2007.

Landsberg, Alison. *Prosthetic Memory. The Transformation of American Remembrance in the Age of Mass Culture*. New York: Columbia University Press, 2004.

Latour, Bruno. "The Recall of Modernity: Anthropological Approaches." Translated by Stephen Muecke. *Cultural Studies Review* 13, no. 1 (2007): 11–30.

——. *We Have Never Been Modern*. Translated by C. Porter. Cambridge, MA: Harvard University Press, 1993.

Lazarus, Emma. "The New Colossus" (1883). In *Selected Poems*, edited by J. Hollander. New York: Library of America, 2005.

Lazarus, Josephine. *The Spirit of Judaism*. Cambridge, MA: John Wilson University Press, 1895.

Lewis, R. W. B. *The American Adam. Innocence, Tragedy and Tradition in the 19th Century*. Chicago: Chicago University Press, 1955.

Loos, Adolf. "Ornament and Crime." In *Ornament and Crime: Selected Essays*, edited by Adolf Opel, translated by Michael Mitchell, 167–76. Riverside, CA: Ariadne Press, 1998.

Lorenz, Chris. "Geschichte, Gegenwärtigkeit und Zeit." In *Phänomen Zeit: Dimensionen und Strukturen in Kulture und Wissenschaft*, edited by Dietmar Goltschigg, 127–35. Tübingen: Stauffenburg, 2011.

——. "Unstuck in Time. Or: The Sudden Presence of the Past." In *Performing the Past, Memory, History, and Identity in Modern Europe*, edited by Karin Tilmans, Frank van Vree, and Jay Winter, 67–105. Amsterdam: Amsterdam University Press, 2010.

——. "Wozu noch Theorie der Geschichte? Über das ambivalente Verhältnis zwischen Gesellschaftsgeschichte und Modernisierungstheorie." In *Kolloguien des Max Weber-Kollegs XV-XXIII*, edited by Wolfgang Schluchter, 75–115. Erfurt: Universität Erfurt, 2001.

Lorenz, C. F. G., and S. Berger. "National Narratives and Their 'Others': Ethnicity, Class, Religion and the Gendering of National Histories." In *Storia della Storiografia/Geschichte der Geschichtsschreibung* 50 (January 2006): 59–98.

Löwith, Karl. *Meaning in History: The Theological Implications of the Philosophy of History*. Chicago: University of Chicago Press, 1949.

Lübbe, Hermann. *Der Fortschritt und das Museum: Über den Grund unseres Vergnügens an historischen Gegenständen*. London: Institute of Germanic Studies, 1982.

——. *Im Zug der Zeit: Verkürzter Aufenthalt in der Gegenwart*. Berlin: Springer, 1992.

——. *Vom Parteigenossen zum Bundesbürger: Über beschwiegene und historisierte Vergangenheiten*, Munich: Fink 2007.

——. *Zeit-Erfahrungen: Sieben Begriffe zur Beschreibung moderner Zivilizationsdynamik, Abhandlungen der Geistes- und Sozialwissenschaftlichen Klasse 5*. Academy of Sciences and Literature, Mainz/Stuttgart: Steiner, 1996.

——. "Zur Identitätspräsentationsfunktion der Historie." In *Identität: Poetik und Hermeneutik VIII*, edited by Odo Marquard and Karlheize Stierle, 277–92. Munich: Fink, 1979.

Luhmann, Niklas. "Das Problem der Epochenbildung und die Evolutionstheorie." In *Epochenschwellen und Epochenstrukturen im Diskurs der Literature- und Sprachhistorie*, edited by Hans Ulrich Gumbrecht and Ursula Link-Heer, 11–33. Frankfurt: Suhrkamp, 1985.

——. "Weltzeit und Systemgeschichte." In Niklas Luhmann, *Soziologische Aufklärung*, vol. 2: *Aufsätze zur Theorie der Gesellschaft*, 103–33. Wiesbaden: Verlag für Sozialwissenschaften, 2009.

Macaulay, Thomas B. "Francis Bacon." In *Critical and Historical Essays, Vol. 2*, 290–398. London: Dent, 1937.

Maier, Charles S. "Two Sorts of Crisis? The 'Long' 1970s in the West and the East." In *Koordinaten deutscher Geschichte in der Epoche des Ost-West Konflikts (Schriften des historischen Kollegs, Band 55)*, edited by Hans Günter Hockerts, 49–62. Munich: Oldenbourg, 2004.

Mann, Thomas. "Disorder and Early Sorrow." In *Stories of Three Decades*, translated by H. T. Lowe-Porter, 500–528. New York: Modern Library, 1934.

Mannheim, Karl. "The Problem of Generations." In *Essays on the Sociology of Knowledge*, edited by Paul Kecskemeti, translated by Paul Kecskemeti, 276–322. New York: Routledge, 1952.

Marinetti, Filippo Tommaso. "The Founding and Manifesto of Futurism." In *Futurist Manifestos*, edited by Umbro Apollonio, translated by R. W. Flint, 19–24. New York: Viking Press, 1973.

Marquard, Odo. "The Age of Unworldliness? A Contribution to the Analysis of the Present." In *In Defence of the Accidental: Philosophical Studies*, translated by Robert M. Wallace, 71–90. Oxford: Oxford University Press, 1991.

——. "Innovationskultur als Kontinuitätskultur." In *Skepsis in der Moderne: Philosophische Studien*. Stuttgart: Reclam, 1994.

——. "Krise der Erwartung—Stunde der Erfahrung: Zur ästhetischen Kompensation des modernen Erfahrungsverlustes." In *Skepsis und Zustimmung: Philosophische Studien*, 70–94. Stuttgart: Reclam, 1994.

——. "Zukunft braucht Herkunft: Philosophische Betrachtungen über Modernität und Menschlichkeit." In *Zukunft braucht Herkunft: Philosophische Essays*, 234–46. Stuttgart: Reclam, 2003.

——. "Zukunft und Herkunft." In *Skepsis und Zustimmung: Philosophische Studien.* Stuttgart: Reclam, 1994.

Marquard, Odo, and Karlheize Stierle, eds. *Identität. Poetik und Hermeneutik VIII.* Munich: Fink, 1979.

Marx, Karl. "The Eighteenth Brumaire of Louis Bonaparte." In *Karl Marx and Frederick Engels: Selected Works in One Volume*, 95–180. New York: International Publishers, 1968.

——. "To Arnold Ruge" (May 1843). In *Early Writings*, translated by R. Livingstone and G. Benton. London: Penguin, 1992.

Mensing, Kolja. *Die Tageszeitung*, August 23, 2006; accessed August 29, 2018, www.perlentaucher.de/buch/24936.html.

Merton, Robert King. *On the Shoulders of Giants: A Shandean Postscript.* New York: Harcourt Brace Jovanovich, 1985.

Miller, Max, and Hans-Georg Soeffner, eds. *Modernität und Barbarei: Soziologische Zeitdiagnose am Ende des 20.Jahrhunderts.* Frankfurt: Suhrkamp, 1996.

Milton, John. *Paradise Lost.* London: Penguin Books, 2000.

Mittelstaedt, Werner. *Das Prinzip Fortschritt: Ein neues Verständnis für die Herausforderungen unserer Zeit.* Frankfurt: Peter Lang, 2008.

Morrison, Toni. "Living Memory: A Meeting with Toni Morrison." In *Small Acts: Thoughts on the Politics of Black Culture*, edited by Paul Gilroy, 175–82. London: Serpent's Tail, 1993.

——. "Rootedness: The Ancestor as Foundation." In *Black Woman Writers (1950–1980): A Critical Evaluation*, edited by Mari Evans, 339–45. New York: Anchor Press, 1984.

Mülder-Bach, Inka, and Eckard Schumacher, eds. *Am Anfar war ... Ursprungsfiguren und Anfangskonstruktionen der Moderne.* Munich: Fink, 2008.

Müller, Jan-Werner, ed. *Memory and Power in Post-War Europe: Studies in the Presence of the Past.* Cambridge, UK: Cambridge University Press, 2002.

Müller, Tim B. "Innenansichten des kalten Krieges: Über ein glückliches Zeitalter." *Zeitschrift für Ideengeschichte* 3 (2013): 26–40.

Nassehi, Armin. *Die Zeit der Gesellschaft: Auf dem Weg zu einer soziologischen Theorie der Zeit.* Wiesbaden: Verlag für Sozialwissenschaften, 2008.

Niethammer, Lutz. *Kollektive Identität: Heimliche Quellen einer unheimlichen Konjunktur.* Reinbeck: Rowohlt, 2000.

Nietzsche, Friedrich. "On the Uses and Disadvantages of History for Life." In *Untimely Meditations*, edited by Daniel Breazeale, translated by R. J. Hollingdale, 57–124. Cambridge, UK: Cambridge University Press, 1997.

——. "Sils-Maria." In *The Gay Science*, translated by W. Kaufmann. New York: Vintage, 1974.

Nussbaum, Martha C. *For Love of Country?* Edited by Joshua Cohen. Boston: Beacon Press, 2002.

"Obama will Marsmission im Jahr 2035." *Frankfurter Allgemeine Zeitung.* April 15, 2010, http://www.faz.net/aktuell/gesellschaft/weltraumprogramm -obama-will-marsmission-im-jahr-2035-1964515.html.

Osten, Manfred. *"Alles veloziferisch" oder Goethes Entdeckung der Langsamkeit: Zur Modernität eines Klassikers im 21. Jahrhundert.* Frankfurt: Insel, 2003.

Osterkamp, Ernst. "Kreative Zerstörung als ästhetisches Verfahren in Richard Wagners 'Meistersingern.'" In *Angst vor der Zerstörung: Der Meister Künste zwischen Archiv und Erinnern,* edited by R. Sollich et al., 11–28. *Recherchen 52.* Berlin: Theater der Zeit, 2008.

O'Sullivan, John. "Introduction." *The United States Magazine and Democratic Review* 1, no. 1 (October 1873): 1–15.

Paine, Thomas. *Complete Works of Thomas Paine: Containing All His Political and Theological Writings.* Edited by Calvin Blanchard. Chicago: Belford & Clarke, 1885.

Palonen, Kari. *Die Entzauberung der Begriffe: Das Umschreiben der politischen Begriffe bei Quentin Skinner und Reinhart Koselleck.* Münster: LIT Verlag, 2004.

Paulun, Simone. *Enacting Cultural Identity: Time and Memory in 20th Century African-American Theater by Female Playwrights.* PhD diss. Konstanz University, 2011.

Platt, Kevin M. F. "History, Social Discipline, and Trauma in Russia." Lecture, "History, Memory, Politics" Seminar, Helsinki Collegium for Advanced Studies, Helsinki, 2011.

Pöppel, Ernst. *Grenzen des Bewusstseins: Über Wirklichkeit und Welterfahrung.* Stuttgart: DVA, 1988.

Raphael, Lutz. "Ordnungsmuster der 'Hochmoderne'? Die Theorie der Moderne und die Geschichte der europäischen Gesellschaften im 20. Jahrhundert." In *Dimensionen der Moderne: Festschrift für Christof Dipper,* edited by Schneider and Lutz Raphael, 73–91. Frankfurt: Peter Lang, 2008.

Raphael, Samuel. *The Theatres of Memory, Vol. I: Past and Present in Contemporary Culture.* London: Verso, 1994.

Reemtsma, Jan Philipp. "Das Implantat der Angst." In *Modernität und Barbarei: Soziologische Zeitdiagnose am Ende des 20. Jahrhunderts,* edited by Max Miller and Hans-George Soeffner, 28–35. Frankfurt: Suhrkamp, 1996.

——. "Wozu Gedenkstätten?" *Aus Politik und Zeitgeschichte* 25–26 (2010): 3–9.

Reichardt, Ulfried. *Globalisierung: Literaturen und Kulturen des Globalen.* Berlin: Akademie Verlag, 2010.

——. "The 'Times' of the New World: Future Orientation, American Culture, and Globalization." *REAL Yearbook of Research in English and American Literature* 19 (2003): 247–66.

Reichert, Klaus. *Fortuna oder die Beständigkeit des Wechsels.* Frankfurt: Suhrkamp, 1985.

Rheinberger, Hans-Jörg. "Über das Ausblenden." In André Blum, *Potentiale des Vergessens.* Würzburg: Königshausen & Neumann, 2012.

Richards, I. A. "Science and Poetry." In *Poetry and Sciences.* New York: W. W. Norton, 1970.

Ricoeur, Paul. *Oneself as Another.* Translated by Kathleen Blamey. Chicago: University of Chicago Press, 1995.

Ritter, Joachim. *Subjektivität: Sechs Aufsätze.* Frankfurt: Suhrkamp, 1974.

Rosa, Harmut. *Beschleunigung: Die Veränderung der Zeitstrukturen in der Moderne.* Frankfurt: Suhrkamp, 2005.

Rosa, Harmut. "Kein Halt auf der Ebene der Geschwindigkeit." *Frankfurter Rundschau* 179, no. 16 (August 2004).

Rosskam, Edwin, and Richard Wright. *12 Million Black Voices: A Folk History of the Negro in the United States.* New York: Thunder's Mouth Press, 1988.

Roth, Philip. *The Facts: A Novelist's Autobiography.* London: Vintage Books, 1988.

Rushdie, Salman. *Fury.* London: Jonathan Cape, 2001.

Said, Edward. *Beginnings: Intentions and Method.* New York: Columbia University Press, 1985.

Salisbury, John of. *Metalogicon: A Twelfth-Century Defense of the Verbal and Logical Arts of the Trivium.* Translated by D. D. McGarry. Gloucester, MA: Peter Smith, 1971.

Scherrer, Jutta. "Russlands neue-alte Errinerungsorte." *Aus Politik und Zeitgeschichte* 11 (2006): 24–28.

Schirrmacher, Frank, ed. *Im Osten erwacht die Geschichte: Essays zur Revolution in Mittel- und Osteuropa.* Stuttgart: Deutsche Verlags-Anstalt, 1990.

Schivelbusch, Wolfgang. *The Railway Journey.* Translated by A. Hollo. Berkeley: University of California Press, 1986.

Schlögl, Rudolf. "Zeit und Ereignisse in der frühneuzeitlichen Vergesellschaftung unter Anwesenden." In *Systemtheorie und Geschichtswissenschaft,* edited by Thomas Kisser. Paris, 2013.

Schmidt-Gernig, Alexander. Review of "Die Entdeckung der Zukunft," by Lucian Hölscher. *H-Soz-u-Kult,* February 10, 2000, hsozkult.geschichte.hu-berlin.de/rezensionen/252.pdf.

Schneider, Christian, et al., eds. *Trauma und Kritik: Zur Generationengeschichte der Kritischen Theorie.* Münster: Westfälisches Dampfboot, 2000.

Schulin, Ernst. "Absage an und Wiederherstellung von Vergangenheit." In *Speicher des Gedächtnisses, Bibliotheken, Museen, Archive,* vol. 1: *Wiederherstellung von Vergangenheit, Kompensation von Geschichtsverlust,* edited by Peter Stachel and Moritz Csákz. Vienna: Passagen, 2000.

Schumpeter, Joseph A. *Capitalism, Socialism and Democracy.* London: Allen and Unwin, 1976.

Shakespeare, William. *Hamlet.* Edited by Cyrus Hoy. New York: W. W. Norton, 1963.

——. *Macbeth.* Edited by Kenneth Muir. London, New York: Routledge, 1996.

Shelsky, Helmut. *Die skeptische Generation: Eine Soziologie der deutschen Jugend.* Düsseldorf: Diederichs, 1963.

Shils, Edward. *Tradition.* Chicago: University of Chicago Press, 1981.

Shklovsky, Viktor. "Art as Device." In *Theory of Prose*, translated by Benjamin Sher, 1–14. Champaign, IL: Dalkey Archive Press, 1991.

Sloterdijk, Peter. *Zur Welt kommen—zur Sprache kommen: Begleitheft zu Peter Sloterdijks öffentlicher Vorlesung.* Frankfurt: Frankfurt City and University Library, 1998.

Steiner, George. *In Bluebeard's Castle: Some Notes Towards the Redefinition of Culture.* London: Faber and Faber, 1971.

Sundermeier, Theo. "Primäre und sekundäre Religionserfahrungen." In *Was ist Religion? Religionswissenschaft im theologischen Kontext: Ein Studienbuch.* Gütersloh, Germany: Chr. Kaiser, 1999.

Swift, Graham. *Waterland.* London: William Heineman, 1983.

Taguieff, Pierre-André. *Du progrès: Biographie d'une utopie modern.* Paris: Librio, 2001.

Taylor, Charles. "Multiculturalism and 'The Politics of Recognition.'" In *The Politics of Recognition*, edited by Amy Gutmann, 25–74. Princeton: Princeton University Press, 1992.

Thoreau, Henry David. "Sounds." In *Walden, or Life in the Woods* (1854). Boston: Houghton Mifflin, 1889.

Torpey, John. *Making Whole What Has Been Smashed.* Cambridge, MA: Harvard University Press, 2006.

——. *Politics and the Past. On Repairing Historical Injustices.* New York: Rowman & Littlefield, 2003.

——. "The Pursuit of the Past: A Polemical Perspective." In *Theorizing Historical Consciousness*, edited by Peter Seixas, 240–55. Toronto: University of Toronto Press, 2004.

Turner, Frederick Jackson. "The Significance of the Frontier." In *The Frontier in American History* (1893), 1–38. New York: Holt, Rinehart & Winston, 1962.

Virilio, Paul. *Polar Inertia.* New York: Sage, 2000.

——. *The Vision Machine.* Translated by J. Rose. Bloomington: British Film Institute and Indianapolis: Indiana University Press, 1994.

Voland, Eckart. "Die Forstschrittsillusion." *Spektrum der Wissenschaft* (April 2007): 108–13.

von Matt, Peter. *Verkommene Söhne, missratene Töchter: Familiendesaster in der Literatur.* Munich: dtv, 2001.

Weber, Max. *Economy and Society.* Edited by Guenther Roth and Claus Wittich. Los Angeles: University of California Press, 1978.

——. *The Protestant Ethic and the "Spirit" of Capitalism.* Edited and translated by Peter Baehr and Gordon C. Wells. London: Penguin, 2002.

Wehler, Hans-Ulrich. *Modernisierungstheorie und Geschichte.* Göttingen: Vandenhoeck & Ruprecht, 1975.

——. "Rückblick und Ausblick, oder: Arbeiten, um überholt zu werden?" Bielefeld, Germany: Universitätsverlag Bielefeld, 1996.

——. "Was uns zusammenhält. Zum Auftakt des mehrbändigen Projekts über 'Deutsche Erinnerungsorte.'" *Die Zeit*, March 22, 2001, 28.

Welskopp, Thomas. "Westbindung auf dem 'Sonderweg': Die deutsche Sozialgeschichte vom Appendix der Wirtschaftsgeschichte zur historischen Sozialwissenschaft." In *Geschichtsdiskurs, Bd. 5: Globale Konflikte, Erinnerungsarbeit und Neuorientierungen seit 1945*, edited by Wolfgang Küttler et al., 191–238. Frankfurt: Fischer, 1999.

Wils, Jean-Pierre. *Wandlungen und Bedeutungen. Reflexionen über eine hermeneutische Ethik*. Freiburg: Herder, 2001.

Winter, Jay. "Foreword: Remembrance as a Human Right." In *Memory and Political Change*, edited by Aleida Assmann and Linda Shortt, vii–xi. Basingstoke: Palgrave Macmillan, 2011.

——. "Introduction. The Performance of the Past: Memory, History, Identity." In *Performing the Past, Memory, History, and Identity in Modern Europe*, edited by Karin Tilmans, Frank van Vree, and Jay Winter, 11–34. Amsterdam: Amsterdam University Press, 2010.

Wittgenstein, Ludwig. *Culture and Value*. Edited by G. H. von Wright. Translated by Peter Winch. Revised 2nd edition. Oxford: Blackwell, 1998.

Wolf, Christa. *A Model Childhood*. Translated by U. Molinaro and H. Rappolt. New York: Farrar, Straus and Giroux, 1980.

Woolf, Virginia. *Orlando: A Biography* (1928). Harmondsworth, 1975.

——. *Mr. Bennett and Mrs. Brown*. London: Hogarth Press, 1924.

——. "A Sketch of the Past." In *Moments of Being*, 61–159. Fort Washington, PA: Harvest Books, 1985.

Zangwill, Israel. "The Melting Pot" (1908). Cited by Werner Sollors. *Beyond Ethnicity: Consent and Descent in American Culture*. Oxford, UK: Oxford University Press, 1989.

Index of Names

Adenauer, Konrad, 26
Adorno, Theodor, 61–62
Anders, Günther, 140
Antin, Mary, 83–84
Assmann, Aleida, 8n9, 100n16, 159n14, 180n8, 228n
Assmann, Jan, 65, 67
Auerbach, Erich, 40n13
Augustine of Hippo, 51, 175, 195

Bachelard, Gaston, 41n15
Bacon, Francis, 42, 136
Bakhtin, Mikhail, 32
Bakunin, Mikhail, 118
Baldwin, James, 88
Bartal, Israel, 146n98
Baudelaire, Charles, 15–20, 30, 46, 51, 98, 134, 147, 158
Bauman, Zygmunt, 62
Bavaj, Riccardo, 56, 60n46, 61n50, 63n

Belyj, Andrej, 35
Benjamin, Walter, 6, 18n6, 25, 61, 144
Beradt, Charlotte, 131n69
Bergmann, Ina, 86n86
Bernard of Chartres, 40n12
Bevernage, Berber, 91n97, 96n7, 215–216, 217n20
Bloch, Ernst, 2, 162, 230, 231n
Blum, André, 41n15
Böhm, Gottfried, 123
Böll, Heinrich, 25–26
Bollas, Christopher, 103n22, 105n28
Borst, Arno, 135
Bredekamp, Horst, 123
Brose, Hanns-Georg, 136n79, 150n
Brumen, Borut, 136n77
Brumm, Ursula, 108n34
Brunner, Otto, 13n
Büchner, Georg, 25–27
Burke, Peter, 70

Cancik, Hubert, 46
Cézanne, Paul, 17, 94
Chakrabarty, Dipesh, 213
Cohen, Joshua, 86n87
Conrad, Christoph, 60nn44–45, 206n
Cromwell, Oliver, 114, 117
Csáky, Moritz, 127n

Danilov, Aleksandr, 223n
Darwin, Charles, 35
Defoe, Daniel, 109–110, 113
Descartes, René, 109
Detmers, Ines, viii, 92n
Domsch, Sebastian, 86n86
Droste-Hülshoff, Annette von,
    133–134, 138, 140, 151, 160, 184
Dux, Günter, 14n

Eichendorff, Joseph von, 138
Eisenstadt, Shmuel N., 100n16
Eliot, George, 138–139
Eliot, T. S., 94
Ellison, Ralph W., 87–88
Elwert, Georg, 136n77
Elysard, Jules (Mikhail Bakunin),
    118n49
Emerson, Caryl, 32n4
Emerson, Ralph Waldo, 74, 77, 79, 82,
    87, 120–121, 133
Evans, Mari, 90n95

Faber, R., 46n2
Fabian, Johannes, 32n2
Faulkner, William, 87n88, 171
Fiedler, Leslie, 80, 101
Filippov, Aleksandr, 223n
Firges, Janine, viii
Frank, Michael, 79n70
Fraund, Philipp, 107n33
Freud, Sigmund, 67, 102, 112, 172
Fuchs, Lawrence H., 76n64

Gall, Lothar, 146n98
Gershenzon, M. O., 224–225
Gide, André, 35
Gilman, W. H., 74n, 120n
Glevarec, Hervé, 184n14

Goethe, Johann Wolfgang von,
    110–111, 142–144, 155, 177
Goettsche, Dirk, 33n5
Gumbrecht, Hans Ulrich, 13, 16, 23,
    26–27, 95n, 98n12, 140n, 164n,
    177, 179–184, 186–191, 196
Gutmann, Amy, 86n87
Guys, Constantin, 15–16

Habermas, Jürgen, 104
Handlin, Oscar, 83n81
Hartog, François, 9, 37n8, 177, 179,
    183–194, 196, 199, 208, 219, 231
Hawthorne, Nathaniel, 134, 135, 141,
    152
Hegel, G. W. F., 42–43, 77, 106
Heidemann, Birte, 92n
Helsper, Werner, 104n24
Henie, Heinrich, 66, 137–138
Herbert, Ulrich, 61
Hesse, Hermann, 106
Hessel, Franz, 18n6
Hettling, Manfred, 59n43
Heubach, Andrea, 102n20
Hitler, Adolf, 214, 218
Hobsbawm, Eric, 60, 206
Hockerts, Hans Günter, 8n10
Hodges, Matt, 32, 131n67
Hollander, John, 82n78
Holquist, Michael, 32n4, 81n76
Hölscher, Lucian, 1n2, 31, 69, 107n32,
    118n50, 124
Hooke, Robert, 41
Horkheimer, Max, 61–62
Horowitz, D. L., 76n64
Hoy, Cyrus, 112n44
Humboldt, Wilhelm von, 142
Huyssen, Andreas, 5–6, 61, 190–191

Illies, Floran, 94n4, 150–151, 152n5,
    156, 157
Ingold, Felix Philipp, 94n4
Ivanov, Vyacheslav, 225–226

Jarausch, Konrad H., 132n70, 227
Jaspers, Karl, 121
Jauß, Hans Robert, 18, 35–36, 73, 94

Jeftic, Karolina, 94n5
Jenkins, Keith, 213n16
Joas, Hans, 158n, 228n
John of Salisbury, 40n12
Jordheim, Helge, 158n
Joyce, James, 22, 34, 94
Jureit, Ulrike, 212n14

Kaschuba, Wolfgang, 142n89
King, Vera, 104n23
Kittsteiner, Heinz D., 61n50
Klinger, Florian, 180n7
Koch, Gertrud, 61n50
Kocka, Jürgen, 56, 59, 199n, 210
Köhler, Horst, 167–170
Koschorke, Albrecht, 36n, 109n37,
    110, 124–126
Koselleck, Reinhart, 1, 36, 37n9,
    42n16, 44n, 49n, 53, 64, 66, 68n57,
    69–71, 77, 96–98, 101, 103,
    112n42, 129, 130n64, 131, 139n,
    140n87, 156, 158n, 165, 171, 210
Kracauer, Siegfried, 144–145
Kraushaar, Wolfgang, 131n68
Krüger, Michael, viii
Küttler, Wolfgang, 59n42

Lachmann, Renate, 79n70, 105,
    196n24, 208n, 224n
Landsberg, Alison, 81n76
Latour, Bruno, 10n, 126, 201, 203–206
Lazarus, Emma, 81–83
Lazarus, Josephine, 82–83
Le Corbusier, 124
Lenoir, Alexandre, 128
Lessing, Gotthold Ephraim, 16
Lewis, R. W. B., 108n34
Link-Heer, Ursula, 95n
Locke, John, 113
Loos, Adolf, 144–145
Lorenz, Chris, 52, 59n41, 60n46,
    96n7, 131n67, 132, 183n, 215–217
Lotman, Yuri, 196, 207–208
Löwith, Karl, 43–44
Lübbe, Hermann, 145, 149, 153–164,
    193
Luhmann, Niklas, 48, 50, 95, 153, 184

Luther, Martin, 111
Lyotard, François, 55–56

Macaulay, Thomas B., 42, 136
Maier, Charles S., 8
Mann, Thomas, 34, 67, 170–171
Mannheim, Karl, 102–103
Mao Zedong, 214
Marinetti, Filippo Tommaso, 78n70,
    135n76
Marquard, Odo, 44–45, 135n75, 140,
    143, 149, 157n11, 162–169, 176,
    203, 205n6, 209–211, 226
Marx, Karl, 25–26, 68, 116–119
Matt, Peter von, 102n19
Maul, Stefan, 193
Mayr, Ernst, 46
McGarry, Daniel D., 40n12
Meier, Christian, 42n16, 96, 101,
    139n86
Mensing, Kolja, 151n4
Merleau-Ponty, Maurice, 101n18
Merton, Robert King, 41n14
Miller, Max, 61n48, 61n50
Milton, John, 114–115
Mitchell, Margaret, 87n88
Mittelstaedt, Werner, 4, 45n23
Monet, Claude, 17
Moritz, Karl Philipp, 122–123
Morrison, Toni, 88nn91–92, 89–90
Muir, Kenneth, 19n
Mülder-Bach, Inka, 111n41
Müller, Jan-Werner, 215n
Müller, Tim B., 57n37

Nassehi, Armin, 53n32
Neumeyer, Harald, 18n6
Newton, Isaac, 41
Niethammer, Lutz, 217
Nietzsche, Friedrich, 27, 46–47, 78,
    105, 117–118, 121, 177–179,
    181–183, 187, 193
Noiriel, Gérard, 76n64
Nussbaum, Martha C., 86n87

O'Sullivan, John, 78, 79
Obama, Barack, 3, 80

Olbertz, Jan-Hendrik, 167
Osten, Manfred, 143n91
Osterkamp, Ernst, 122–123, 124n58

Pagliarulo, Magdalena, 145n95
Paine, Thomas, 107–108
Palonen, Kari, 49n
Park, Robert E., 85n84
Paulun, Simone, 90n94
Pearce, Roy H., 135n74
Plato, 51
Platt, Kevin M. F., 223n
Pöppel, Ernst, 155n
Pound, Ezra, 226
Proust, Marcel, 35, 180
Putin, Vladimir, 2–3

Raphael, Lutz, 57n39, 99n, 136n80
Raphael, Samuel, 152n6
Reemtsma, Jan Philipp, 61n50,
    209n10, 211–212
Reichardt, Ulfried, 75–79, 87
Reichert, Klaus, 98n13
Rheinberger, Hans-Jörg, 41n15
Richards, I. A., 140, 164
Ricœur, Paul, 209
Rippl, Gabriele, 79n70
Ritter, Joachim, 97–98, 149, 166, 203
Rosa, Hartmut, 9n11, 146
Rosskam, Edwin, 88n90
Roth, Guenther, 100n16
Roth, Philip, 81n77
Ruse, Michael, 39n
Rushdie, Salman, 90–91

Sabrow, Martin, 132n70
Saez, Guy, 184n14
Said, Edward, 109–111
Scherrer, Jutta, 3n4
Schirrmacher, Frank, 173n
Schivelbusch, Wolfgang, 87n88,
    138n84
Schlögl, Rudolf, 48n28, 50–52, 93n2,
    130, 132, 182
Schluchter, Wolfgang, 53n32
Schmidt-Gernig, Alexander, 69n
Schmitt, Carl, 214

Schneider, Christian, 105n27
Schneider, Ute, 57n39
Schulin, Ernst, 127, 152
Schumacher, Eckhard, 111n41
Schumpeter, Joseph Alois, 118–120
Scott, Walter, 132
Seixas, Peter, 177n2
Shakespeare, William, 19, 112–113,
    228
Shils, Edward A., 48n29, 100n15
Simmel, Georg, 140
Šklovskij, Viktor, 21–22
Sloterdijk, Peter, 112
Smitek, Zmag, 136n77
Soeffner, Hans-Georg, 61n48, 61n50
Sollich, Robert, 122n55
Sollors, Werner, 83n80
Stachel, Peter, 127n63
Stalin, Josef, 2, 214, 218
Steiner, George, 79n71, 187n
Stierle, Karlheinz, 135n75, 157n11
Sundermeier, Theo, 108n35
Svevo, Italo, 35
Swift, Graham, 1

Taguieff, Pierre-André, 42n16
Taylor, Charles, 86n87
Thoreau, Henry David, 137
Tilmans, Karin, 183n12, 220n
Tolstoy, Leo, 21
Torpey, John, 177, 179, 188–191, 227
Torstendahl, Rolf, 9n12, 37n8
Turner, Frederick Jackson, 137, 159

Ušpenskij, Boris, 196, 207–208

Veit-Brause, Irmline, 9n12, 37n8
Virilio, Paul, 101, 147n
Vogt, Peter, 158n
Voland, Eckart, 39n, 46nn24–25
Volodikhin, Dmitry, 223n

Wagner, Richard, 122n55, 123n56
Wallerstein, Immanuel, 56n36
Weber, Max, 14–15, 50, 67, 100
Wehler, Hans-Ulrich, 56–60, 71, 210
Welskopp, Thomas, 59n42

Whitman, Walt, 77
Williams, Tennessee, 87n88
Wils, Jean-Pierre, 38n
Winter, Jay, 220n, 228n
Wittgenstein, Ludwig, 24
Wittich, Claus, 100n16
Wolf, Christa, 171

Woolf, Virginia, 18n6, 21–22, 28,
   34–35, 93–96, 130
Wright, Georg Henrik von, 24n
Wright, Richard, 88

Zangwill, Israel, 80n74, 82–83
Zitelmann, Rainer, 124